Thomas Gräupl

L-DACS1

Thomas Gräupl

L-DACS1

Analysis, Design and Evaluation of the Quality-of-Service Protocols of the Future Aeronautical Communication System

Südwestdeutscher Verlag für Hochschulschriften

Impressum/Imprint (nur für Deutschland/only for Germany)
Bibliografische Information der Deutschen Nationalbibliothek: Die Deutsche Nationalbibliothek verzeichnet diese Publikation in der Deutschen Nationalbibliografie; detaillierte bibliografische Daten sind im Internet über http://dnb.d-nb.de abrufbar.
Alle in diesem Buch genannten Marken und Produktnamen unterliegen warenzeichen-, marken- oder patentrechtlichem Schutz bzw. sind Warenzeichen oder eingetragene Warenzeichen der jeweiligen Inhaber. Die Wiedergabe von Marken, Produktnamen, Gebrauchsnamen, Handelsnamen, Warenbezeichnungen u.s.w. in diesem Werk berechtigt auch ohne besondere Kennzeichnung nicht zu der Annahme, dass solche Namen im Sinne der Warenzeichen- und Markenschutzgesetzgebung als frei zu betrachten wären und daher von jedermann benutzt werden dürften.

Coverbild: www.ingimage.com

Verlag: Südwestdeutscher Verlag für Hochschulschriften GmbH & Co. KG
Heinrich-Böcking-Str. 6-8, 66121 Saarbrücken, Deutschland
Telefon +49 681 37 20 271-1, Telefax +49 681 37 20 271-0
Email: info@svh-verlag.de

Approved by: Salzburg, Paris Lodron Universität, Diss. 2011

Herstellung in Deutschland (siehe letzte Seite)
ISBN: 978-3-8381-3330-0

Imprint (only for USA, GB)
Bibliographic information published by the Deutsche Nationalbibliothek: The Deutsche Nationalbibliothek lists this publication in the Deutsche Nationalbibliografie; detailed bibliographic data are available in the Internet at http://dnb.d-nb.de.
Any brand names and product names mentioned in this book are subject to trademark, brand or patent protection and are trademarks or registered trademarks of their respective holders. The use of brand names, product names, common names, trade names, product descriptions etc. even without a particular marking in this works is in no way to be construed to mean that such names may be regarded as unrestricted in respect of trademark and brand protection legislation and could thus be used by anyone.

Cover image: www.ingimage.com

Publisher: Südwestdeutscher Verlag für Hochschulschriften GmbH & Co. KG
Heinrich-Böcking-Str. 6-8, 66121 Saarbrücken, Germany
Phone +49 681 37 20 271-1, Fax +49 681 37 20 271-0
Email: info@svh-verlag.de

Printed in the U.S.A.
Printed in the U.K. by (see last page)
ISBN: 978-3-8381-3330-0

Copyright © 2012 by the author and Südwestdeutscher Verlag für Hochschulschriften GmbH & Co. KG and licensors
All rights reserved. Saarbrücken 2012

Table of Contents

1 Introduction 3
2 Acronyms and Abbreviations 7
3 Background 12
   3.1   Development of B-VHF, B-AMC and L-DACS 1 14
   3.2   The Aeronautical Telecommunications Network 18
   3.3   Design Goals 18
4 Related Work 22
   4.1   VHF Digital Link Mode 2 22
   4.2   VHF Digital Link Mode 3 22
   4.3   AeroMACS 23
   4.4   L-DACS 2 23
   4.5   Iris 24
   4.6   NEWSKY and SANDRA 24
   4.7   ICAO WG-I and IETF 24
5 Methodology 26
   5.1   Overview 26
   5.2   Service Oriented Simulation Architecture 28
   5.3   Simplified Evaluation Scenarios 29
   5.4   Detailed Evaluation Scenarios 32
       5.4.1   Air Traffic 34
       5.4.2   Data Traffic 38
   5.5   Protocol Simulation 47
   5.6   Evaluation 49
6 Future Terrestrial Digital Aeronautical Communication Systems 54
   6.1   Broadband-VHF 55
       6.1.1   System Architecture 56
       6.1.2   Physical Layer Overview 57
       6.1.3   Medium Access Sub-Layer 59
       6.1.4   Discussion of B-VHF 64
   6.2   Broadband Aeronautical Multicarrier Communication 65

- 6.2.1 System Architecture 67
- 6.2.2 Physical Layer Overview 70
- 6.2.3 Medium Access-Sub Layer 85
- 6.2.4 Logical Link Control Sub Layer 98
- 6.2.5 Performance Evaluation 111
- 6.2.6 Discussion of B-AMC 128
- 6.3 L-DACS 1 135
  - 6.3.1 System Architecture 135
  - 6.3.2 Physical Layer Overview 139
  - 6.3.3 Medium Access Sub-Layer 146
  - 6.3.4 Logical Link Control Sub-Layer 155
  - 6.3.5 Performance Evaluation 173
  - 6.3.6 Discussion of L-DACS1 190
- 6.4 Summary 195
- 7 Conclusion 197
- 8 References 203
- 9 Appendix 210
  - 9.1 SOA Simulation Service Interface 210
    - 9.1.1 Simplified Evaluation Scenarios 212
    - 9.1.2 Detailed Evaluation Scenarios 214
    - 9.1.3 Evaluation 214
  - 9.2 DIN1319-3 Confidence intervals 217
  - 9.3 Jain's Fairness Index 217
  - 9.4 Analysis of Slotted ALOHA and RDLC B-VHF sRA Access 218
    - 9.4.1 Definitions 218
    - 9.4.2 Slotted ALOHA Medium Access 219
    - 9.4.3 Random Delay Counter Medium Access 224
    - 9.4.4 Conclusion 226

1 Introduction

The VHF COM band currently used for air-ground communications is becoming congested and is rapidly approaching its capacity limits. Future Air Traffic Management *ATM*[1] concepts will, however, require more intensive use of data communications than today. Seeking to define a future communication system providing the capacity and quality of service required for planned ATM operations, the Federal Aviation Administration *FAA* and EUROCONTROL initiated a joint study in the frame of Action Plan 17 *AP17* to investigate suitable technologies and provide recommendations to the ICAO[2] ACP Working Group T (formerly called WG-C) [1].

The final outcome of AP17 activities was that no single technology could be fully recommended yet, primarily due to concerns about interference between the new system and different already deployed systems. However, AP17 activities identified several desirable features which the future system should fulfill. Based on these features, two initiatives for the development of the L-band[3] Digital Aeronautical Communication System *L-DACS* were started at the end of AP17. The first system, L-DACS 1, is based on broadband technologies while the second system, L-DACS 2, is based on narrowband technologies.

This thesis presents the author's analysis, design, and evaluation of the user plane quality of service protocols of B-AMC (the technology proposal from which L-DACS 1 was derived after AP17 was concluded in 2007) and L-DACS 1. It was the objective of the author's work to develop a protocol design providing the quality of service required for future ATM operations. His work was constrained by the current capabilities of industrial implementation and the expected operational environment.

Quality of service is an essential feature for sub-network technologies in future aeronautical networks. Air traffic service applications expect the network to forward data according to its priority and traffic class. Priority has the essential role of ensuring that high priority operational data is not delayed by low priority non-operational data, even when the network is overloaded with low priority data. Service classes ensure that data is conveyed by appropriate transport services. However, link layer quality of service is not only determined by the implementation of differentiated traffic classes and priorities. In the case of aeronautical data links it is necessary to take the additional requirements of safety critical systems into account. The main focus of the author's

---

[1] Acronyms and abbreviations are defined in chapter 2.

[2] The International Civil Aviation Organization (ICAO) is a specialized agency of the United Nations.

[3] The use of the L-band for future terrestrial aeronautical communication was decided in AP17.

work lay therefore on the notions of responsiveness, reliability, efficiency, scalability, and resilience.

The research presented in this thesis concentrates on the analysis, design and evaluation of user plane protocols suitable for safety related aeronautical communication systems. The design was guided by extensive analytical and simulation based evaluations according to the requirements indicated above. The desired behavior of core parts of the data link layer design was proven analytically and the overall performance of the system was evaluated using large scale computer simulations.

B-AMC was based on B-VHF, a project co-funded by the European Commission within the 6th framework program and finalized in late 2006. Within the B-VHF project the feasibility of aeronautical multi-carrier based wideband communication was demonstrated in the VHF COM band [2]. The results of the project were evaluated positively by EUROCONTROL and FAA, and B-VHF was put on the future communications study shortlist as one of the most promising candidates. However, later developments showed that it is more likely that the future aeronautical communication system for 2020 and beyond will be implemented in the L-Band. Therefore EUROCONTROL funded an investigation for a B-VHF-like system in this radio spectrum. The main contribution of the author to B-VHF was the critical analysis of the B-VHF medium access protocols.

The aim of the B-AMC study was to adapt the B-VHF system to L-Band conditions while maintaining design principles developed in B-VHF. Special concern was given to the different interference situations mainly caused by systems currently deployed in the L-Band such as DME, UAT, SSR Mode S, and the military Joint Tactical Information Distribution System JTIDS. On the one hand, out-of-band emissions of the B-AMC transmit signal had to be kept at a minimum in order not to interfere with existing L-Band systems. On the other hand, the B-AMC signal has to be robust against strong interference from existing systems in the aeronautical L-Band. This is especially challenging as the B-AMC system should be operated in the spectral gap between two adjacent DME channels.

The author's major contribution to the B-AMC research was the analysis and design of the medium access approach. The author devised a protocol design providing dependable medium access to a high number of users without any dependency of the access latency on the data traffic pattern. This was realized by the introduction of a dedicated and periodic control channel for each aircraft-station. This decouples the medium access algorithm from the data traffic pattern and makes medium access contention-free.

L-DACS 1 was derived from B-AMC, TIA-902 P34[4], and WiMAX IEEE 802.16e in a joint cooperation with EUROCONTROL and FAA. The presented work, which was performed in two EUROCONTROL funded studies and one nationally funded FFG project within the TAKEOFF program, aimed at developing an initial system specification for L-DACS 1. This system specification shall enable prototyping activities to clarify system compatibility issues that could not be covered analytically or via modeling [3]. The L-DACS 1 design inherited its main features from the B-AMC system design. Especially the medium access concepts devised by the author for B-AMC were retained. Like B-AMC, the air-ground mode of the L-DACS 1 data link is a multi-application cellular broadband system capable of simultaneously providing various kinds of Air Traffic Services *ATS* and Aeronautical Operational Control *AOC* communication services via deployed ground-stations. Note that ATS and AOC are communication services related to the safety and regularity of the flight i.e. they are considered as safety critical.

The author's major contribution to the development of L-DACS 1 was the complete re-design of the user plane logical link control protocols. The author replaced the HDLC based sliding window protocol of B-AMC with a two-layer credit-based ARQ protocol. The sending window management was simplified by coupling it to the central resource management of the ground-station making near to optimal flow management possible. In addition to the improved flow management, the protocol now operates in fixed timing relations to the MAC frame structure to achieve near to optimal timer management.

The author's work resulted in an initial protocol specification which is considered complete, evaluated and ready for prototyping by the relevant authorities (EUROCONTROL and FAA supported by NASA, MITRE and ITT). The relevance of the author's innovations is further underlined by the adoption of key concepts of his work within the competing L-DACS 2 technology proposal.

The outline of this thesis is as follows: Chapter 3 describes the background for the development of new ATM concepts and technologies. Chapter 4 looks at projects performing related work. Chapter 5 gives a description of the methodology applied in the presented research. Chapter 6 analyses the findings of the B-VHF study which provided the motivation for the further work. Chapter 6.2 discusses the design and evaluation of the B-AMC protocol. Chapter 6.3 discusses the analysis, design, and evaluation of L-DACS 1. Chapter 7, the conclusion, sums up the most important results of this research.

---

[4] TIA-902 P34 is an American public safety radio system similar to the European TETRA and TETRAPOL systems.

The work discussed in this thesis was performed within the B-VHF, B-AMC, L-DACS 1, and CoLB projects[5]. Selected results were therefore already published within the official project documentation. However, a significant amount of work was performed in addition and complementary to the project work.

---

[5] B-VHF was co-funded by the European Commission within the 6th framework program. B-AMC and L-DACS 1 were funded by EUROCONTROL. CoLB was funded by the Austrian research promotion agency FFG within the TAKEOFF program.

2 Acronyms and Abbreviations

1090ES	1090 MHz Extended Squitter
3GPP	3rd Generation Partnership Project
ACK	Acknowledgement
ADS-B	Automatic Dependent Surveillance Broadcast
AOC	Aeronautical Operational Control
AP17	Action Plan 17
APT	Airport
ARQ	Automatic Repeat Request
AS	Aircraft Station
ATC	Air Traffic Control
ATM	Air Traffic Management
ATN	Aeronautical Telecommunications Network
ATN/IPS	Aeronautical Telecommunications Network over Internet Protocol Suit
ATN/OSI	Aeronautical Telecommunications Network over OSI Protocol Suit
ATS	Air Traffic Services
B-AMC	Broadband Aeronautical Multicarrier Communication
BC	Broadcast Control
BCCH	Broadcast Control Channel
BER	Bit Error Rate
BSS	B-AMC Special Services
CC	Common Control
CCCH	Common Control Channel
CNES	Centre National d'Études Spatiales

CO	Control Offset
COCR	Communication Operating Concept and Requirements for the FRS
COE	Control Offset End
COS	Control Offset Start
CoLB	Consolidated L-DACS 1 based on B-AMC
CRC	Cyclic Redundancy Check
DAMA	Demand Assigned Multiple Access
DC	Dedicated Control
DCCH	Dedicated Control Channel
DCH	Data Channel
DLS	Data Link Service
DLR	Deutsches Zentrum für Luft- und Raumfahrt
DME	Distance Measuring Equipment
ENR	En-Route
FAA	Federal Aviation Agency (USA)
FCI	Future Communication Infrastructure
FDD	Frequency Division Duplex
FER	Frame Error Rate
FFG	Forschungsförderungsgesellschaft (Austrian research promotion Agency)
FIS-B	Flight Information Services Broadcast
FL	Flight Level *or*
FL	Forward Link
FRS	Future Radio System
GBN	Go-Back-N
GNSS	Global Navigation Satellite Systems

GS	Ground Station
GSM	Global System for Mobile Communications
IATA	International Air Transport Association
ICAO	International Civil Aviation Organization
IEEE	Institute of Electrical and Electronics Engineers
IFF	Identification Friend or Foe
ILS	Instrument Landing System
ITU	International Telecommunication Union
JTIDS	Joint Tactical Information Distribution System
L-DACS	L-band Digital Aeronautical Communication System
LLC	Logical Link Control
LME	Link Management Entity
LTE	3GPP Long Term Evolution
MAC	Medium Access Control
MF	Multi-Frame
MGM	Management
MLS	Microwave Landing System
NAK	Negative Acknowledgement
NAVSTAR GPS	NAVSTAR Global Positioning System
NextGen	Next Generation Air Transportation System
OFDM	Orthogonal Frequency-Division Multiplexing
OFDMA	Orthogonal Frequency-Division Multiple Access
QoS	Quality of Service
ORP	Oceanic, Remote, Polar
PDU	Protocol Data Unit
PHY	PHYsical layer

PIAC	Peak Instantaneous Aircraft Count	
QAM	Quadrature Amplitude Modulation	
QPSK	Quadrature Phase-Shift Keying	
RA	Random Access	
RACH	Random Access Control Channel	
RL	Reverse Link	
RNAV	Random NAVigation	
SA	Synchronized Access	
SACH	Synchronized Access Control Channel	
SaR	Segmentation and Reassembly	
SDU	Service Data Unit	
SESAR	Single European Sky ATM Research	
SF	Super Frame	
SNDCP	Sub-Network Dependent Convergence Protocol	
SOA	Service Oriented Architecture	
SOAP	Service Oriented Architecture Protocol	
SSR	Secondary Surveillance Radar	
sRA	synchronized Random Access	
TACAN	TACtical Air Navigation	
TCAS	Traffic alert and Collision Avoidance System	
TDMA	Time Division Multiple Access	
TIS-B	Traffic Information Service Broadcast	
TMA	Terminal Maneuvering Area	
UAT	Universal Access Transceiver	
UMTS	Universal Mobile Telecommunications System	
VDL2	VHF Digital Link Mode 2	

VDL4		VHF Digital Link Mode 4
VI		Voice Interface
VOR		VHF Omnidirectional Range
WiMAX		Worldwide Interoperability for Microwave Access
WSDL		Web Services Description Language
XML		eXtensible Markup Language

3 Background

Air transportation is an important factor for the economic growth of the European Union, however, the current system is already approaching its capacity limits and needs to be reformed to meet the demands of further sustainable development [4]. These limitations stem mainly from the current European air traffic control system.

Air traffic control within Europe is fragmented due to political frontiers into regions with different legal, operational, and regulative contexts. This fragmentation decreases the overall capacity of the European air traffic control system and, as the system is currently approaching its capacity limits, causes significant congestion of the airspace. According to the European Commission airspace congestion and the delays caused by it cost airlines between €1.3 and €1.9 billion a year [5]. For this reason, the European Commission agreed to adopt a set of measures on air traffic management to ensure the further growth and sustainable development of European air transportation.

The key enabler of this transformation is the establishment of a Single European Sky[6] *SES*. The objective of the SES is to put an end to the fragmentation of the European airspace and to create an efficient and safe airspace without frontiers. This will be accomplished by merging national airspace regions into a single European Flight Information Region FIR within which air traffic services will be provided according to the same rules and procedures.

In addition to the fragmentation of the airspace the second limiting factor for the growth of European air transportation lies within the legacy Air Traffic Control *ATC* concept. In the current ATC system, which has been developed during the first half of the twentieth century, aircraft fly on fixed airways and change course only over navigation waypoints (e.g. radio beacons). This causes non-optimal paths as aircraft cannot fly directly to their destination and results in a considerable waste of fuel and time[7]. In addition, it concentrates aircraft onto airways requiring ATC controllers to ascertain their safe separation.

The tactical control of aircraft by ATC controllers generates a high demand of voice communication which is proportional to the amount of air traffic. As voice communication puts a considerable workload on the human controller the air traffic cannot be increased arbitrarily without compromising the safety of the system. This situation is made worse by the fact that the radio spectrum dedicated to aeronautical voice communication is becoming increasingly saturated i.e. even if the human

---

[6] Regulation (EC) No 549/2004 of the European Parliament and of the Council of 10 March 2004.

[7] On average, flight routes within Europe are 49 kilometers too long [3]. EUROCONTROL reported 9,916,000 IFR (Instrument Flight Rules) flights in 2007 [91] resulting in 485,884,000 unnecessary flight kilometers over Europe.

controllers could cope with more air traffic safely, there would not be enough voice frequencies to do so. Excessive controller workload and voice frequency depletion are therefore the main technical problems of the current air traffic control system.

An alternative approach to the legacy ATC system is to let all aircraft fly directly (i.e. on great-circle routes) to their destination airports without using airways. This concept is known as free flight or direct-to operations. The extremely high number of possible departure and arrival airports, departure times, cruising altitudes and flight speeds would then produce a semi-random distribution of aircraft supporting their safe separation outside of airport areas [6][8]. The free flight concept is therefore also known under the term Random NAVigation *RNAV*[9].

Using RNAV it is sufficient if aircraft cruising in the en-route phase of the flight are monitored by automatic systems. Human intervention is only required if a separation conflict is detected. If the situation cannot be resolved by the aircrews or the airline dispatchers themselves, the air traffic controller takes over and advises the involved aircraft to change their course or altitude. This concept does not longer *control* air traffic, but rather *manages* it. It is therefore called Air Traffic Management *ATM*, and is expected to supersede ATC in the Single European Sky. ATM is already implemented in today's air transportation system to a limited extent. However, there is currently little capability for online System Wide Information Management *SWIM* and Collaborative Decision Making *CDM*. Most of today's ATM procedures are carried out offline in preparation of the flight. These concepts will therefore be further developed in the SESAR Joint Undertaking of the European Commission [7].

Free flight and the Single European Sky will allow airlines to choose the shortest and most cost efficient routes (called 4D-business trajectories). The introduction of advanced ATM procedures and automated support tools will significantly decrease the controller workload. However, free flight and advanced ATM require aircraft to be equipped with accurate position determination and collision avoidance equipment as well as data communications to integrate them into the ATM, SWIM and CDM process [8].

Position determination and collision avoidance will be implemented on the basis of a technology called Automatic Dependent Surveillance Broadcast *ADS-B* combining

---

[8] [3] reports that the direct-to concept would reduce the number of separation conflicts by approximately 20% within the German air space and suggests a proportional reduction of the control workload.

[9] Note that the abbreviation RNAV is also used for Radio Navigation. Radio Navigation is not discussed in this thesis.

Global Navigation Satellite Systems[10] *GNSS* (e.g. NAVSTAR GPS or Galileo) with surveillance data links (e.g. UAT or 1090ES).

Data communications is required as ATM transfers parts of the decision making from air traffic controllers to cockpit crews supported by automated procedures and algorithms (e.g. self-separation). The aircrews must now be provided with timely, accurate and sufficient data to gain the situational awareness necessary to effectively collaborate in the collaborative decision making process of ATM. This requires the availability of sufficiently capable data links. However, the data link solutions available today cannot provide the capacity and quality of service required for the envisaged system wide information management [**9**]. Improved air-ground communication has therefore been identified as one key enabler in the transformation of the current air transportation system to the Single European Sky.

3.1 Development of B-VHF, B-AMC and L-DACS 1

Today's air-ground communication system is based on analogue VHF voice transmission and is used for tactical aircraft guidance. It is supplemented by several types of aeronautical data links that are also operated in the VHF COM band, most notably ACARS (FANS 1/A) and VHF Digital Link Mode 2.

However, these data links are scarcely deployed. Their further deployment is blocked by the fact that the VHF band is already heavily used by voice communication and is anticipated to become increasingly saturated in high density areas [**10**]. Introducing additional communication systems into the same frequency band will therefore increase the pressure on the existing infrastructure even further. ACARS and VDL Mode 2 can therefore not provide a viable upgrade path to ATM.

At the eleventh ICAO Air Navigation Conference in 2003 it has therefore been agreed that the aeronautical air-ground communications infrastructure has to evolve in order to provide the capacity and quality of service required to support the evolving air traffic management requirements [**9**]. The roadmap of the transformation to ATM was formulated in three relevant recommendations[11]:

Recommendation 7/3 - Evolutionary approach for global interoperability of air-ground communications. This recommendation promotes the continuing use of already implemented systems (supporting voice as well as data), the optimisation of the available spectrum utilisation, and the consideration of transition aspects.

---

[10] Position determination may also be based on other technologies (e.g. VOR and DME, or inertial navigation). However, GNSS is the most common proposal with regard to future aeronautical navigation.

[11] This summary of the rather lengthy recommendations in [**7**] is quoted from [**9**]. Recommendations 7/1 and 7/2 are out of the scope of this thesis and therefore omitted.

Recommendation 7/4 - Investigation of future technology alternatives for a/g communications. This recommendation addresses the need for investigations to identify the technology candidates to support the future aeronautical communications, and

Recommendation 7/5 - Standardization of aeronautical communication systems. Finally this recommendation emphasises the need for standardisation activities for technically proven technologies which provide proven operational benefits.

Recommendation 7/3 expresses the intention of ICAO to maintain the existing communication system preserving current investment into data link technology. In the short term the system shall be further optimized to prolong its life time, while the long term goal is its preparation for the transition to new technologies. Recommendation 7/4 and 7/5 address the development and standardization of suitable future technologies for air-ground communication.

It was the position of the airlines (represented by IATA) that the "air-ground infrastructure should converge to a single globally harmonized, compatible and interoperable system" [11]. Thus FAA and EUROCONTROL, representing the regions feeling the most pressure to reform their air-ground communication infrastructure, initiated the Action Plan (AP17) activity to jointly identify and assess candidates for future aeronautical communication systems [12]. This activity was coordinated with the relevant stakeholders in the U.S. (Joint Planning and Development Office Next Generation Air Transportation System *NextGen*) and in Europe (Single European Sky ATM Research *SESAR*).

Action Plan 17 concluded in November 2007 and comprised six technical tasks and three business tasks [12]. The business tasks are not of relevance in the context of this thesis, however, the technical tasks were:

- Task 1: Improvements to current systems - frequency management
- Task 2: Identify the mobile communication operational concept
- Task 3: Investigate new technologies for mobile communication
- Task 4: Identify the communication roadmap
- Task 5: Investigate feasibility of airborne communication flexible architecture
- Task 6: Identify the Spectrum bands for new system

The data link technologies discussed in this thesis (B-VHF[12], B-AMC and L-DACS1) were developed in response to Recommendation 7/4 and as input to AP17 Task 3 and its follow-up activities.

---

[12] B-VHF is only touched briefly where it provided input to its successors B-AMC and L-DACS1.

The generic name for all technology proposals to recommendation 7/4 and AP17 technical task 3, including systems not discussed in this thesis, is Future Radio System *FRS*. The subject of this thesis is therefore the design and development of one of the two remaining technology options considered for the terrestrial future radio system: L-DACS 1, which builds upon B-VHF, B-AMC, P-34 and IEEE 802.16e.

Broadband-VHF (B-VHF) [13][14][15][16][17][18] was a system concept developed from 2004 to 2006 in a research project co-funded by the European Commission. The project investigated and demonstrated the feasibility of a multi-carrier based wideband communication system to support aeronautical communications while operating as an overlay system in the VHF COM band. An overlay system utilizes unused frequencies of other systems operating in the same band. It does not require dedicated spectrum on its own. B-VHF did therefore not decrease the resources of the VHF voice system.

B-VHF demonstrated good potential for satisfying the needs of future aeronautical communications. Following an initial investigation of promising technologies, it emerged on the AP17 shortlist as one of the most promising candidate technologies[13]. However, the overlay implementation option in the VHF COM band was considered elaborative and costly and the L-band was identified as more suitable frequency band for communication in the En-Route and TMA airspace (cf. [9] 7.5.1.2 b and [12] Technical Task 6). For that reason, EUROCONTROL funded the investigation of a B-VHF-like system in the aeronautical L-band (960-1164 MHz). This new technology proposal was given the generic name: Broadband Aeronautical Multicarrier Communication (B-AMC).

The aim of the B-AMC project [19][20][21][22][23][24] was to adapt the B-VHF system to L-band conditions while maintaining existing design principles developed in B-VHF. A particular challenge was the different interference situation caused by systems currently deployed in the L-Band such as DME/TACAN, UAT, SSR/Mode S, and the military Joint Tactical Information Distribution System (JTIDS): On the one hand, out-of-band emissions of the B-AMC transmit signal had to be kept at a minimum in order not to interfere with existing L-Band systems. On the other hand, the B-AMC signal had to be robust against strong interference from other systems.

In contrary to B-VHF, B-AMC was not designed as an overlay system, but as an inlay system i.e. it was designed to operate in the gaps between used L-band frequencies.

These new channel conditions required several adaptations of the physical layer. Not surprisingly, the revision of the physical layer required a radical redesign of the data link layer protocols as well. In addition, the key design goals of B-AMC were shifted to primarily support data communication and only to optionally support digital voice communication which was the main design goal of B-VHF.

---

[13] In the final version of the technology short list B-VHF was replaced by B-AMC (see below).

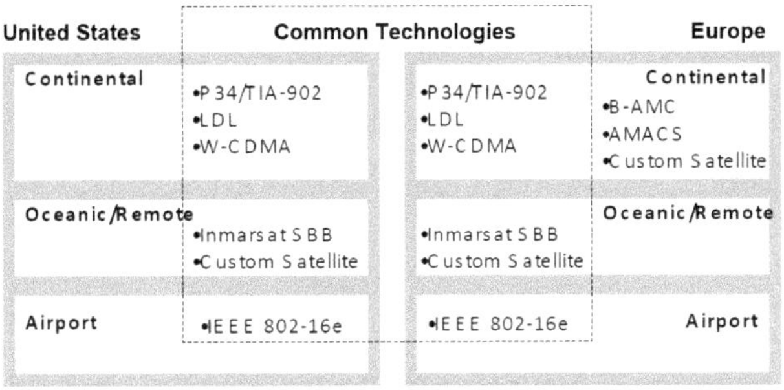

United States	Common Technologies		Europe
Continental	•P34/TIA-902 •LDL •W-CDMA	•P34/TIA-902 •LDL •W-CDMA	Continental •B-AMC •AMACS •Custom Satellite
Oceanic/Remote		•Inmarsat SBB •Custom Satellite	Oceanic/Remote
Airport	•IEEE 802-16e	•IEEE 802-16e	Airport

Figure 3-1: AP17 final shortlist of evaluated technologies. Reproduced from [12][14].

Action plan 17 was finalized in late 2007 and the final report [12] concluded that none of the considered technology proposals (see Figure 3-1) could be fully recommended for all airspace domains. The future system will therefore be a system of systems integrating existing technologies as well as new communication systems. This Future Communications Infrastructure *FCI* shall comprise at least three data links: A system for the communication on the airport surface, a terrestrial continental communications system, and a satellite communications system for remote and oceanic areas. Within this thesis only the terrestrial (or continental) component of the future communications infrastructure is discussed.

The AP17 technology assessment led to the identification of suitable technology features and to the selection of two promising candidate sets for the terrestrial continental communication system. This system was termed L-band Digital Aeronautical Communication Systems *L-DACS*: The first set of options (L-DACS 1) is based on broadband technologies (B-AMC, TIA-902 P34), while the second set of options (L-DACS 2) is based on narrowband technologies (LDL, AMACS).

B-AMC was identified as the most promising L-DACS 1 candidate by EUROCONTROL. Together with another L-DACS 1 candidate (TIA-902 P34 [25]) and IEEE 802.16e WiMAX [26] it was selected to provide the technological basis for the development of a consolidated L-DACS 1 system.

As one follow-up activity to AP17, EUROCONTROL funded the development and first specification of the L-DACS 1 system [1] on the basis of a revised B-AMC system in 2008 and 2009 [27][28][29][30]. In addition to several protocol changes resolving issues identified during the AP17 technology assessment, the B-AMC proposal was

---

[14] Note that this figure is slightly misleading. P34/TIA-902, LDL, and W-CDMA were actually solely proposed by the United States. The column presenting B-AMC, AMACS, and the custom satellite (which were the European proposals) might be in the wrong position and belong into the center column.

supplemented with features from the TIA-902 P34 [**25**] and IEEE 802.16e WiMAX standards [**26**].

Although there was no formal cooperation between EUROCONTROL and FAA at this point (AP17 had already been concluded) the development of L-DACS 1 was observed and advised by FAA and its sub-contractors NASA, ITT and the MITRE cooperation.

After the end of the EUROCONTROL funded initial specification the development of the L-DACS 1 technology was continued in the "Consolidated L-DACS 1 based on B-AMC" CoLB project of the Austrian research promotion agency FFG as part of the TAKEOFF program. This project produced an updated specification and extensive guidance material [**31**][**32**]. The overview paper [**10**] provides an independent summary of the development of the L-DACS systems up to the year 2010.

The author's contributions to the B-VHF, B-AMC, and L-DACS 1 design process are the main topic of this thesis and are presented in the following chapters.

3.2 The Aeronautical Telecommunications Network

Within AP17 it has become apparent that none of the new data link technologies will be capable to satisfy the needs of all upcoming services on their own. This raised the need for the integration of different technologies into an aeronautical inter-network on the basis of the future communications infrastructure.

In the past there has already been an attempt to integrate different aeronautical communication technologies in an Aeronautical Telecommunication Network *ATN* based on ISO/OSI technology *ATN/OSI* [**33**][**34**][**35**]. This approach never came into the position to develop its full potential as the ISO/OSI networking technology has never been adopted by the industry to any significant extent. ATN/OSI has therefore not been deployed widely. Thus the tendency to move the ATN to another technological basis emerged soon. Most importantly there have been considerations towards the implementation of an ATN on top of the IP Protocol Suit *ATN/IPS* [**36**].

For the fixed (i.e. ground-ground) communication infrastructure a decision for migration to the IPS is about to be adopted at ICAO level, while the subject is still being studied for mobile communication. In the view of EUROCONTROL the implementation of a Pan European Network *PEN* based on IP technology will be an important element of the FCI and therefore justify the investigation of the feasibility of IP based solutions for the air-ground communications (i.e. mobile) segment as well. For this reason the FRS candidate technologies have been designed to operate within an IP context from the beginning.

3.3 Design Goals

The primary design goals of all FRS technology proposals were defined by the high level objectives formulated in AP17 [**37**]:

- *The system development shall be facilitated and expedited through the choice of appropriate components and mature standards.*
- *The new system should be capable to operate in the L-band without interfering with existing users of the band.*
- *The system performance should meet the requirements defined in AP17 technical task 2.*

The reason for the first design goal was the target deployment year of the FRS, 2020. The aeronautical industry has comparatively long deployment cycles: In the past the deployment of safety related communication systems has taken between 8 to 15 years [**12**] i.e. it is required that any FRS candidate system has already achieved a sufficiently high maturity by now, if its initial deployment shall begin by 2015. Starting deployment in 2015 shall allow for a period of pre-operational use before operational service starts in 2020.

The L-DACS 1 family of protocols fits quite well into the established development cycle considering that development started with B-VHF in 2004. In addition to the experience with B-VHF and B-AMC, the L-DACS 1 design incorporated inputs and several mature concepts found in the TIA-902 P34 and IEEE 802.16e standards to further increase the technology readiness level.

The L-band was identified as the best candidate band for the deployment of the FRS due to its propagation characteristics and potential spectrum availability. However, the FRS will not be the only user of the L-band. There is significant number of existing systems deployed in this band (e.g. DME, TACAN, JDITS/MIDS, SSR, TCAS, UAT, GNSS, and others) that must not be disturbed in their operation. Suppressing interference towards other systems is not only a physical layer task. It requires the data link layer to support the physical layer by avoiding harmful usage patterns of the radio channel to maintain a low duty-cycle.

Provisions to achieve a low duty-cycle were introduced with the B-AMC protocol, where they were built directly into the system. Within L-DACS 1 this design was modified, making the desired duty-cycle a configurable parameter of the resource reservation algorithm.

Meeting the requirements defined in AP17 technical task 2 requires to support operational aeronautical communication i.e. Air Traffic Services *ATS* and Aeronautical Operational Control *AOC* communications. ATS communication provides navigation, control and situational awareness, while AOC communication is used to perform the business operations of the airline. The system shall be capable to provide simultaneous

ATS and AOC communication with adequate performance as of 2020 and beyond. Passenger communication is out of the scope of the FRS.

These three high level objectives of AP17 were augmented by a number of non-technical, legal and political requirements, which are, however, not discussed extensively here. Within this thesis only the design aspects and evaluation criteria related to the quality of service of the user plane performance of the system are discussed in detail.

Note that the L-DACS 1 notion of "quality of service" is broader than in most other cases. This is due to the fact that the naive notion of quality of service emerged from the design and operation of multimedia networks for the delivery of entertainment content. However, in the case of aeronautical data links it is necessary to follow a different approach to reflect the quality of service requirements of a safety critical system. This was reflected in the identification of five relevant design goals by the author. These design goals define the target parameters (see section 5.6) of the protocol design.

Responsiveness is the capability of the system to react quickly to communication demand. This comprises the ability to deliver data traffic within specified delays and to provide swift voice service with minimum latency. The required level of responsiveness depends on the service class of the data traffic and requires a prioritized approach to medium access.

Reliability is the ability of the system to perform its functions under stated conditions for a specified period of time i.e. to transmit data without losing or duplicating information. The required level of reliability is expressed in terms of service continuity.

Efficient resource usage of the new system is dictated by the scarcity of the available spectrum. This implies avoiding unnecessary protocol overhead (e.g. finding the right balance between forward error correction and backward error correction) and fair distribution of channel resources among users with the same priority.

Scalability is required for the FRS in order to handle growing amounts of data traffic and users i.e. the technology should support as many of the defined use cases as possible with acceptable quality of service.

Resilience is the ability of the FRS to provide and maintain an acceptable quality of service even under adverse conditions. In particular this refers to periods of excessive load and high numbers of users. The system shall behave predictable and, if it fails, this must be detected early and reported immediately.

An additional aspect of resilience is that safety related systems have to undergo certification. Certification is a costly and elaborative process[15]. The system design should therefore avoid unnecessary complexities to make the system certifiable with economically reasonable effort.

---

[15] The certification costs of safety related software have been estimate with $1,000 per line of code.

4 Related Work

B-VHF, B-AMC and L-DACS 1 are neither the only proposals for future radio systems nor the only research efforts developing aeronautical communication systems. The envisaged transformation of the European air transportation system has spawned a considerable number of projects in this area. Not all projects can be mentioned here, but this section provides a short overview of projects related to L-DACS 1 and its predecessors. Most of these projects have to be seen in the context of the Single European Sky ATM Research Programme *SESAR* [7] founded by the European Commission and EUROCONTROL although they are not all part of it.

There are two relevant legacy data link technologies, two projects developing complementary or alternative data link technologies, and several other projects and standardization bodies concerned with the integration of existing and future data links. With exception of VDL Mode 2, VDL Mode 3, and L-DACS 2[16] the author has been involved in all projects and standardization efforts mentioned in this section. 1090ES, UAT, and VDL Mode 4 which are technologies primarily used for surveillance communication, are briefly described in section 6.2.2.1.

4.1 VHF Digital Link Mode 2

Very High Frequency Digital Link Mode 2 *VDL Mode 2* is a legacy VHF digital communication system for the aeronautical environment. It supports ATS and AOC data communication. Its physical layer uses 25 kHz VHF channels and 8-phase shift keying modulation. This provides a shared data rate of 31.5 kbit/s for each 200 nautical miles cell. VDL Mode 2 medium access is based on a simple carrier sense multiple access CSMA scheme without support for priorities. The logical link control protocols have been designed to be compatible with X.25.

VDL Mode 2 is currently being implemented in Europe via an implementation rule[17] of the European Commission in the framework of the Single European Sky.

4.2 VHF Digital Link Mode 3

Very High Frequency Digital Link Mode 3 *VDL Mode 3* is another legacy VHF digital communication system for the aeronautical environment. It uses 25 kHz VHF channels and provides simultaneous access to (digital) voice and data services with a single aircraft transceiver. VDL3 uses time division multiple access to multiplex different voice and data connections onto a single radio channel. A second level of TDMA is used to support duplex communication with the ground station. This approach is also

---

[16] There were however two meetings of the author with HELIOS, who contributed to the L-DACS 2 data link layer design (Meeting with HELIOS, 12th June 2008, Farnborough; Meeting with HELIOS July 14th 2009, Oberpfaffenhofen).

[17] Commission Regulation 29/2009

known as time division duplex. In the course of the development of VDL Mode 3 the AMBE ATC10B vocoder was certified. At the time of this writing it is still the only digital vocoder certified for operational use in the aeronautical environment.

The implementation of VDL Mode 3 was abandoned by the FAA in 2004.

4.3 AeroMACS

AeroMACS is derived from IEEE 802.16 also known as WiMAX. It shall be capable of supporting current and future ATS applications as well as AOC applications on the airport surface. The base technology of AeroMACS, WiMAX, was initially developed for stationary wireless communication and later adapted for mobile wireless communication. The WiMAX standard itself consists of a huge set of options and provides only a technology framework. This makes interoperability between different implementations is difficult. Consequently the WiMAX Forum™ was formed to provide certification of conformity and verification of interoperability. Certificates are given for so called "profiles", where a profile defines a subset of options from the IEEE 802.16 standard. The main idea of using WiMAX for airport communications in the form of an AeroMACS profile is to benefit from existing technologies and from industrial vendor support.

As of this writing the AeroMACS profile is being developed in the frame of the SESAR JU and the SANDRA project.

4.4 L-DACS 2

L-DACS 2 is an alternative proposal for a terrestrial FRS. "L-DCAS2 is considered for operation in the L band, and has been developed from material for AMACS, UAT, DME and VDL Mode 4. GSM technical elements have also been used as basic technical background [38][39]." L-DACS 2 is a narrow band system based on time division duplex within 200 kHz radio channels. Its main advantage is claimed to lie in the re-use of GSM technology which should expedite the certification of the system. In contrast, the focus of L-DACS 1 lies on enabling re-use of radio spectrum by use of 500 kHz inlay channels in frequency division duplex. L-DACS 2 requires dedicated spectrum.

L-DACS 2 was specified after L-DACS 1 and refined several design concepts introduced in B-AMC and L-DACS 1. Especially the concept of deterministic, contention-free medium access devised by the author and presented in this thesis was adopted in the updated specification [38]. A performance evaluation of L-DACS 2 can be found in [40].

4.5 Iris

The Iris[18] Programme [41] for Air Traffic Management of the European Space Agency aims to develop a satellite communications link for operational aeronautical communication, complementing existing and future terrestrial systems. The envisaged launch date of the Iris satellites is around the year 2015. It is therefore likely that the Iris system will be operational before L-DACS. Iris is designed to offer sufficient capacity for 2025 and beyond. L-DACS and Iris may thus co-exist for a considerable amount of time.

The co-existence of terrestrial and satellite based data links is addressed by SESAR with the "dual link" concept. This concept foresees the simultaneous availability of at least two independent data link solutions for increased resilience. The mode of operation (simultaneous use of two data links, or use of a single data link with a back-up) is not yet defined. Among economic considerations (i.e. pricing model for data link usage) this depends on the availability of technological solutions for the integration of multiple data links.

4.6 NEWSKY and SANDRA

The NEWSKY [42] project of the European Commission developed the concept of a global mobile communication network for aeronautical communications. The project pursues the vision of "Networking the Sky" by integrating a range of data links based on different communication technologies (ground based, satellite-based, aircraft-to-aircraft) as well as different application classes (air-traffic services, airline operational and administrative communication, aeronautical passenger communication) into a single, seamless network based on Internet Protocol IP technology. By integrating non-operational data traffic into the network (i.e. airline administrative communication and aeronautical passenger communication) it goes already one step beyond the SESAR dual link concept. The NEWSKY work is continued in the follow-up project SANDRA since 2009. SANDRA includes also the development of an IEEE 802.16e based airport surface data link technology (i.e. AeroMAX prototype) in cooperation with the SESAR JU.

4.7 ICAO WG-I and IETF

The use of IP based protocols in aeronautical networks is standardized by ICAO WG-I [36] under the term Aeronautical Telecommunications Network/Internet Protocol Suit *ATN/IPS*. It is expected that ATN/IPS will replace the current ATN/OSI technology which uses the OSI internet protocols. The WG-I standardization efforts are less detailed than the NEWSKY or SANDRA research. There have however been several contributions to WG-I from NEWSKY (including several contributions by the author).

---

[18] "Iris" is not an acronym.

The Internet Engineering Task Force *IETF* has also indicated its interest to contribute to the standardization of an IP based ATN solution[19].

---

[19] MEXT ad hoc meeting for NEMO route optimization for aviation with the author, July 29th 2008, IETF 72, Dublin.

5 Methodology

The main topic of this thesis is the design and development of the B-AMC and L-DACS 1 protocols by the author with the focus on the quality of service features. Designing a communications protocol is an iterative task requiring the constant evaluation and re-evaluation of the protocol. The frequent assessment of design alternatives has the purpose to support the design process when taking design decisions, to detect design deficiencies early, and to assess the expected protocol performance[20]. The author used analytical treatment and computer simulations to support the design process of the work presented in this thesis.

The analytical treatment applied standard methods commonly used to describe and analyze the behavior of dynamic systems: queuing theory and Markov chains. A rigid treatment of these methods can be found in Kleinrock's seminal work [43].

The computer simulations were event driven simulations. They were implemented from scratch by the author to avoid introducing hidden assumptions on the protocol implementation adopted by external developers. They are described in the remainder of this section.

5.1 Overview

The aeronautical environment is demanding to simulate. This is due to its high complexity, which, in the context of the evaluation of aeronautical communication technologies, relates to the mobility of aircraft, the properties of the telecommunication protocols, and the simulated aeronautical applications. It is the multi-faceted nature of this simulation task that requires a simulation approach reflecting these properties. Within this thesis an approach based on a Service Oriented Architecture *SOA* has been applied to simulate B-AMC and L-DACS 1. This approach and its interface protocol were devised by the author for the Iris project [41] and later reused in other contexts[21] including this thesis.

The SOA approach is a flexible and simple approach to create simulations that are adaptable to changing requirements and can be extended easily. It is an additional benefit of this methodology to foster the integration of existing simulation tools into new simulation trials. In the case of the assessment of aeronautical wireless communication technologies this allows the generation of complex evaluation scenarios in a comprehensible and straight-forward manner.

---

[20] "Design decisions have to be based on measurements." Dr. H. Clausen, SatNEx Summer School 2009.

[21] The application of this approach to the simulation of B-AMC is described in [51]. Note, however, that [51] describes a different set of simulations than discussed in this document. The same approach was also used in the Iris, CoLB and NEWSKY projects.

The service oriented architecture approach originated from network centric warfare concepts. It did not take long until these concepts were successfully adopted within the civil domain under the notion of network enablement. However, the central ideas of the approach remained unchanged, as they proved to be valid in both application domains. Civil SOA concepts have been found to be especially successful when employed to create synergy effects from distributed business services.

The adoption of SOA as business methodology is naturally reflected in the structure of the underlying software implementation. However, the SOA concept is not confined to business software and can be applied to any environment where services shall be accessed without knowledge of their internal operation. Although this approach has not yet been applied widely to technical engineering, this methodology offers great potential to support the decomposition of complex simulation and design tasks according to domain specific concepts.

The information centric concept of SOA is based on the loose coupling of different services; each service contributes its specific capabilities to create an overall solution. From a more technical point of view, service providers can be seen as producers, offering locally available resources or abilities to their customers (i.e. consumers) through well-known interfaces. A benefits chain leading to the ultimate solution is being built by the information flow from service to service independently of the underlying implementation. Thus, each consumer may autonomously utilize any collection of services from one or several providers to create the effects he or she desires.

The main effect from applying SOA to technical simulations is the shaping of the information flow of the technical design process by decentralized services; where a decentralized service is understood as a simulation or decision support tool. This effect results in a series of benefits.

Due to the distribution of the workload each service or tool has to deal with only one particular aspect of the simulation, making the overall solution less constraint by computational limitations and thus more scalable. In a certain sense this scalability extends to the software development process: The decomposition of the simulation task into independent services makes the software management far less complex. It is well known that development time does not grow linearly with the complexity of the problem [**44**]; therefore decomposition into several less challenging sub-tasks offers over-proportional reductions in development cost.

Keeping in mind that development times are usually several orders of magnitude larger than the runtimes of a simulation a significant reduction in development time usually outweighs other performance gains over the complete project cycle by far.

It is an additional benefit that the flexible combination of existing services supports the quick formulation of new solutions. This is especially valuable in a dynamic context where the involved (i.e. simulated) technologies change quickly. If adaptations (e.g. protocol changes) become necessary only the affected service (e.g. protocol simulator) has to be modified, while all other components of the solution remain as they are. By this the SOA concept offers an elegant way to reuse existing capabilities in new contexts.

5.2 Service Oriented Simulation Architecture

The straight-forward approach to simulate a communication technology like B-VHF, B-AMC or L-DACS 1 would be to evaluate only the layer two (data-link layer) communication protocols. Although technically sufficient, this classical approach would evaluate the protocol performance without taking influences from the airspace situation into account.

Thus, in order to validate the network capabilities in a given aeronautical scenario, as it is required by EUROCONTROL, the simulation framework has to include additional properties of the environment. In the context of this thesis this means the air-space situation and the data communication patterns of operational aeronautical communication.

The resulting decomposition of the simulation according to domain specific concepts is illustrated in Figure 5-1. The simulation services shaded in grey are not discussed in detail in this thesis. The simulation services with white background were implemented by the author.

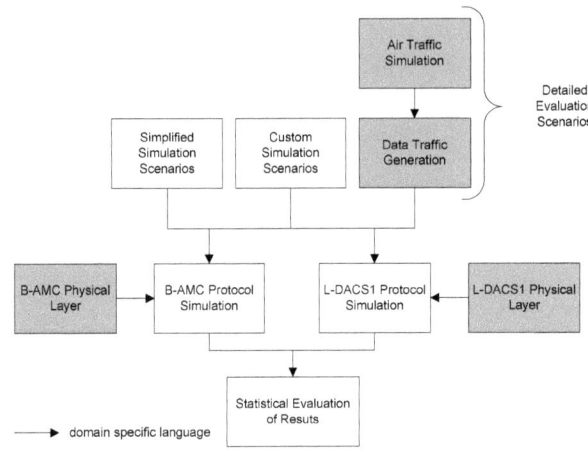

Figure 5-1: Service oriented simulation tool chain.

The evaluation scenarios are based on two EUROCONTROL defined approaches: The simplified evaluation scenarios described in the FCI evaluation scenario document [**45**] and the detailed scenarios based on the COCR report [**46**].

The author's implementation of the simplified scenarios is described in section 5.3. The implementation of the detailed simulation scenarios is outlined in the same section. The methods applied to extrapolate the current air traffic to the deployment time-frame of the FRS (i.e. the air traffic simulation) and the implementation of the data traffic patterns defined in [46] (i.e. the data traffic generation) are published by the author in [47], [48], and [49].

In addition to the EUROCONTROL based scenarios it is sometimes useful to define custom scenarios. These scenarios are designed to test particular properties of the protocol that are not covered by the simplified or detailed scenarios. Custom scenarios are protocol dependent and described in detail where they are used.

The protocol simulation is the author's implementation of the B-AMC or L-DACS 1 protocol (or one of its versions) in a computer program. It accepts the simulation scenario as input from the respective simulation service. Its output is forwarded to the evaluation service. Note that the performance of the physical layer has been assessed in separate simulations conducted by the institute for communication and navigation of the German aerospace center (Deutsches Zentrum für Luft und Raumfahrt DLR) [21] [50] [29] during the B-AMC and L-DACS 1 projects and Frequentis AG [40] during the CoLB project.

The statistical evaluation of the simulation results is performed by the evaluation service. It analyzes the raw simulation data according to the evaluation criteria defined in section 5.6. This analysis is summarized in HTML reports containing tables and figures.

During simulation runs this simulation services are synchronously linked; the output of each service provides the input for the next service. Information exchange between services is performed using a domain specific modeling language. The interaction between the different services is organized in sessions (displayed as arrows in Figure 5-1). A session may either be established directly between simulation services running at the same time (e.g. using a TCP connection or UNIX pipe) or be saved in trace files for later use. Saving sessions to trace files is the preferred approach as it fosters the reuse of intermediate results. The service interface is described in appendix 9.1.

5.3 Simplified Evaluation Scenarios

The evaluation of the B-VHF, B-AMC and L-DACS 1 quality of service features in this thesis was performed on the basis of the data traffic profile (also called "mobile communication operational concept") defined in the COCR report [46] and the air traffic volumes defined in the companion document to the COCR [45].

The COCR mobile communications operational concept is very detailed and is described on the basis of a set of anticipated (i.e. hypothetical) data link services. These services are divided into three categories: Air Traffic Control *ATC*, Aeronautical

Operational Control *AOC* and Network Management Services *NET*. Each of these services is described in great detail: The events triggering the generation of a data packet, size and quantity of the packet, expected reaction of the peer entity (i.e. responses or acknowledgements), and the expected class of service (cf. Table 5-12 and Table 5-13).

It was recognized by the authors of the COCR report that this elaborate model is non-trivial to implement, in particular, as it requires a detailed air traffic model. Therefore the COCR report was augmented with the companion document [**45**] containing a set of simplified evaluation scenarios.

These evaluation scenarios are "simplified" in the sense that the scenarios of the companion document are easier implemented by the evaluator. The simplified scenarios were created using the same data link service descriptions as in the detailed scenarios. However, they were already based on synthetic air traffic situations (i.e. artificial air traffic provided by the authors of the COCR report) referred to as "air traffic volumes".

Table 5-1: Traffic volumes (cited from [45]).

Ref.	Type	Dimensions	Height Range	Number of aircraft (PIAC)
TV 1.1	APT Zone	Cylinder, 10 NM[22] diameter	0 – FL[23]50	26
TV 1.2	APT Surface	Cylinder, 5 NM diameter	0	264[24]
TV 2.1	TMA Small	Cuboid, 49 x 49 NM	FL50 – FL245	44
TV 2.2	TMA Large	Cuboid, 75.0 x 75.0 NM	FL50 – FL245	53
TV 3.1	ENR Small	Cuboid, 55 x 55 NM	FL245 – FL450	45
TV 3.2	ENR Medium	Cuboid, 100.0 x 100.0 NM	FL245 – FL450	62
TV 3.3	ENR Large	Cuboid, 200.0 x 200.0 NM	FL245 – FL450	204
TV 3.4	ENR Super Large	Cuboid, 400.0 x 400.0 NM	FL245 – FL450	522

---

[22] Nautical Miles.

[23] Flight Level FL expresses the aircraft altitude (above mean sea level) in steps of 100 ft (e.g. FL50 corresponds to an aircraft altitude of 5000 ft above mean sea level). Note that the abbreviation FL is also used for the Forward Link FL (i.e. ground-to-air) transmission direction depending on the context.

[24] The APT Surface traffic volume contains all aircraft on the ground. The other traffic volumes contain only airborne aircraft.

An excerpt of the relevant air traffic volumes is cited in Table 5-1. The "APT Surface" traffic volume has been left aside in this thesis as this communication domain is covered by the dedicated IEEE 802.16e based airport surface data link [12]. The "ENR Super Large" traffic volume covers an area larger than the area that could be covered using the theoretical maximum range of B-VHF, B-AMC or L-DACS1, which is 200 nautical miles. It is therefore left aside too.

Except for the APT Zone traffic volume, which is cylindrical, all traffic volumes are cuboids of different sizes. The TMA and ENR traffic volumes have constant heights of 19,500 feet (5,943.6 meters) and 20,500 feet (6,248.4 meters), respectively. Each traffic volume has a Peak Instantaneous Aircraft Count value *PIAC* reporting the maximum number of aircraft observed within this volume at the same time.

In addition to the introduction of synthetic air traffic, data traffic is no longer presented at the packet level, but aggregated into average user data rates (i.e. offered load) as displayed in Table 5-2. The user data rates are split into four scenarios: Either ATS traffic alone or ATS and AOC traffic combined, with or without the very demanding A-EXEC[25] service. The most challenging scenario is the ATS+AOC scenario with A-EXEC service.

Table 5-2: Simplified evaluation scenarios.

Scenario	PIAC	Average User Data Rate (kbit/s)							
		ATS Only, with A-EXEC		ATS + AOC, with A-EXEC		ATS Only, without A-EXEC		ATS + AOC, without A-EXEC	
		FL[26]	RL	FL	RL	FL	RL	FL	RL
APT Zone	26	-	-	-	-	3	10	3	15
APT Surface	264	-	-	-	-	30	30	150	30
TMA Small	44	30	30	30	30	30	30	30	30
TMA Large	53	30	30	30	30	30	30	30	30
ENR Small	45	30	30	150	30	30	30	80	30
ENR Medium	62	30	30	150	30	30	30	100	30
ENR Large	204	30	40	300	40	30	40	200	40
ENR Super Large	522	40	50	500	50	40	50	500	50

---

[25] "The A-EXEC service provides an automated safety net to capture situations where encounter-specific separation is being used and a non-conformance FLIPINT event occurs with minimal time remaining to resolve the conflict. [...] When non-conformance occurs, triggering an imminent loss of separation, the ground automation system generates and sends a resolution to the aircraft for automatic execution without the Flight Crew or Controller in the loop." [41]

[26] In this table FL and RL denote Forward Link (ground-to-air) and Reverse Link (air-to-ground) directions.

At the start of each simplified evaluation scenario the air traffic volume is populated with aircraft. The simplified scenarios do not require the simulation of cell entry and cell exit therefore it is assumed that the number of aircraft is constant at the PIAC during the complete simulation time. The position of the aircraft within the traffic volume is not simulated as the physical layer simulations covered the influence of the aircraft's position already with worst case assumptions.

5.4 Detailed Evaluation Scenarios

The B-VHF and B-AMC performance evaluations published in [16], [18], [19], [20], [21] and [50] were performed using the simplified evaluation scenarios from [45]. However, these scenarios have significant drawbacks: Due to the aggregation of the data traffic into user data rates information on individual packets is lost and they are no longer suitable for the evaluation of quality of service features. There is no information available on the size or service class of individual packets. In fact, the size of the messages may be chosen freely by the evaluator, which led to diverging evaluation results in some cases ([23] and [24]).

For these reasons the evaluations presented in this thesis are based on the original COCR specifications i.e. the evaluation scenarios were generated by the combination of realistic air traffic simulations with detailed COCR [46] based packet generation. Each scenario consists of one hour of air traffic and data traffic in rectangular traffic volumes defined by the author analogue to the simplified scenarios. The traffic volumes are centered over the Paris Charles de Gaulle airport and the air traffic is extrapolated to the year 2025 using the tools and methodologies described by the author in [47] [51]and [49], respectively[27].

Table 5-3: APT Zone + TMA evaluation scenarios.

Reference	Description	Comment
TMA.15	Cuboid, 15 x 15 NM + APT Zone	
TMA.30	Cuboid, 30 x 30 NM + APT Zone	
TMA.45	Cuboid, 45 x 45 NM + APT Zone	APT Zone + TMA Small from [45] is 49 x 49 NM
TMA.60	Cuboid, 60 x 60 NM + APT Zone	
TMA.75	Cuboid, 75 x 75 NM + APT Zone	APT Zone + TMA Large from [45]

---

[27] The extrapolation is based on the High-A scenario discussed in [42]. It is therefore a worst case extrapolation. The more recent results of [43] are not used here as they are based on a different air traffic forecast than the COCR report.

An overview of the evaluation scenarios is displayed in Table 5-3 and Table 5-4. For reference the equivalent simplified scenarios are indicated in the comment column of the tables. However, it should be noted that the detailed evaluation scenarios, although chosen analog to the simplified scenarios, are not absolutely identical.

The TMA.x evaluation scenarios include the airport zone i.e. the TMA.x scenarios are analog to the combination of the APT Zone traffic volume (TV 1.1) and the analog TMA traffic volume (TV 2.x) from [45]. This combination was necessary as the transition between the APT and TMA domains were implemented in different ways in both air traffic models[28]. This is also the border between the use of the airport surface data link technology and L-DACS. In addition, the cylindrical APT Zone traffic volume was approximated by a rectangular traffic volume of the same area. However, as we will see, these approximations lead to comparable evaluation scenarios.

Table 5-4: ENR evaluation scenarios.

Reference	Description	Comment
ENR.25	Cuboid, 25 x 25 NM	
ENR.50	Cuboid, 50 x 50 NM	ENR Small from [45] is 55 x 55 NM
ENR.75	Cuboid, 75 x 75 NM	
ENR.100	Cuboid, 100 x 100 NM	ENR Medium from [45]
ENR.125	Cuboid, 125 x 125 NM	
ENR.150	Cuboid, 150 x 150 NM	
ENR.175	Cuboid, 175 x 175 NM	
ENR.200	Cuboid, 200 x 200 NM	ENR Large from [45]
ENR.225	Cuboid, 225 x 225 NM	
ENR.250	Cuboid, 250 x 250 NM	

The ENR.x evaluation scenarios were chosen analog to the ENR traffic volumes of the simplified scenarios, however, without taking the ENR Super Large traffic volume (TV 3.4) into account. This scenario has a size of 400x400 nautical miles, covering an area larger than the area that could be covered using the theoretical maximum range of B-VHF, B-AMC or L-DACS1, which is 200 nautical miles. The largest rectangular sector that could be completely covered with this radio range has a size of approximately 282x282 nautical miles. Thus the maximum en-route scenario has been chosen to be 250x250 nautical miles (ENR.250) requiring up to 90% of the maximum radio range.

The relationship between the simplified scenarios of [45] and the detailed evaluation scenarios defined in this thesis is illustrated in Figure 5-2.

---

[28] The simplified evaluation scenarios of [40] assume that the transition between the APT and TMA domain is performed at a fixed height. In the detailed evaluation scenarios the APT/TMA transition is based on actual ATC sectors.

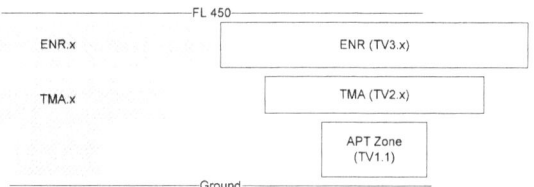

Figure 5-2: Detailed evaluation scenarios and simplified scenarios from [45].

5.4.1 Air Traffic

The air traffic volumes of this evaluation were chosen to be rectangular by the author so that the evaluation results could be compared to analogue results produced on the basis of the simplified evaluation scenarios. The airport Paris Charles de Gaulle was selected as center of the traffic volumes for two reasons. The first reason is that Paris Charles de Gaulle is the airport of the European core area with the highest number of flights over the year, the second reason is, that it is located in the region with the highest density of DME stations in Europe. As B-AMC and L-DACS 1 are both susceptible to DME interference (cf. section 6.2.2) this coincides with the worst case scenario of the physical layer evaluations [52].

The air traffic simulations were based on air traffic records from 31st August 2007, which was the peak day (in terms of aircraft movements) of that year. This data was extrapolated to the target deployment year of the FRS, 2025 [12], on the basis of the EUROCONTROL long term forecast [53][29]. The method of extrapolation is described in detail in [47]. Without going into any detail, it should be noted here that the extrapolation approach does not only take the increase of air traffic into account, but does also model aircraft routes according to the RNAV concept i.e. both quantitative and qualitative changes of the air traffic pattern are taken into account.

The complete air traffic model comprises an area much greater than the area of interest in this thesis [30]. Therefore the flights within the defined evaluation scenarios had to be extracted by the author. Each evaluation scenario contains only the relevant parts of the complete flight. For example: ENR.250 contains all flights in the En-Route phase within a 250 nautical miles square around Paris Charles de Gaulle. If a flight leaves the area or changes to the TMA flight phase it is removed from the scenario and vice versa. The distribution of the air traffic density within the TMA.75 and the ENR.250 scenario is plotted in Figure 5-3.

---

[29] Both, the detailed evaluation scenarios described in this document and the simplified evaluation scenarios of [40] are based on the long term forecast [53] from 2006. Other issues of the EUROCONTROL long term forecast may yield different results.

[30] The area of interest of the complete air traffic model is described in detail in [42]. It comprises the area from W80 to E80 and N80 to S80.

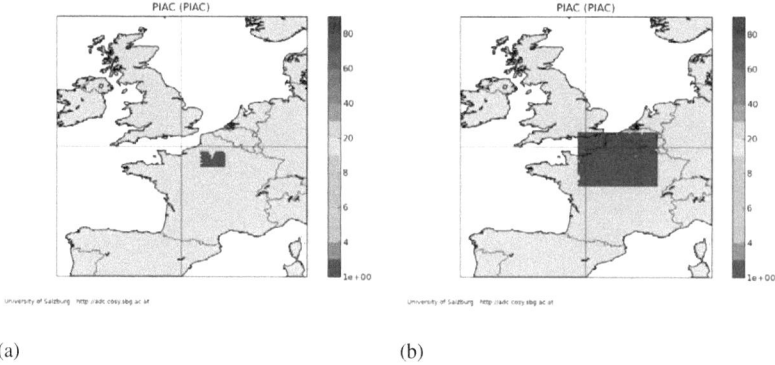

(a)   (b)

Figure 5-3: Geographic distribution of PIAC density TMA.75 and ENR.250.

The density is plotted using the PIAC value for each 0.1x0.1 degree area. As the PIAC assumes almost always the value 1 there is usually not more than one aircraft within each 0.1x0.1 degree area at any instant of time. At the given latitude this corresponds approximately to less than one aircraft per 5x5 nautical miles and indicates that the RNAV approach can indeed provide the safe separation of aircraft in most cases[31] (cf. [6]).

The runways of Paris Charles de Gaulle are in east-west direction, which is reflected in the TMA.75 plot as there are no approaches from the north. Paris Charles de Gaulle cannot be approached from the south either, however, Le Bourget airport (which is mainly used by business aviation) has a runway in the north-south direction and is located directly south of Paris Charles de Gaulle. This is reflected by the aircraft density plot of the TMA scenario.

The TMA.x scenarios include also the airport zone. Note that the definition of the APT zone traffic volume of [45] (cylindrical, 10 nautical miles in diameter) covers only Paris Charles de Gaulle. The airport zone of Le Bourget, which is more than 5 nautical miles apart from Paris Charles de Gaulle, is therefore not included in the TMA.x evaluation scenarios. The TMA sector covering both airports is however included. While it might be argued, that the deployment of a terrestrial communication technology would most likely cover both airports, the definition of the APT Zone traffic volume is retained in this thesis for the sake of comparable results.

Figure 5-4 displays the evolution of the air traffic of TMA.75 and ENR.250 over the chosen hour of simulation time. The time interval is 12:00 UTC to 13:00 UTC as its one of the busiest periods of the day in Paris Charles de Gaulle.

---

[31] Note that the success of RNAV in most cases (20% less separation conflicts according to [3]) does not invalidate the need for air traffic control for the remaining separation conflicts.

Note that the air traffic population of the TMA.75 scenario shows significant variations, while the aircraft population of the ENR.250 scenarios remains quite stable. The perturbations of the aircraft population of the TMA.75 scenario are mainly caused by aircraft entering and leaving the TMA zone. The number of aircraft at the airport remains relatively stable.

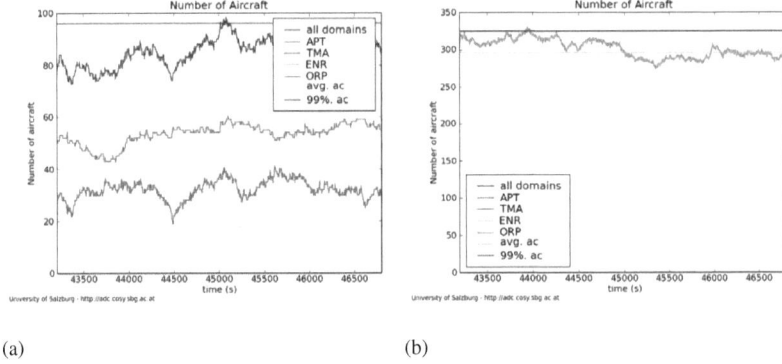

(a)   (b)

Figure 5-4: Air traffic[32] TMA.75 and ENR.250 vs. simulation time[33].

Table 5-5 displays the statistical characteristics of the air traffic in the TMA.x scenarios. In Figure 5-5 the number of aircraft is plotted against the scenario size in square nautical miles. Note that the TMA.x scenarios correlate very well with similar sized air traffic volumes of the simplified evaluation scenarios [45].

Table 5-5: Air traffic in TMA scenarios.

Scenario	TMA.15	TMA.30	TMA.45	TMA.60	TMA.75
Aircraft min	0.00	0.00	0.00	0.00	0.00
Aircraft avg	52.00	58.37	65.77	73.43	82.47
Aircraft 95%	62.70	70.00	78.00	84.00	93.00
Aircraft 99%	65.00	72.00	81.00	86.00	96.00
Aircraft max (PIAC)	67.00	73.00	83.00	86.00	98.00
Aircraft stdev	13.27	13.06	13.58	13.43	13.98

---

[32] Note that although all air traffic domains are plotted in the graph some of them contain no aircraft and coincide therefore with the x-axis (ENR and ORP in Figure 5-4 (a) and APT, TMA, and ORP in Figure 5-4 (b)).

[33] The simulation contains the air traffic during the peak hour of the day (12:00 – 13:00 GMT).

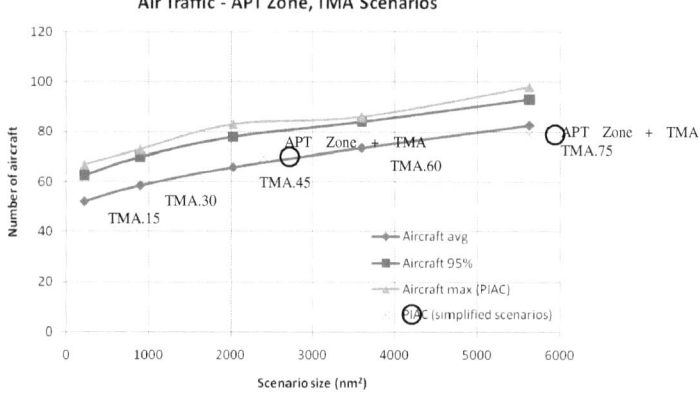

Figure 5-5: Air traffic in TMA scenarios.

Figure 5-6, Table 5-6, and Table 5-7 display the statistical characteristics of the ENR scenarios. The PIAC predictions of the simplified scenarios of [45] and the realistic scenarios are again almost identical with the notable exception of the ENR Small volume, which shows some deviation.

Table 5-6: Air traffic in ENR scenarios (part I).

Scenario	ENR.25	ENR.50	ENR.75	ENR.100	ENR.125
Aircraft min	0.00	0.00	0.00	0.00	0.00
Aircraft avg	4.60	15.39	30.88	49.44	74.49
Aircraft 95%	7.00	21.00	36.00	59.00	86.00
Aircraft 99%	8.00	22.00	38.00	62.00	88.00
Aircraft max (PIAC)	8.00	23.00	38.00	63.00	88.00
Aircraft stdev	1.65	3.68	5.35	7.40	10.12

Table 5-7: Air traffic in ENR scenarios (part II).

Scenario	ENR.150	ENR.175	ENR.200	ENR.225	ENR.250
Aircraft min	0.00	0.00	0.00	0.00	0.00
Aircraft avg	104.35	140.49	187.33	240.88	296.16
Aircraft 95%	113.00	153.00	206.00	263.00	320.00
Aircraft 99%	115.00	155.00	208.00	267.00	325.00
Aircraft max (PIAC)	115.00	156.00	209.00	268.00	329.00
Aircraft stdev	12.55	16.63	22.83	28.64	34.73

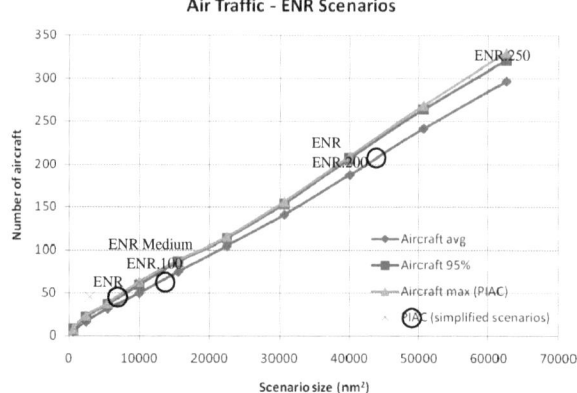

Figure 5-6: Air traffic in ENR scenarios.

The detailed simulation scenarios use the same service interface protocol format as the simplified simulation scenarios.

5.4.2 Data Traffic

On the basis of the air traffic extrapolation data packets were generated for each aircraft. The data generation included all data services defined in the COCR report [46] with the exception of some services identified not suitable for the transmission over the B-VHF, B-AMC or L-DACS 1 air-ground data link: Broadcast packets originating from the aircraft were not included[34]. Broadcast packets transmitted by the ground-station were assumed to provide TIS-B like services (cf. section 6.2.2.1).

The COCR report defines triggers for each packet exchange with regard to the flight phase (departure or arrival), ATC-sector, and domain (APT, TMA, ENR, or ORP). These data packet exchanges were generated for each aircraft according to its current flight phase, sector and domain, and were characterized with the number, size and service class of each packet. Additional service interface elements and attributes that are used by the data traffic simulation to determine the flight phase, sector and domain of each aircraft are documented by the author in [54].

---

[34] The services included into evaluation scenarios are: NETKEEP, NETCONN, WXTEXT, WXRT, WXGRAPH, UPLIB, TECHLOG, SWLOAD, POSRPT, OOOI, NOTAM, MAINTRT, MAINTPR, LOADSHT, GATES, FUEL, FREETEXT, FLTSTAT, FLTPLAN, FLTLOG, ENGINE, CABINLOG, AOCDLL, URCO, SURV-ATC, SAP (modified; non-periodic), PPD, PAIRAPP, M&S ACL, ITP ACL, FLIPINT, FLIPCY, DYNAV, D-TAXI, D-SIGMENT, D-SIG, DSC, DRV-R, D-OTIS, D-ORIS, DLL, D-FLUP, DCL, D-ATIS, D-ALERT, COTRAC-W, COTRAC-I, C&P SURV, C&P ACL, ARMAND, AMC, A-EXEC, ACM, ACL.

The generation of data packets is best illustrated using an example service: D-OTIS provides the air crew with information derived from ATC, ATIS, METAR and other flight information services.

According to the mobile operational concept of [46] the D-OTIS service is only used by 30% of the aircraft in the APT, TMA and ENR domains. A typical D-OTIS dialogue between the aircraft and the air traffic controller comprises eleven 193 byte packets in the forward link and three 107 byte packets in the reverse link. Table 5-8 provides an excerpt from Table 6-15 on p. 111 of [46] summarizing the quantities and sizes of the D-OTIS packet exchange. The description of the trigger events for this service is given in Table 6-2 of [46] and cited in Table 5-9.

Table 5-8: Excerpt from Table 6-15 [46]

Services	Uplink Qty x Size (bytes)	Downlink Qty x Size (bytes)
D-OTIS	11 x 193	3 x 107

Table 5-9: Excerpt from Table 6-2 [46]

Service	APT	TMA	ENR	ORP
D-OTIS	1 (in ramp position), departure only for 30 % of aircraft	1 per domain, arrival only for 30 % of aircraft	1 per domain for 30 % of aircraft	-

The individual data packets of the service dialogue are assumed to be exchanged in turns by the aircraft and the controller[35]. The occurrence of trigger events for packet exchanges during a typical flight is illustrated in Figure 5-7.

Note that within the OSI reference model COCR user data packets correspond, strictly speaking, to application layer messages. However, the overhead introduced by the layers below the application layer has already been statistically included by the authors of [46]. Thus it is not necessary to take additional higher layer overhead into account. COCR application layer messages will therefore be identified with user data packets in

---

[35] According to comments received by the author from EUROCONTROL (mail from Danny van Roosbroek; May 13th 2008) on this implementation of the COCR mobile operational concept (1 message RL, 1 FL, 1 RL, 1 FL, 1 RL, 9 FL) the D-OTIS packet sequence was actually assumed to be performed differently. Rather, a demand with a subsequent report and cancellation is assumed. These reports contain four packet uplinks each (1 RL, 4 FL, 1 RL, 4 FL, 1 RL, 1 FL). However, this is not documented in [41]. In the comment it is left open whether the order of the packets is actually relevant for the hypothetical services of [41] and that *"These assumptions were made in order to estimate a reasonable load for D-OTIS, and are not intended to constrain the communication solution."*

the simulations. Note, however, that this does not take the effects of network layer or transport layer fragmentation into account.

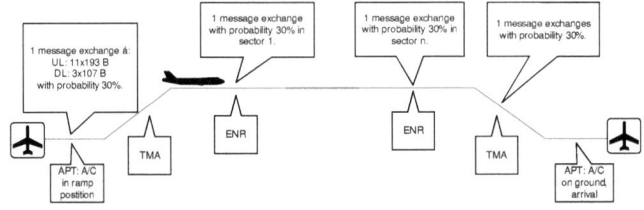

Figure 5-7: Trigger events for D-OTIS message exchanges.

Figure 5-8 displays the statistics of the number of generated data packets per second for the TMA.x scenarios. These statistics were derived over 3 second intervals[36]. Note that the number of packets to be transmitted on the reverse link is significantly lower at approximately the third of the forward link packet generation rate. The peak of the maximum on the RL is caused by an outlier value.

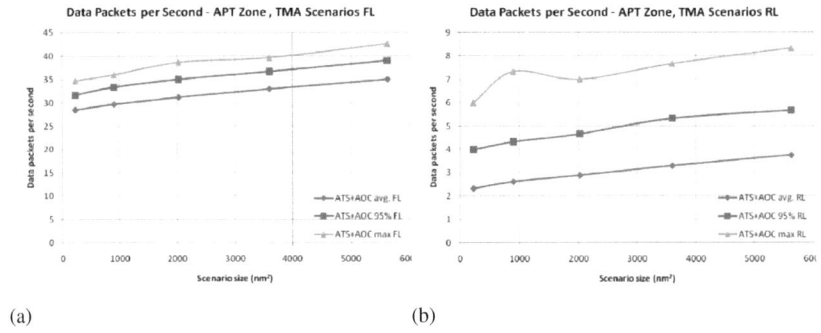

(a) (b)

Figure 5-8: Data packets per second – TMA scenarios.

If the geographic density of the packet generation events is plotted, the shape of the terminal maneuvering area *TMA* of Paris Charles de Gaulle airport and Paris Le Bourget airport becomes visible.

Note that the reveres link plot in Figure 5-9 uses the current position of the aircraft generating the packet to determine the geographic distribution, while the forward link plots use the position of the destination aircraft instead of the ground-station position which actually generates the packet, but does not move.

---

[36] Making the statistical analysis using 3 second intervals was originally requested by ESA as this was in the order of magnitude of the expected round-trip time for aeronautical data link services. The approach was kept in all further analyses for comparability.

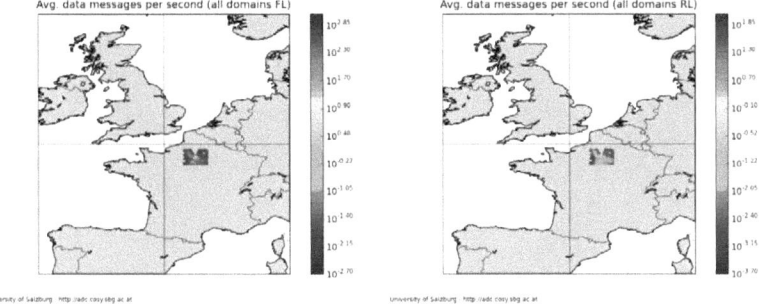

Figure 5-9: Distribution of data packets in space – TMA scenarios.

Inspecting the packet generation rates of the ENR scenarios in Figure 5-10 we can identify a significant growth of the packet generation rate with the scenario size. It is notable that the reverse link packet generation rate reaches less than a fifth of the forward link rate.

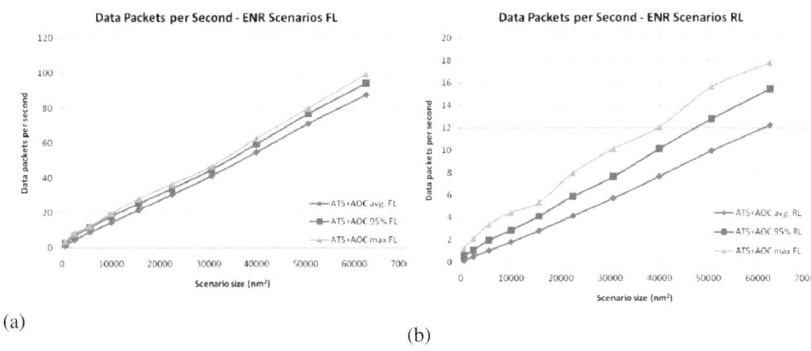

(a)   (b)

Figure 5-10: Data packets per second – ENR scenarios.

Figure 5-11 displays the geographic distribution of the data message generation events for the ENR.250 scenario. The great-circle RNAV routes between major airports are clearly discernible in both plots.

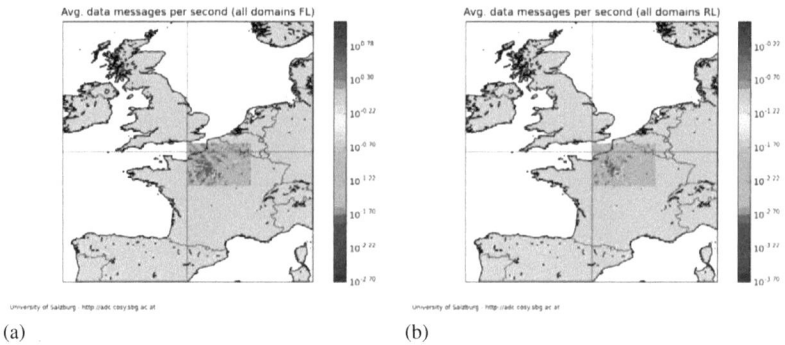

Figure 5-11: Distribution of data packets in space – ENR .250.

The user data rate (i.e. offered load) of the TMA.x and ENR.x scenarios is displayed in Figure 5-12 and Figure 5-13. It is noticeable that the user data rate of the detailed evaluation scenarios deviates from the user data rate of the simplified scenarios. This is not surprising as the detailed scenarios employ a different application mix than the simplified scenarios. In particular, many RL surveillance services have been left aside.

If the user data rate of the APT Zone traffic volume (TV 1.1) and the TMA traffic volumes (TV2.x) are combined we get an aggregate average user data rate of 33 kbit/s on the FL and 40-45 kbit/s on the RL. While the average FL user data rate of the detailed evaluation scenarios is comparable to the average user data rate of the simplified scenarios (cf. Figure 5-12; left), the user data rate of the RL is significantly lower.

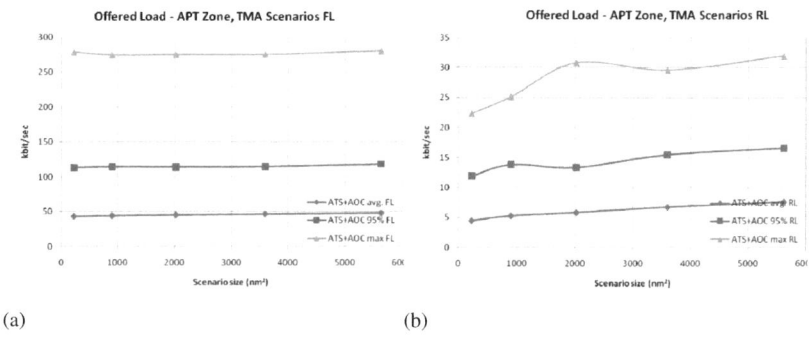

Figure 5-12: Offered load – TMA scenarios.

For the detailed ENR.x scenarios the 95% percentile of the FL user data rate correlates nicely with simplified scenarios. The user data rates of the detailed RL ENR.x scenarios are however on average significantly lower than the user data rates of the simplified scenarios, too.

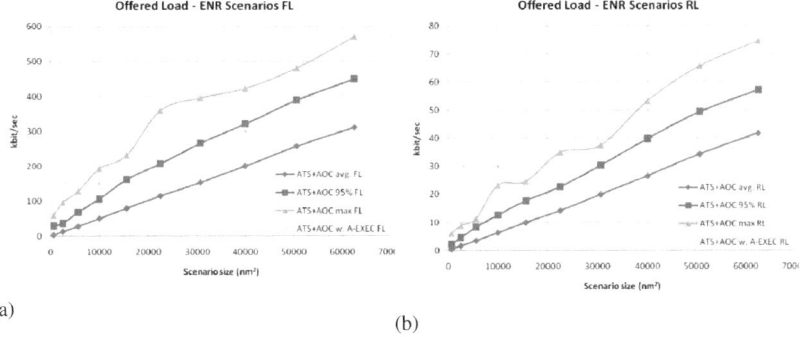

Figure 5-13: Offered load – ENR scenarios.

The deviation of the RL average user data rate in the detailed scenarios and the simplified scenarios is caused by the exclusion of the RL surveillance services from the data profile. This is also confirmed by independent implementations of the COCR mobile operational concept performed by HELIOS and CNES[37] which yield similar results in this case [23] [55][38].

The strong correlation of the 95% percentile of the FL user data rate of the detailed scenarios with the average FL user data rate of the simplified scenarios indicate that the simplified scenarios were constructed as worst case scenarios. Indeed [45] states that the aggregate user data rate U was computed according to the formula

$$U = \sum_{s \in S} \frac{P \, m_s}{TT_{95,s}}$$

where S is the set of COCR data link services, P is the PIAC of the scenario, m_s is the message size of service s, and $TT_{95,s}$ is the simplified 95% percentile latency requirement of service s[39] i.e. no statistical multiplexing was taken into account. (In a more optimistic setting it might be assumed that not all P aircraft want to transmit at the same time and P could be replaced by $P' < P$.)

Consequently, the most significant difference between the user data traffic of both evaluation scenarios lies in the different burstiness of the traffic pattern. The COCR based data traffic of the detailed evaluation scenarios displays strong variations of the traffic load within a short time. The peak to average ratio of the offered load in the

---

[37] Centre National d'Études Spatiales. The French space agency.

[38] Within [54] the implementation of the mobile operational concept discussed in this document is referred to as "ESA results" as it was produced under an ESA contract.

[39] The TT_{95} requirement of the simplified scenarios is derived from the TD95-FRS requirement of the detailed scenarios [40].

TMA.75 scenario is 5.85 on the FL and 4.19 on the RL if measured over 3 second intervals i.e. while the average offered load on the FL is approximately 55 kilobits per second, it may have peaks up to 300 kilobits per seconds. This effect is not captured in the simplified scenarios. The graph of the offered user data rate is plotted in Figure 5-14 below.

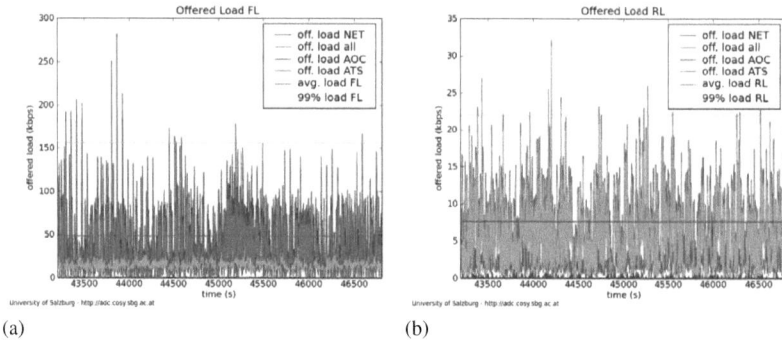

(a)   (b)

Figure 5-14: User data rate vs. time TMA.75.

The variance of the offered data traffic is not quite as strong in the ENR.250 scenario. The peak to average ratio of the offered load is 2.38 on the FL and 1.96 on the RL. Its graph is displayed in Figure 5-15. The offered load was measured over 3 second intervals.

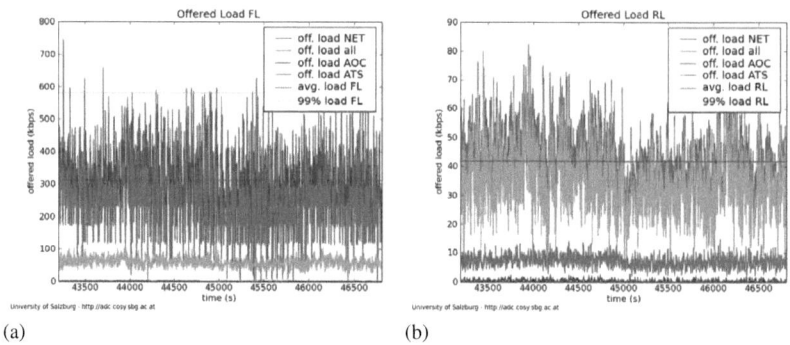

(a)   (b)

Figure 5-15: User data rate vs. time ENR.250.

Table 5-10 displays the contribution of the different service classes and packet sizes to the offered load on the FL and RL. Each service class has a required minimum latency labeled TD95-FRS and indicated on the left. The TD95-FRS requirements are discussed in detail in section 5.6. Figure 5-16 displays the distribution and contribution of each packet size and service class to the total amount of traffic in the TMA.75 scenario in terms of traffic volume and number of packets.

On the FL there are only three main contributors to the offered load. More than 90% of all FL packets are contributed by surveillance services and have a size of 34 bytes or less (DB-D, DB-E). However, these packets contribute only approximately 20% of the traffic volume. The bulk of the remaining traffic is contributed by larger packets. The remaining two significant contributions are made by AOC services (DG-K, ≤ 4,077 bytes) and the graphical weather service (DG-J, ≤ 21,077 bytes).

On the RL the distribution of the packet size is less pronounced, but follows a similar pattern. Most of the packets are small in size, but the bulk of the traffic is contributed by a few high volume services with large packets. The main contributions to the offered load on the RL are made by the DG-C (≤ 222 bytes), DG-D (≤ 2,763 bytes), DG-K (≤ 727 bytes) and DG-J (≤ 148 bytes) service classes. Note that approximately 50 % of the packets are smaller than 222 bytes.

Table 5-10: Contributions to TMA.75 offered load.

Class of Service		TD95–FRS (s)	Avg. Offered Load (%)		Avg. Number of Packets / Sec (%)		Max. Packet Size (Byte)	
			FL	RL	FL	RL	FL	RL
DB-D	SURV	1.2	14.50	-	73.13	-	34	-
DB-E		1.2	3.79	-	19.12	-	34	-
DG-A	NET	9.8	0.17	1.01	0.21	2.00	154	148
DG-C	ATS	1.4	1.03	5.34	1.40	13.46	491	222
DG-D		2.4	9.63	65.49	2.60	29.46	1969	2763
DG-F		4.7	2.08	0.95	0.27	1.88	1340	129
DG-J	AOC	13.6	48.48	15.98	1.79	40.04	21077	148
DG-K		26.5	20.32	11.22	1.48	13.15	4077	727

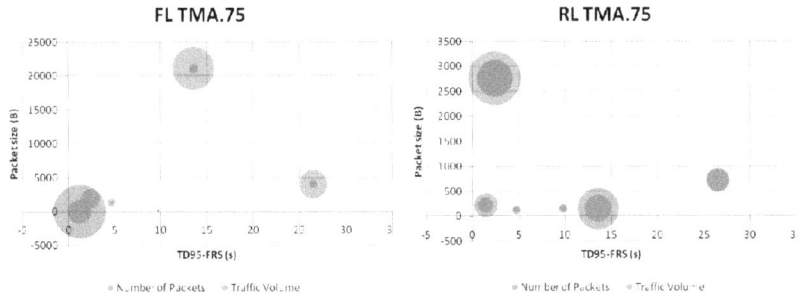

Figure 5-16: Contributions to TMA.75 offered load.

In the ENR.250 scenario the situation is similar. There are, however, only two main contributors to the FL traffic as the DG-F service class (i.e. the corresponding data link application) is not used in the ENR air space. The RL data traffic pattern is almost the same.

Table 5-11: Contributions to ENR.250 offered load.

Class of Service		TD95–FRS (s)	Avg. Offered Load (%)		Avg. Number of Packet / Sec (%)		Max. Packet Size (Byte)	
			FL	RL	FL	RL	FL	RL
DB-B	SUR	1.2	1.58	-	20.73	-	34	-
DB-E	V	1.2	5.27	-	68.90	-	34	-
DG-A	NET	9.8	0.13	0.96	0.44	3.16	154	148
DG-C	ATS	1.4	0.24	1.36	0.91	6.50	126	93
DG-D		2.4	11.82	80.47	4.05	32.86	1969	2763
DG-J	AO	13.6	80.23	9.95	3.08	42.72	21077	233
DG-K	C	26.5	0.72	7.26	1.90	14.76	377	727

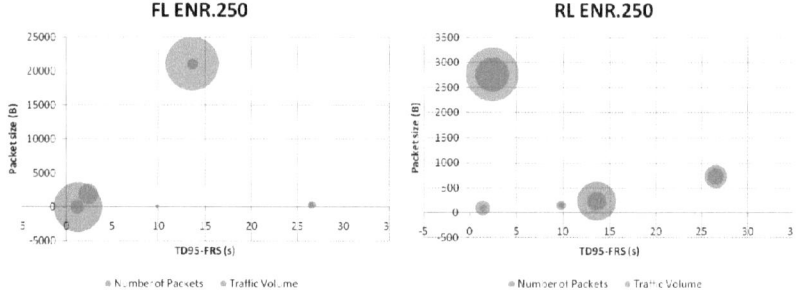

Figure 5-17: Contributions to ENR.250 offered load.

Note that the maximum application layer packet sizes observed in the data traffic pattern need not result in network layer packets of the same size. It is highly probable that large higher layer packets would commonly be fragmented by transport layer and network layer protocols. Assuming Ethernet derived on-board networks maximum fragment sizes between one and two kilobits have to be expected. However, even if the actual packet sizes were smaller the burst size of the application layer services (i.e. the load of the system) would still remain the same. Burst size and packet size are therefore identified with each other in the evaluation scenarios. No transport layer flow control or fragmentation is assumed in order to capture the worst case traffic profile.

The properties of the COCR data traffic profile have been summarized in [56] as follows: *"ATM data traffic consists predominantly of very short messages (message body between ~20 and a few hundred bytes), spaced by intervals of several seconds to several minutes. A few longer messages (up to a few kilobytes) are also present.*

Messages are triggered by events related to the progress of the flight or, for a few message classes, by the passing of time. In other words, the traffic is inelastic, consisting of mainly short, infrequent messages occurring at unpredictable, irregular intervals."

5.5 Protocol Simulation

The simulation of the protocols discussed in this thesis has been split into two simulation tasks: The assessment of the physical layer and the evaluation of the data link layer. These tasks were performed in independent simulations.

The simulation of the physical layer (interference, modulation, and coding) was performed by the institute for communication and navigation of the German aerospace center (Deutsches Zentrum für Luft und Raumfahrt ***DLR***). The results of these simulations (e.g. bit error rate, frame size, etc.) were used as input to the data link layer simulations discussed in this thesis.

Although the physical layer and the data link layer were simulated independently, the overall performance of the system is determined by the combined operation of both layers. For this reason, the performance of the data link layer was evaluated with different settings (e.g. bit error rate) to determine the optimal working point of the physical layer. The harmonization of the physical layer and the data link layer was therefore one iterative process during the development of the B-AMC and L-DACS 1 systems.

The author's simulation of the data link layer was not only used to assess the performance of the system, but also as a design tool to support design decisions during protocol development. For this reason the computer simulation of the protocols was implemented "near the specification" without introducing additional levels of abstraction. It is therefore based on the same formal model as employed in protocol specifications: Protocol entities interacting via protocol primitives and protocol data units.

A protocol entity may either be a functional block (e.g. Data Link Service ***DLS***) or a sub-layer (e.g. MAC sub-layer). Protocol entities located higher in the protocol stack request services from protocol entities located lower in the protocol stack. A protocol entity may issue indications of certain events to protocol entities located above it in the protocol stack.

There are two pairs of primitive operations between protocol entities: Request (.req) and confirmation (.conf), and indication (.ind) and response (.resp). A service is requested from a protocol entity via a .req primitive. The request and its result may be confirmed with a .conf primitive. Within a computer simulation the relationship between .req and .conf is naturally modeled with function calls and return values if an imperative programming language is used.

Events raised by protocol entities are indicated to other protocol entities with .ind primitives. There may be a response to an indication via a .resp primitive. Implementing indications and responses is slightly less trivial. An accepted approach is to model this relationship in computer simulations is using the observer pattern [**57**].

The formal term for a data packet accepted by one protocol entity from another protocol entity located higher is the protocol stack is Service Date Unit *SDU*. A protocol entity may modify (e.g. fragment) the SDU or add Protocol Control Information *PCI* (e.g. a header) to the SDU. This creates the Protocol Data Unit *PDU* of this protocol entity. Protocol entities of the same type communicate via the exchange of PDUs. This exchange may be realized using requests and indications of protocol entities located lower in the protocol stack. A PDU of layer *n* is a SDU for layer *n-1*.

The use of protocol primitives and PDUs within the protocol simulation is illustrated in Figure 5-18. The "higher layers" protocol entity of the protocol stack implements the interface to the simulation scenario and the evaluation service. If the simulation scenario indicates the generation of a new data packet, the "higher layers" entity requests its transmission from the data link layer. If a data packet is received, its status is indicated to the evaluation service. Lost packets may be indicated to the evaluation service directly by the data link layer entity (e.g. if they are discarded by the data link layer protocol).

The data link layer may comprise several protocol entities connected via protocol primitives itself. However, this is protocol dependent and therefore not displayed. For better readability .conf and .resp primitives have been omitted in Figure 5-18. Note also, that the figure presents a simplified view. In the actual protocol simulations several sender and receiver entities may be present.

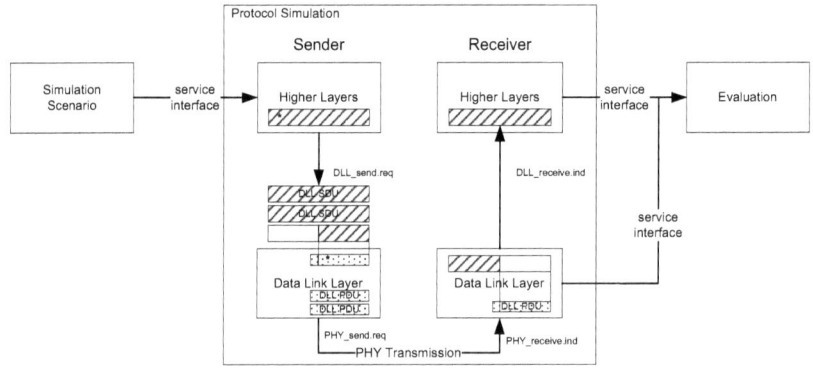

Figure 5-18: Use of primitives and PDUs in the protocol simulation.

The evaluation of the protocol performance is partially influenced by the air traffic model and the protocol implementation. Sending and receiving data packets takes a finite amount of simulation time. An aircraft may leave the simulation within this interval, that is, during an ongoing transmission. For this reason the simulation scenarios were extended by a lead time and follow-up time to capture such packets. The lead time was chosen long enough to allow the aircraft-stations to join the network. The follow-up time was chosen to be the highest latency requirement of Table 5-12. Packets received after this time interval would be expired in any case.

5.6 Evaluation

Evaluation criteria for design goals can either be quantitative and measurable criteria or objective qualitative criteria. The Communications Operating Concepts and Requirements *COCR* document [46], which was an output of AP17 technical task 2, defined measurable criteria for one-way latency (TD95-FRS), continuity, integrity, and availability. These criteria define the target parameters of the FRS design.

The TT95-FRS latency criterion can be applied directly here: The availability criterion refers to the reliability of the hardware, the integrity criterion refers to the strength of the applied error detection, and the continuity criterion refers to the reliability of the communication service.

Measuring the reliability of hardware is clearly out of the scope of this thesis. Measurement results on the strength of the B-AMC error detection are published in [50]. Availability and integrity are therefore not discussed in this thesis.

The evaluation criteria for *responsiveness* are defined in the COCR document for the detailed simulation scenarios as TD95-FRS [46]. They are defined in terms of requirements for the 95% percentile of the one-way latency of the different service classes. One-way latency is measured as the time from the submission of a packet to the FRS by the higher layers of the sender to the reception of the packet by the higher layers of the receiver. This includes the delays caused by possible retransmissions in the FRS due to lost packets as well as queuing.

In addition to the required maximum 95% percentile of the one-way latency [46] states an expiration time for each service: The expiration time is the interval of time after which a message should be considered as lost even if it is successfully received later. Within Table 5-12 the requirements for the "DG" service classes, covering unicast air-ground communication, are cited.

Table 5-12: DG one-way latency requirements (cited from [46]).

Class of Service (CoS)	Expiration Time (ET) (s)	95% percentile (TD95-FRS) (s)	Service Type
DG-A	-	9.8	NET
DG-B	1.6	0.74	ATS air-ground data
DG-C	5.0	1.4	
DG-D	7.8	2.4	
DG-E	8.0	3.8	
DG-F	12.0	4.7	
DG-G	24.0	9.2	
DG-H	32.0	13.6	
DG-I	57.6	26.5	
DG-J	-	13.6	AOC air-ground data
DG-K	-	26.5	
DG-L	-	51.7	

Analogue to the unicast service classes [46] defines broadcast service classes. Broadcast can either mean air-to-air broadcast (service class "DA") or ground-to-air broadcast (service class "DB"). Only the ground-to-air broadcast service classes will be considered in the presented evaluations. The requirements for the DB service classes are cited in Table 5-13.

Table 5-13: DB one-way latency requirements (cited from [46]).

Class of Service (CoS)	Expiration Time (ET) (s)	95% percentile (TD95-FRS) (s)	Service Type
DB-A	3.2	0.4	ATS ground-to-air broadcast
DB-B	4.8	1.2	
DB-C	8.0	1.2	
DB-D	3.2	1.2	
DB-E	8.0	1.2	
DB-F	16.0	1.2	

The "DA" service classes, identifying requirements for air-to-air broadcast, are out of the scope of our evaluations and thus omitted here.

It should be noted, that there is no further definition of the term "service classes" in the COCR report [46] than the displayed latency and continuity requirements below. In fact, the service classes are defined according to these.

The TD95-FRS requirements can also be applied to each COCR service separately. The relevant tables mapping services to service classes can be found [46] are not cited here. The fulfillment of per-service requirements is indicated where appropriate.

From these requirements we can derive two quantitative and one qualitative evaluation criterion:

- Ground-to-air (FL) one-way latency of user-data.
- Air-to-ground (RL) one-way latency of user-data.
- Do the 95%-percentile values of the one-way latency satisfy the requirements of Table 5-12 and Table 5-13: yes/no?

The quantitative evaluation criteria for *reliability* are defined in [46] and [45] in terms of service continuity. Service continuity is defined as the probability that a data transfer will be completed without experiencing anomalous behavior. Possible anomalous behavior includes the loss or duplication of messages or the delivery of messages after the stated expiration time which is counted as a logical loss. For the detailed evaluation scenarios the COCR report states continuity requirements for each class of service as displayed in Table 5-14 and Table 5-15. Note that service classes with the same continuity requirement may differ in other requirements (e.g. latency).

Table 5-14: DG continuity requirements (cited from [46]).

Class of Service (CoS)	Continuity (%)	Service Type
DG-A	-	NET
DG-B	99.999992	ATS air-ground data
DG-C	99.96	
DG-D	99.96	
DG-E	99.96	
DG-F	99.96	
DG-G	99.96	
DG-H	99.96	
DG-I	99.96	
DG-J	-	AOC air-ground data
DG-K	-	
DG-L	-	

Just like in the case of the TD95-FRS requirements the continuity requirements are given separately for the unicast and broadcast service classes.

Table 5-15: DB continuity requirements (cited from [46]).

Class of Service (CoS)	Continuity (%)	Service Type
DB-A	99.996	ATS ground-to-air broadcast
DB-B	99.96	
DB-C	99.96	
DB-D	99.996	
DB-E	99.996	
DB-F	99.996	

From these requirements the author derived two quantitative and one qualitative evaluation criterion:

- Continuity of addressed user-data.
- Continuity of broadcast user-data.
- Does the system continuity satisfy the requirements of Table 5-14 and Table 5-15: yes/no?

There are no qualitative requirements defined for *efficiency* in [46]. Thus it is measured only quantitatively: Channel utilization is defined as the fraction of time, the physical channel is either completely or partially occupied. Channel efficiency is defined as the ratio of the number of bits that can be transmitted over the channel (which is defined by the net rate of the physical layer) to the transmitted user data in bits without taking FRS overhead into account. The interface queue length indicates the amount of data that has not yet been transmitted. High queue lengths indicate congestion. Fairness of the resource distribution algorithm is evaluated quantitatively according to Jain's fairness index [58].

- Ground-to-air (FL) channel utilization.
- Air-to-ground (RL) channel utilization.
- Ground-to-air (FL) channel efficiency.
- Air-to-ground (RL) channel efficiency.
- Interface queue length.
- Resource distribution fairness.

Scalability is evaluated according to the simplified evaluation scenarios defined in section 5.3 and the quality of service requirements defined in section 4.6 of [45]. The quality of service requirements are defined in terms of continuity and the 95% percentile of the one-way latency for each traffic volume type.

Table 5-16: Quality of Service Requirements for simplified evaluation scenarios (cited from [45]).

Scenario	Without A-EXEC		with A-EXEC	
	TT_{95}-1 way (s)	Continuity (%)	TT_{95}-1 way (s)	Continuity (%)
APT	1.4	99.96	-	99.999992
TMA	1.4	99.96	0.74	99.999992
ENR	1.4	99.96	0.74	99.999992
ORP	5.9	99.96	-	99.999992
AOA	1.4	99.96	-	99.999992

The following qualitative evaluation criteria can therefore be derived:

- Does the system fulfill the latency requirements of Table 5-16 in all applicable scenarios: yes/no?
- Does the system provide the required level of continuity of Table 5-16 in all applicable scenarios: yes/no?

Resilience is particularly hard to measure. For this reason it is necessary to resort to a qualitative analysis of the system behavior in this case. This analysis was performed according to the two questions formulated below:

- How does the system performance change with rising numbers of users?
- How does the system performance change under rising user data load?

Responsiveness, reliability and efficiency are evaluated using the detailed evaluation scenario defined in section 5.4. Scalability is evaluated using the simplified simulation scenarios of section 5.3. Resilience is evaluated using custom simulation scenarios taking critical values of the protocol into account.

Each simulation is performed ten times with different random seeds. All values of interest are estimated by the mean of these ten measurements. 95% confidence intervals are calculated according to DIN 1319-3 (see appendix 9.2). The evaluation service measures the following values:

Offered load: The offered load is measured as the amount of data or the number of packets that shall be transmitted by the system.

Throughput: Throughput is measured as the amount of data or the number of packets that were successfully received. Expired packets are not included.

Loss: Loss is measured as the amount of data or the amount of packets that were not successfully received i.e. loss is the difference between offered load and throughput.

Latency: The one-way latency of a data packet is calculated as the time between the creation of the packet and its successful reception.

Continuity: The percentage of packets that is not lost, duplicated or expired.

Channel utilization: Channel utilization is defined as the ratio to which the physical channel is occupied.

Channel efficiency: Channel efficiency is defined as the ratio of the user data throughput to the physical layer offered load not including forward error correction.

Queue length: The queue length is measure as the amount of data or the number of packets waiting in the interface queue of the FRS.

6 Future Terrestrial Digital Aeronautical Communication Systems

This chapter presents the main results of the author's research. It is divided into three parts: Section 6.1 analyses the findings of the B-VHF study which provided the motivation for the further work. Chapter 6.2 discusses the analysis, design and evaluation of the B-AMC protocol. Chapter 6.3 discusses the analysis, design, and evaluation of L-DACS 1.

The author's main contribution to the B-VHF research was the formal analysis of the medium access protocols and the identification of serious design issues of the approach for safety related systems.

The author's major contribution to the development of B-AMC was the analysis and design of the medium access approach. The B-AMC medium access approach built on the lessons learnt from the analysis of the B-VHF protocol. The B-VHF approach was based on random access slots. However, in order to cope with significant numbers of users B-VHF required high numbers of slots, but even so the latency would rise sharply under high load. In addition to the poor performance the second problem of the random access based approach was that it was essentially non-deterministic, which posed a major problem for a safety-related system. The medium access latency depended on the number of medium access attempts of the aircraft-stations i.e. the system performance was determined by the application's data traffic pattern, which is neither predictable nor under the control of the system. B-AMC medium access was therefore based on a new approach devised by the author to solve these problems. It was designed to provide dependable medium access to a high number of users without any dependency of the access latency on the data traffic pattern. This was realized by the introduction of a dedicated and periodic control channel for each aircraft-station. The aircraft-stations use this channel to provide the ground-station with periodic updates on their resource needs. This decouples the medium access algorithm from the data traffic pattern. Providing dedicated resources for each control channel makes medium access contention-free. The medium access latency is therefore only coupled to the number of aircraft-stations served by the ground-station.

The author's major contribution to the L-DACS 1 research was the complete re-design of the user plane LLC protocols[40]. The HDLC based sliding window protocol of B-AMC was replaced by a two-layer credit-based ARQ protocol. The sending window management was simplified by coupling it to the central resource management of the ground-station. The ground-station has a complete view of all resource needs in the system as it collects the resource requests of all users. Consequently the size of the resource allocation is also the optimal DLS transmission window size making near to

---

[40] Note that the original B-AMC LLC user plane protocols were also designed by the author. This is discussed in section 6.2.4.

optimal flow management possible. In addition to the improved flow management, the DLS protocol operates now in fixed timing relations to the MAC frame structure to achieve near to optimal timer management.

The author's contributions to the B-VHF, B-AMC and L-DACS 1 protocol design resulted in an initial protocol specification which is considered ready for prototyping. The relevance of the author's innovations is further underlined by the adoption of key concepts of his work within the competing L-DACS 2 technology proposal.

6.1 Broadband-VHF

This section intends to give a motivation for the development of the B-AMC and L-DACS 1 medium access algorithms by reviewing the B-VHF medium access approach. The analysis of the reasons behind the failure of B-VHF to provide reliable data communication with the quality of service characteristics required for a safety related system provided the basis for the later protocol designs.

The main goal of the B-VHF project [13][14][15][16][17][18] was to verify the feasibility of a multi-carrier based overlay system for future voice-based air traffic control *ATC* communications in the VHF band. This concept was later superseded by the data-based ATM concepts supported by B-AMC and L-DACS 1. The B-VHF system concept aimed to coexist with existing VHF systems in the same frequency band. This approach should enable an in-band transition from the current to a future ATC communications system and the reuse of the protected VHF band.

B-VHF supported two types of communication: The protocol was designed to provide native support for digital voice communication and optionally to provide a general purpose digital data link, too. While each of these transmission modes can be used on its own, the protocol supported the simultaneous operation of both modes. This was accomplished by combining the multi-carrier characteristic of the B-VHF system with a time-division multiple-access *TDMA* scheme. The TDMA framing was under the control of a ground-station managing all B-VHF communication within a designated area, called a B-VHF cell. Within this cell direct communication occurs only between aircraft and the ground-station. Aircraft to aircraft communication is established indirectly via the ground-station using a relay mechanism.

The primary design goal of B-VHF was to transparently support digital voice communication in entire ATC sectors. If a sector is covered by a single cell the B-VHF data link directly supported this mode of voice communication. In the case that an ATC sector is covered by more than one B-VHF cell, the logically equivalent voice channels of all relevant cells had to be interconnected via permanent virtual circuits in the ground network.

The secondary design goal for the B-VHF system was to support existing data link applications and to be adaptable to new data protocols. Consequently, the B-VHF interface to the upper layers was designed to support the ATN/OSI and ATN/IPS protocol stacks. However, the data link layer protocol was not optimized for this type of operation.

The author's main contribution to the B-VHF research was the formal analysis of the medium access protocols and the identification of serious design issues (non-determinism, dependence on the data traffic pattern) of the approach for safety related communication.

6.1.1 System Architecture

The B-VHF protocol stack is displayed in Figure 6-1. It is structured into a medium access control sub-layer and a logical link control sub-layer.

The Medium Access Control *MAC* entity in the medium access control sub-layer provides access to the physical layer. The MAC entity employs a centralized reservation approach where the ground-station coordinates and administrates aircraft-station access to the shared medium. The B-VHF Special Service *BSS* entity provides scheduling and resource management for data transmissions.

The Data Link Service *DLS* entity in the logical link control sub-layer is responsible for frame exchange, frame processing, error detection and recovery. The DLS uses the HDLC protocol [59]. The Link Management Entity *LME* controls link establishment and maintenance between peer DLS sub-layers. It coordinates cell-entry, cell-exit, automatic handover, manual ATC sector handover, and failure handling procedures.

The Voice Interface *VI* provides support for digital voice channels. It communicates directly with the MAC entity i.e. the BSS can only manage quality of service between different data applications.

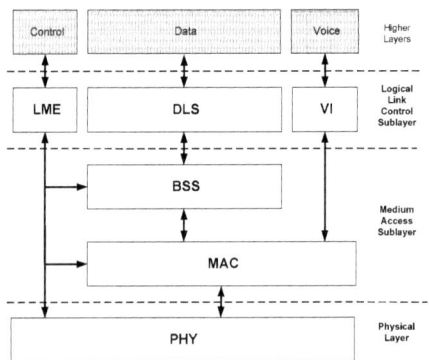

Figure 6-1: B-VHF protocol stack.

6.1.2 Physical Layer Overview

B-VHF investigated and demonstrated the feasibility of a multi-carrier based wideband communication system to support aeronautical communications while operating as an overlay system in the VHF COM band. An overlay system utilizes unused frequencies of other systems operating in the same band. It does not require dedicated spectrum on its own. This section provides a high-level overview of the B-VHF physical layer. Further documentation can be found in [60].

6.1.2.1 Overlay Co-Existence in the VHF-Band

For realizing the coexistence of the B-VHF system and legacy VHF systems in the same frequency band the B-VHF system employed an *overlay concept* as illustrated in Figure 6-2 and explained below.

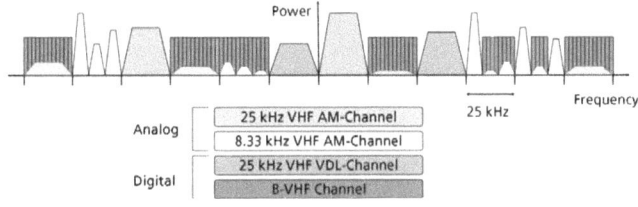

Figure 6-2: B-VHF overlay concept. [18]

The motivation for this overlay approach was, that spectral measurements showed that not all channels in the VHF band are occupied at all times and locations [61]: The frequency planning for the legacy VHF systems introduces a certain amount of unused channels. This frequency gaps could be used by the B-VHF system.

This was realized with orthogonal frequency division multiplexing *OFDM* based modulation techniques[41]. With OFDM, the B-VHF spectrum could be flexibly adapted to the changing spectrum allocations by turning on and off OFDM subcarriers (cf. Figure 6-2). For a more detailed description of the overlay concept and the applied transmission techniques refer to [62].

6.1.2.2 Modulation

The key parameters of the B-VHF system are summarized in [18]. It used up to 480 OFDM sub-carriers within one 1 MHz VHF channel. Not all of these sub-carriers were used for data or voice transmission. Several sub-carriers were used as guard bands or cancellation carriers to reduce the interference towards the legacy systems in the VHF band. Assuming that all 480 subcarriers are available for the B-VHF system (i.e. there are no legacy VHF systems in the area) and considering all overheads in an OFDM transmission frame as well as in the B-VHF frame structure the provided data rate can

---

[41] The B-VHF reverse link used OFDM. The forward link (which is not relevant in this context) used MC-CDMA.

be calculated. If uncoded voice is transmitted a total data rate of 312 kbit/s can be achieved in each direction (FL and RL) using QPSK modulation (i.e. sixty 5.2 kbit/s voice channels).

6.1.2.3 B-VHF Laboratory Test-Bed

For demonstration purposes a laboratory test-bed of the B-VHF physical layer with 128 subcarriers was implemented by the Institute for Communication and Navigation of the German Aerospace Center (Deutsches Zentrum für Luft und Raumfahrt *DLR*). 112 subcarriers were used for transmission and 8 subcarriers on each side of the transmission spectrum served as a guard band. Figure 6-3 shows on the left side measurements of the spectrum of the B-VHF system with a 50 kHz wide frequency gap for a legacy VHF system. The right side of the figure shows the time alteration of the spectrum, beautifully displaying the frame structure with the synchronization symbols and the pilot symbols.

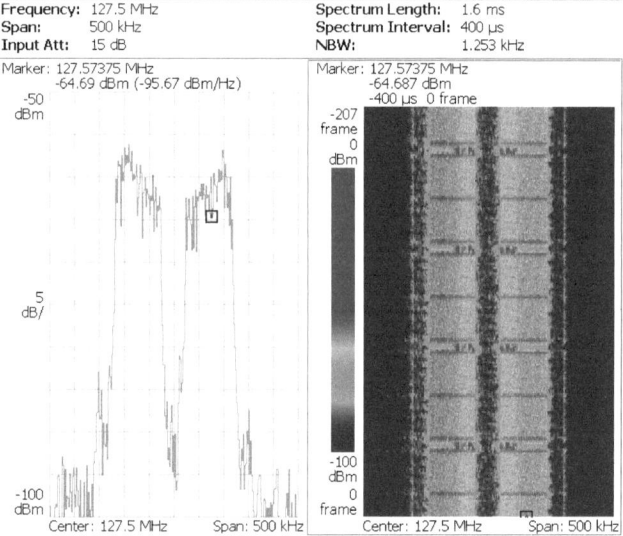

Figure 6-3: B-VHF physical layer demonstrator [18]. Note the frequency gap for a legacy VHF system.

On top of the physical layer test-bed a hardware implementation of the AMBE ATC10B vocoder[42] was used to demonstrate the voice communication capabilities of the B-VHF system. An in depth discussion of the B-VHF laboratory test-bed can be found in [63].

---

[42] The author contributed the voice protocol stack to this work.

6.1.3 Medium Access Sub-Layer

The remainder of this chapter provides an analysis of the B-VHF medium access algorithm. This analysis was performed by the author with the focus on data transmissions in order to identify the deficiencies of the B-VHF medium access approach that were later addressed in his work on B-AMC and L-DACS 1. Voice circuit[43] setup is not discussed here.

6.1.3.1 Frame Structure

The B-VHF timing structure is organized as a sequence of super frames. Each super frame (Figure 6-4) has a length of 240 milliseconds and starts with a broadcast slot *BC* followed by two odd and two even multi frames *MF*. The BC slot is used by the ground-station for the public announcement of management data related to its cell. The multi-frames consist of three different slot types. Each slot type is associated with a link direction. The Forward Link *FL* slot is used for ground to air communication, the Reverse Link *RL* slot for air to ground transmission. The length of the B-VHF super-frame was set to 240 milliseconds to be compatible with the frame length of the AMBE-ATC10B vocoder (60 milliseconds; i.e. three 20 millisecond samples).

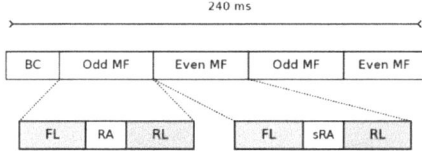

Figure 6-4: B-VHF super-frame.

Each multi-frame contains a FL slot and a RL slot. These slots are reserved for user data and extra management information not transmitted in the BC slot. Both of these slots are under the authority of the ground-station: An aircraft-station wishing to send data frames has to make a reservation with the ground-station first.

Each odd multi-frame contains a random access *RA* slot, used for the synchronization of newly arriving aircraft by the exchange of net entry messages between the aircraft-station and ground-station. The even multi-frames contain a synchronized random access *sRA* slot, which is used for medium access on the RL. Aircraft-stations have to request resources in this slot before they are allowed to transmit data. If the aircraft-station succeeds in issuing a resource request in this slot, the ground-station may grant the desired resources by sending a resource grant message in one of the FL slots. The internal structure of the sRA is discussed below.

---

[43] Voice circuits were realized by reserving OFDM sub-carriers, reducing the size of the channel available for data transmissions.

For each of the time slots different kinds of physical channels are used. If the available spectrum (i.e. number of active sub-carriers, which is determined by the size of the VHF spectrum gaps) allows the usage of multiple physical channels, appropriate channels may be combined to increase the total capacity of the respective time slot (i.e. each slot combines as many sub-carriers as possible).

6.1.3.2 Medium Access Approach

The B-VHF system follows a bandwidth on demand scheme. Aircraft-stations have to request channel resources from the ground-station before sending on the RL. In order to receive a resource allocation an aircraft-station has to issue a reservation requests in one of the sRA slots using a random delay counter algorithm (described in the next section). The ground-station centrally coordinates all received resource requests for the RL according to their priority and issues grants on the FL.

Each sRA is internally decomposed into R random access slots. The exact number of random access slots per sRA and their physical layer representation were not specified in the B-VHF project and depend on the number of available sub-carriers. Thus the original focus of the author's analysis of the medium access performance was to determine the MAC protocol behavior in the general case, to determine possible working points for the data mode of B-VHF.

6.1.3.3 Medium Access Algorithm

The B-VHF medium access algorithm collects information on required resources in each aircraft. Once the aircraft has determined its needs it waits for the next super-frame to issue a resource request. This may be a request for a reserved allocation or for on-demand resources.

In this super-frame the aircraft-station selects a sRA random access slot according to the random delay counter algorithm and puts the resource request on the channel. In case of successful reception of the resource request by the ground-station the aircraft will receive an answer in the same or the next super-frame in one of the four forward link slots. If a "resource granted" message was not received within the specified time, the aircraft has to wait for the next super-frame before it can start another attempt. The medium access algorithm of the B-VHF data mode is illustrated in Figure 6-5.

For better performance each aircraft is assigned to one of two user groups. Each group is holding the exclusive right to use one particular sRA slot (sR1 or sR2), which effectively halves the number of users competing for sRA random access slots. Figure 6-5 displays how user groups are mapped to the channels. The first RL and FL slot in the super-frame are not directly preceded by a sRA slot and may be used to process queued resource requests (labeled "extra response" and "extra resources" in the figure).

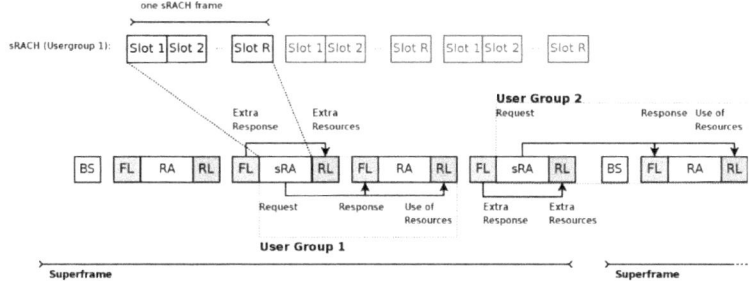

Figure 6-5: B-VHF medium access algorithm.

6.1.3.4 Medium Access Performance Analysis

The random delay counter algorithm is a variant of the slotted ALOHA algorithm. Slotted ALOHA is one of the simplest medium access algorithms. An aircraft wishing to send just transmits its message. If it was not successful, it waits for a random number of slots, but not longer than an upper bound of R slots, and then it tries again.

The random delay counter algorithm RDLC is only slightly more complex. This algorithm is organized in rounds of R slots. Each aircraft willing to send is allowed to do so only once per round. For this purpose it randomly chooses one specific slot r of the R slots and uses it for transmission. In all other slots of the round it has to remain silent.

In the case of B-VHF the number of random access slots R per sRA was investigated. The project did not make a final recommendation on this parameter. However, the author's analytical model to derive the number of random access slots R for a given traffic pattern with u competing users is given in section 9.4 in the appendix. It was the original goal of this derivation to relate the number of random access slots to the B-VHF medium access performance in order to derive the minimum number of random access slots necessary to fulfill the latency requirements. The same analytical model provides also a motivation for the use of RDLC instead of standard slotted ALOHA.

In order to analyze the impact of the number of random access slots R on the medium access performance we need a formal model of the B-VHF medium access algorithm: First it is needed to calculate the probability of sending a resource request successfully in the presence of u competing aircraft (1 specific aircraft + u others). In order not to suffer from a collision, no other aircraft may be sending in the same slot. As the probability to find one other aircraft sending in a specific slot is 1/R for RDLC by design we define

$$p_{succ}(u) = \left(1 - \frac{1}{R}\right)^u \text{ and}$$

$$p'_{succ}(u) = 1 - p_{succ}(u) \text{ for } u \in N$$

where p_{succ} is the probability of sending a resource request successfully in the presence of u competing aircraft, and p'_{succ} is the probability of sending a resource request unsuccessfully in the presence of u competing aircraft.

This gives the probabilities for sending successfully or not (if the aircraft decided to send) [44] assuming that all aircraft use the same setting for the parameter R and that the number of competing users u is constant. Note that the number of aircraft competing for resources u is not necessarily equal to the number of aircraft per cell n, although $u \leq n$ certainly.

Let X_t be a random variable describing the state of the RDLC process of the selected aircraft after each round of R slots (*Successful, Collision*). The probability of this variable assuming the state *Successful* is the completion rate ρ_t at time t.

$$\rho_t = P(X_t = Successful) \text{ for } 1 \leq t.$$

The completion rate can be calculated by

$$\rho_t = \sum_{1 \leq i \leq t} p_{succ} \, (p'_{succ})^{i-1}$$

which is the probability for exactly $t - 1$ unsuccessful attempts and one successful RDLC attempt.

Let Y be a random variable yielding the round (i.e. sRA slot) in which the aircraft sends successfully. Then $P(Y = t)$ is the probability that the aircraft sends successfully in round t and ρ_t becomes the distribution function $\rho_t = F_Y(t) = P(Y \leq t)$ of Y.

The average medium access latency l (i.e. expected waiting time until success) is then

$$l(u, R) = E(Y) = \sum_{1 \leq t} t \, P(Y \geq t) \approx \sum_{1 \leq t} t \, (1 - \rho_t) = \sum_{1 \leq t} t \, (1 - P(X_t = Successful))$$

Note that the time is given in discrete rounds of R slots, but can be mapped to real time easily using the frame structure. If the length of the B-VHF super frame is given by S (where $S=240$ ms) the average medium access latency is then given by

---

[44] This is analog to computing the probability of sending successfully in one round, which can be calculated by

$$p_{succ}(u) = \left(\frac{R - 1}{R}\right)^u$$

being the probability that all competing users chose one of the $R - 1$ other slots (i.e. not my slot).

$$l(u,R)S + S/2$$

The last term accounts for the average waiting time until the start of the next sRA slot.

The right side of Figure 6-6 presents the results of this model for an "En Route 2015" scenario[45] with high (PIAC 250; $u=19$), medium (PIAC 175; $u=9$), and low (PIAC 100; $u=3$) cell population from [64]. The calculation of u from the PIAC for the given traffic pattern is also described in this document. The expected medium access delay increases almost exponentially when the amount of available slots decreases. Comparison with the left side of the figure shows that the analytical results and simulation results correlate very well (over 0.94 correlation).

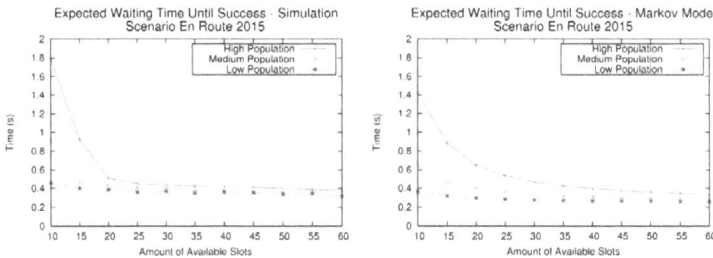

Figure 6-6: B-VHF medium access latency $l(u,R)$ (simulation and analytical model).

These results show clearly that the performance of the RDLC medium access algorithm degrades significantly under excessive load. In addition, the B-VHF simulation results of [64] and [65] indicate that the bandwidth utilization (i.e. the usable bandwidth) drops significantly, if the expected waiting time for successful medium access exceeds a certain threshold. This increases the end-to-end latency significantly. The simulation based protocol evaluation in [64] and [65] showed that B-VHF did indeed not fulfill the quality of service requirements in all scenarios[46].

Figure 6-7 shows the calculated expected waiting time until successful medium access (the time it takes until a sRA message is delivered successfully from aircraft-station to ground-station; the data transmission time is not taken into account) for up to 250 users split into two user groups. This calculation was conducted assuming 216, 108, 54, and 26 access slots per super-frame (i.e. $R=108, 54, 27, 13$). 108 random access slots was the maximum number of random access slots considered per sRA in the B-VHF

---

[45] The B-VHF performance evaluation did not use the evaluation scenarios defined in [41] and [40] that are described in section 5.3 and section 5.4 as they were not available at that time.

[46] The simulation results of [64] indicated that the effective drop in usable bandwidth requires the use of advanced modulation schemes like QAM-64, which may not always be possible under interference.

project[47] i.e. *l(u, 108)* gives the optimal B-VHF medium access performance. The x-axis shows the number of users *u* trying to transmit concurrently.

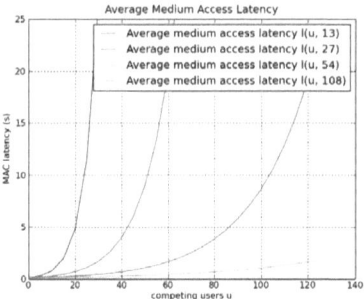

Figure 6-7: B-VHF medium access latency *l(u,R)* for R=108, 54, 27, and 13.

Although the average number of concurrent medium accesses was rather low in the investigated evaluation scenarios (less than 20), it should be noted that *u* is not constant in realistic traffic patterns with high peak to average ratios (up to 4 on the RL cf. section 5.4.2). During bursts of activity *u* may rise significantly above the average value i.e. the B-VHF medium access algorithm performs worst, where it is needed most.

6.1.4 Discussion of B-VHF

In order to cope with significant numbers of users B-VHF requires high numbers of random access slots, which may not always be available due to spectrum constraints. But even with the maximum number of random access slots the medium access latency may rise sharply under high load.

From the perspective of resilience and reliability the main problem of B-VHF medium access is that it is essentially non-deterministic. This poses a major problem for a safety-related system. The B-VHF medium access latency depends on the number of medium access attempts made by the aircraft-stations i.e. the system performance is determined by the application's data traffic pattern, which is hardly predictable and (even more importantly) not under the control of the system.

This result is not surprising if it is taken into account that B-VHF was primarily designed as a digital voice system (where it did deliver excellent performance). However, in order to support the data-link based ATM concepts of the future a different approach to medium access was necessary.

---

[47] It should be noted, however, that the spectrum measurements indicated that 50% of this value is more realistic (due to channels occupied by legacy systems). In addition the width of the channel would be further reduced by sub-carriers reserved for voice circuits.

6.2 Broadband Aeronautical Multicarrier Communication

After the B-VHF project it became clear that the future European ATM system would require broadband data communications rather than additional voice services. In addition, EUROCONTROL favored the L-band over the VHF band now (cf. section 3.1) therefore it was the primary design goal of the Broadband Aeronautical Multicarrier Communication **B-AMC** study to adapt the B-VHF system to L-band conditions and to redesign the data link layer to optimally support data communications. Both tasks were performed on the basis of the lessons learnt from B-VHF.

B-AMC was designed to support air-ground communication as well as direct air-air communication, a feature which did not exist in B-VHF. Air-ground communication is managed by a master ground-station while direct air-air communication is performed without using a ground relay. These two communication capabilities have different scopes[48] and are realized in two separate radio modes. In this thesis, only the air-ground mode is discussed. The key design objective of the air-ground mode was the optimization of B-AMC for data communication while keeping support for digital voice. The operation of the system should be completely transparent with automatic handovers between radio cells. The system should support operational aeronautical communication i.e. Air Traffic Services **ATS** and Aeronautical Operational Control **AOC** communications.

The B-AMC study covered a wide range of activities not all of which are discussed within this thesis. The main subjects of the B-AMC redesign in the context of this thesis are the issue of medium access and user plane quality of service. Details on other aspects of the system can be found in the B-AMC project documentation [50][52][66][67][68][69][70][71][72][73] and the relevant publications [19][20][21][22][23][24]. Note that B-AMC was a design study concentrating on critical issues and did not intend to create a complete system specification i.e. several non-critical aspects of the system were only covered by working hypotheses and not investigated in detail.

The B-AMC physical layer operates in the in the L-band from 960 MHz to 1215 MHz[49]. It is a broadband multi-carrier system using Orthogonal Frequency-Division Multiplexing **OFDM**. Like B-VHF B-AMC was designed to share its radio spectrum with other, already existing systems i.e. B-AMC does not need the allocation of new blocks of spectrum, but can be used in already assigned ones. However, contrary to B-

---

[48] The focus of the air-ground mode is the support of ATN/OSI and ATN/IPS addressed data communication. The air-air mode focuses on broadcast surveillance transmissions and a few related addressed services which are expected for the distant future [41].

[49] The term L-band is sometimes used to denote slightly different parts of the radio spectrum. Within this document it will always be used to denote the range form 960 MHz to 1215 MHz that has been assigned to Aeronautical Radio Navigation by the ITU [77].

VHF, which employed an OFDM based overlay approach, B-AMC is an inlay system (see section 6.2.2).

In the data link layer the B-AMC medium access protocol was the author's major innovation in this development step. The B-AMC data link layer protocol was designed to provide deterministic contention-free medium access for resource requests, to support deterministic centralized resource allocations with several levels of priority, and to allow for link layer multiplexing of transmissions to avoid head of line blocking.

The split of the medium access procedure into request and allocation in B-VHF was retained in the B-AMC design. This concept, known as bandwidth-on-demand or Demand Assigned Multiple Access DAMA (although this term is more common in the context of satellite systems), is widely deployed in contemporary packet radio networks. However, the need for contention-free deterministic medium access (which is new in this context) was a lesson learnt from the B-VHF project: The resource request latency should be controllable by the system and not depend on the data traffic pattern. Instead, the B-AMC resource request latency should only depend on number of registered users. Note that the number of users in the cell can be controlled by the ground-station via the cell-entry procedure.

Bandwidth-on-demand systems require the coordinated allocation of resources. This coordination can either be distributed or centralized. Centralized resource allocation is simpler to implement and supports deterministic resource allocations. However, it is not possible for the aircraft-station to send detailed resource requests to often without unreasonably increasing the management overhead. Thus, a distributed system may have more accurate and newer information on the current resource needs. In the B-AMC protocol design the author made the decision to follow a hybrid approach: The resource allocation between different users shall be performed centralized by the ground-station. The resource distribution between packets of different priorities shall be performed locally by each user[50].

The existence of large AOC messages posed an additional problem: A large message of low priority may block the data link for a significant time preventing the timely delivery of high-priority ATM messages. This issue is known as head-of-line-blocking. To avoid head-of-line-blocking it was decided that the B-AMC protocol should offer the possibility to transparently multiplex several on-going user data transmissions (i.e. to suspend low priority transmission for high priority transmissions).

---

[50] This requires the airborne stations to transmit only the aggregated resource needs of each priority, which is possible with small messages. Sending resource requests per packet was deemed too bandwidth intensive and in contradiction to the independence of medium access from the data traffic pattern.

6.2.1 System Architecture

B-AMC is a point-to-multipoint system. It is deployed via dedicated ground-stations, each one controlling air-ground communication on its assigned radio channels and within its radio range. This is called a B-AMC cell. The air-ground mode of the B-AMC system is thus a cellular radio system.

Prior to utilizing the system an aircraft-station has to register with a ground-station and to establish dedicated logical channels for user and control data. Control channels have statically allocated bandwidth, while user channels have dynamically assigned bandwidth according to the current demand.

The B-AMC link layer topology is star shaped: Logical channels exist only between the ground-station and the aircraft. Direct transmissions between aircraft of the same cell cannot be performed without routing in the network layer. The B-AMC network topology is illustrated in Figure 6-8. Note that although the B-AMC data link layer employs some connection oriented design principles, the system was nevertheless designed for connectionless higher layer protocols.

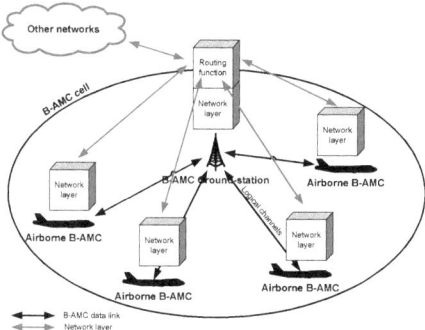

Figure 6-8: B-AMC network topology.

The B-AMC system architecture defines five major functional blocks: Link Management Entity, Data Link Service, Voice Interface, B-AMC Special Services, and Medium Access. These entities are present in the aircraft and the ground-station and communicate over logical channels as illustrated in Figure 6-9.

The Link Management Entities *LME* perform the registration (cell-entry) and deregistration (cell-exit) of aircraft with a ground-station. During cell-entry the identity and authorization of an aircraft is verified. This is conducted over the logical broadcast control channel *BCCH* (ground-station to aircraft) and the logical random access channel *RACH* (aircraft to ground-station). These two channels are special in the sense that they are permanently available to all aircraft within a cell. They do not even require the prior synchronization of the physical layer. A special case of (re-)registration is the handover form one ground-station to another, which is performed over the same logical channels as above. When there are no registration events, the link management entity uses the logical common control channel *CCH* (ground-station to aircraft) and the logical dedicated control channel *DCCH* (aircraft to ground-station) for the exchange of housekeeping information (signal power reports, etc.).

Bidirectional exchange of user data between the ground-station and the aircraft is performed by the Data Link Services **DLS** entities. Each class of service is represented by one distinct data link service entity. Different classes of service may vary in their priority, reliability and resource requirements. All DLS entities use the logical data channel **DCH** for user plane transmissions and the logical dedicated control channel **DCCH** for control plane transmissions (e.g. acknowledgements if the DLS uses ARQ for increased reliability). B-AMC offers a built in class of service for the transmission of voice streams. This service is provided by the Voice Interface **VI** entity. Voice streams are transmitted over the logical voice channel **VCH**, which is functionally equivalent to the data channel but may be shared by several users to emulate partyline communication.

The dynamic assignment of physical layer resources to logical data channels is provided by the Medium Access **MAC** entity. For ground-to-air transmissions this assignment is performed locally in the ground-station. However, air-to-ground transmissions resources have to be requested by the airborne MAC entity and are assigned by the ground-station. The air-to-ground resource allocation mechanism of the MAC entity uses the logical synchronized access channel **SACH** (aircraft to ground-station) and the common control channel **CCCH** (ground-station to aircraft) for the exchange of control information (i.e. resource requests and resource grants).

The DLS and the VI are connected to the MAC entity by the B-AMC Special Services **BSS** entity which actively manages the DLS and VI transmission queues to provide multiple classes of service. The transmission queues of the relevant logical channels are mapped to transport channels. Transport channels[51] are an abstraction for the physical layer resources that are provided by the MAC entity. The BSS provides the mapping between the VCH, DCH, and DCCH logical channels to transport channels. As this task can be performed locally, the BSS does not communicate over logical channels itself.

Note that the DCH, DCCH and SACH logical channels are point-to-point channels and require one protocol instance per aircraft in the ground-station. The voice interface VI and its logical channel VCH are shared by all aircraft, but may be present in multiple instances if more than one voice channel is configured.

---

[51] LTE uses the term "transport block" for the same concept [**84**]. L-DACS 1 uses the term PHY-SDU. Although the other terminologies are clearer, the B-AMC terminology is retained in this document for consistency with the rest of the B-AMC literature.

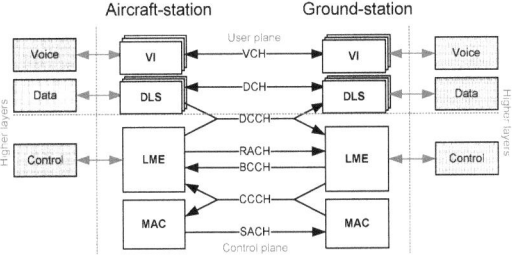

Figure 6-9: B-AMC logical channel structure.

The five functional blocks of the B-AMC data link layer architecture are organized in two sub-layers: The medium access sub-layer and the logical link control sub-layer. The logical link control sub-layer contains the Link Management Entity LME, the Data Link Services DLS, and the Voice Interface VI. The medium access sub-layer comprises the B-AMC Special Services BSS entity and the Medium ACcess MAC entity.

In order to provide its services within the stack each protocol entity performs a specific set of tasks: The LME performs the management *MGM* of the aircraft-station or ground-station. The DLS performs the segmentation and reassembly *SaR* of higher layer PDUs and provides enhance reliability using an ARQ based DLS protocol. The BSS entity provides active queue management for the MAC transmission queues enforcing quality of service *QoS*. In addition it segments and reassembles DLS PDUs to transport channels. The mapping of protocol functions to protocol entities is displayed in Figure 6-10.

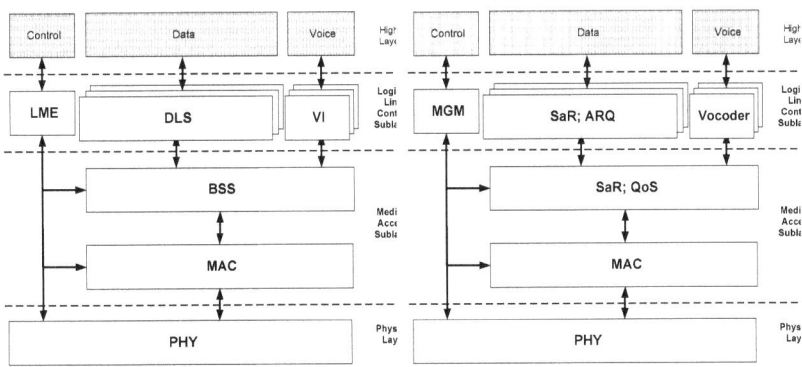

Figure 6-10: B-AMC protocol stack and functional architecture.

The VI digitizes analog speech using the AMBE ATC10B vocoder.

6.2.2 Physical Layer Overview

The B-AMC physical layer operates in the in the L-band from 960 MHz to 1215 MHz. Like many other contemporary wireless network systems it uses OFDM based radio technology. However, its particular configuration is rather unusual. As this has consequences for the design of the data link layer, the B-AMC physical layer shall be discussed in some detail here.

6.2.2.1 Radio Spectrum

The most characteristic property of the B-AMC physical layer is that it has been designed to share its radio spectrum with other, already existing systems i.e. B-AMC does not need the allocation of new blocks of spectrum, but can be used in already assigned ones. Currently there are several other systems operating in the L-band: DME, TACAN, MIDS/JTIDS, SSR/Mode-S (including TCAS and ADS-B), UAT and GNSS. These systems must not be disturbed in their operation, thus the co-existence with existing systems was an important design goal. In fact, the provisions for spectrum co-existence had such a profound impact on the whole system that they have influenced the design at all layers. In order to understand this design it is therefore helpful to have some basic knowledge of the existing L-band infrastructure.

Distance Measuring Equipment ***DME*** is an L-band radio technology used to determine the distance of an aircraft to a DME site. The system comprises two main components: an airborne interrogator unit and a ground-based transponder site. The airborne interrogator queries the transponder which replies after a predefined time interval. The airborne unit then calculates the slant distance to the transponder site form the elapsed time between interrogation and reply. There are two types of DME, DME/N and DME/P. DME/N is widely deployed today and allows determining the distance with an accuracy of ±185 meters (± 0.1 nautical miles). DME/N transponder sites are often collocated with VHF Omnidirectional Range ***VOR*** beacons which provide bearing information to aircraft. In this case the DME frequency is coupled to the VOR frequency so that the pilot has to select only the VOR frequency. The combined VOR/DME system then allows aircraft to determine their position relative to the VOR/DME sites at up to 200 nautical miles range. Complementary to the long range VOR/DME system DME transponder sites are also used as part of the Instrument Landing System ***ILS***. In this case the DME frequencies are coupled to the ILS frequencies and the approach DME transponder is configured to have a reduced range of about 40 nautical miles. The second type of DME system, DME/P was intended as an integral part of the Microwave Landing System ***MLS*** which should have superseded the ILS. It provides distance information with a higher accuracy of ± 30 meters. However MLS was never widely deployed and ILS and MLS are now both expected to be replaced by satellite based navigation systems (abbreviated Global Navigation Satellite Systems ***GNSS***). Thus hardly any DME/P sites exist.

TACtical Air Navigation *TACAN* is the military version of the VOR/DME system. The VOR component of the system uses two frequencies instead of one providing its users with higher accuracy bearing information. The DME part of the TACAN system is compatible to the civil system. If a TACAN station is collocated with a civil VOR facility (as is often the case), it is referred to as VORTAC facility. In this case an additional DME unit is not necessary, as civil aircraft can use the DME component of the TACAN station. TACAN transponders are sometimes installed on mobile units like air refueling tankers. DME and the DME component of TACAN both operate between 962 MHz and 1213 MHz.

The Multifunctional Information Distribution System *MIDS* is another military system operating in the L-band. MIDS is a NATO term, in the United States the system is known as Joint Tactical Information Distribution System *JTIDS*. It is used as the communications component of the Link-16 NATO data exchange format. Technically MIDS/JTIDS is a TDMA-based high speed (ca. 115 kbit/s) data link system, designed to be secure and resistant against jamming. It operates in 51 designated channels between 969 and 1206 MHz. (The same region as DME.) The channel allocations are not in accordance with ITU radio resource allocations and thus subject to peacetime restrictions to avoid interference with DME. There are two gaps of 45 MHz and 48 MHz in the otherwise regular channel structure (channels are allotted every 3 MHz) to protect the safety critical SSR and TCAS systems at 1030 MHz and 1090 MHz. MIDS/JTIDS itself is not sensitive to interference as it implements a sophisticated frequency hopping scheme.

Secondary Surveillance Radar *SSR* is a radar technology used in air traffic control. Aircraft are equipped with transponders that are interrogated by ground-based SSR interrogators at 1030 MHz. The transponder answers at 1090 MHz and the reply is then interpreted by the interrogator unit to determine the range and bearing of the aircraft. (As SSR uses directed interrogation beams it can be envisaged as a reverse VOR/DME system.) Content and sophistication of the reply depend on the mode of the transponder. In civil aviation the modes A, C and S are used. Military aircraft commonly use other modes for Identification Friend or Foe *IFF* purposes. A Mode-A transponder reply contains an octal four digit aircraft identification code previously assigned by the controller. Mode-C replies contain the pressure altitude of the aircraft. Mode-S is the currently most advanced transponder mode. It allows interrogating specific aircraft according to their 24 bit ICAO address. (S stands for "selective".) This allows more reliable operation of SSR in congested air-space as not all aircraft in the interrogation beam will reply at the same time corrupting each other's signals. A Mode-S message may contain additional information like the aircraft position and velocity. This data is then presented to the air traffic controller as additional information on the radar screen. As much of the situational awareness of the air traffic controllers depends on the proper function of SSR, the system is regarded as safety critical.

The Traffic alert and Collision Avoidance System II *TCAS II* uses the aircraft transponder in a similar way as SSR to avoid mid-air collisions. The transponders of nearby aircraft (about 40 nautical miles range) are interrogated in regular intervals to determine a three-dimensional picture of the air traffic situation. If the system detects danger of collision the pilot is warned acoustically.

If the aircraft transponder is configured to transmit identification (24 bit ICAO aircraft address), position and velocity (both derived from GNSS) in regular intervals without being interrogated, the system can be used for cooperative surveillance. This mode of operation is called Mode-S extended squitter (also referred to as 1090ES). 1090ES is planned as physical layer for Automatic Dependent Surveillance Broadcast *ADS-B*. In Europe no official decision for 1090ES as ADS-B physical layer has been made yet. However, EUROCONTROL's CASCADE[52] program is exclusively based on 1090ES. In the United States the decision has been made to deploy ADS-B on top of two physical layers: 1090ES and UAT. The usage of 1090ES is envisaged for large aircraft operating in high altitudes. UAT shall be used in lower air spaces and by general aviation.

The Universal Access Transceiver *UAT* is a TDMA based data link specifically developed to support surveillance broadcast. Currently it supports ADS-B, TIS-B and FIS-B. It operates in single channel at 978 MHz. The introduction of ADS-B is going to be a gradual process. While new aircraft will be equipped with 1090ES or UAT transponders at the time of deployment, older aircraft will have to be retrofitted over time. To complicate matters several types of transitional ADS-B equipment exist. "ADS-B in" is only suitable to receive signals from other aircraft, while "ADS-B out" equipment will only transmit surveillance signals without receiving them. Therefore it is expected, that there will be a transition period where aircraft with different levels of ADS-B awareness have to share the air-space. However, even after the transition has been completed, ADS-B equipped aircraft will not be able to receive surveillance signals from all other aircraft nearby as they might use different physical layers (i.e. 1090ES or UAT). To alleviate this situation Traffic Information System Broadcast *TIS-B* has been devised. TIS-B is a ground based service collecting surveillance data from all available sources. This does not only include 1090ES and UAT signals, but may also include other resources like SSR and primary radar. The combined picture of the air traffic situation is then broadcast by a TIS-B ground-station to all nearby aircraft. This arrangement allows aircraft that are equipped with ADS-B in (or better) to gain complete situational awareness of the air traffic situation. Note that TIS-B need not use the same radio link as ADS-B. Flight Information System Broadcast *FIS-B* is a similar service used to broadcast additional situational information to aircraft. It contains

---

[52] The CASCADE program coordinates the deployment of ADS-B in Europe.

mostly weather reports. UAT has been specifically designed as radio link for ADS-B, TIS-B and FIS-B[53].

The upper regions of the L-band contain spectrum allocations for Global Navigation Satellite Systems *GNSS*. The frequency 1176.45 MHz is shared between the American GPS and the European GALILEO system. GALILEO has a second frequency allocation at 1207.14 MHz for enhanced accuracy. However, both signals are wideband signals, effectively covering the whole range from 1164 MHz to 1214 MHz.

A comprehensive picture of L-band radio spectrum usage is summarized in Figure 6-11. The multitude of existing systems and spectrum allocations makes it difficult to find spectrum for the safe deployment of a new system. Taking away frequencies used by safety critical surveillance systems (SSR/Mode-S and its variants at 1030 MHz and 1090 MHz; UAT at 978 MHz) and other applications of high public interest (GNSS from 1164 MHz to 1214 MHz) only spectrum regions already used by DME and MIDS/JTIDS remain. MIDS/JTIDS is a military system designed to be robust against jamming, it can therefore be expected not to suffer from B-AMC interference. Thus the main concern of the B-AMC physical layer design was the co-existence with DME.

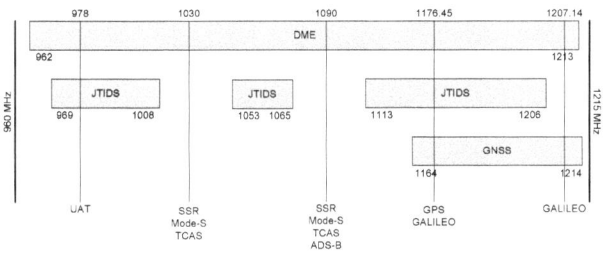

Figure 6-11: Spectrum allocations in the L-band.

6.2.2.2 Inlay Co-Existence in the L-Band
DME and the DME component of TACAN do not use the allocated spectrum en-block, but define a channel structure on it. DME channels are located at 1 MHz offsets between 962 MHz and 1213 MHz, therefore in total 252 channels are available. However, these channels are never used alone, but in a pair-wise configuration for interrogation and reply. The reply channel is always separated from the interrogation

---

[53] There are other systems that have been designed to support ADS-B and its supplements, too. However, they are either deployed in different radio bands or under development. VHF Digital Link Mode 4 *VDL4* has been designed to support ADS-B in the VHF spectrum. Currently it is deployed in several Scandinavian countries and Russia, but its deployment is not planned in other parts of the world. The list of systems under development that claim to offer some degree of ADS-B, TIS-B and FIS-B support is extensive: AMACS/L-DACS2, LDL, P34, B-AMC/L-DACS1 and several others. It should be noted that as of now UAT has not seen extensive deployment outside of the USA either.

channel by an offset of 63 MHz. Whether it is 63 MHz below or above the interrogation channel depends on the channel type. DME knows four channel types X, Y, W and Z. The channel type defines the signaling scheme and the direction of the frequency offset. DME channels are therefore designated by a channel number from 1 to 126 and the channel type (e.g. 123X). Tables for the translation form this notation to frequency pairs can be found in [**74**]. W and Z channels are only used by DME/P.

B-AMC is intended to operate in 500 KHz wide cannels located in the 1 MHz gaps between adjacent DME channels. This type of design is called an inlay system. Inlay systems and similar methods of utilizing "white"-space spectrum are an approach to frequency allocation receiving increased interest, as finding free ("green") spectrum becomes progressively more difficult. B-AMC shall cover the needs for aeronautical data communication well beyond the year 2030. Therefore it is necessary to make as much bandwidth as possible available to the system. As the L-band is already crowded by other aeronautical and military systems, an inlay concept not requiring any green spectrum is an attractive approach. A simulated B-AMC signal between two adjacent DME channels is illustrated in Figure 6-12. Note that the DME signal is pulsed and therefore not always present.

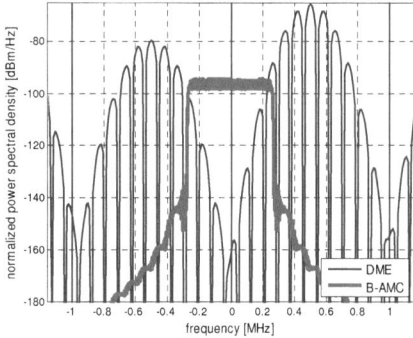

Figure 6-12: Simulated spectrum of B-AMC between two adjacent DME channels [21].

However, designing and deploying an inlay technology is a non-trivial matter as the co-existence with the legacy systems has to be ensured. The problem of co-existence can be decomposed into two parts: Interference from the inlay system towards the legacy systems and interference from the legacy systems towards the inlay system.

Naturally the new system must not disturb the operation of the existing infrastructure. The legacy systems can however not be modified, thus, the inlay system has to carry most of this burden. B-AMC uses a powerful combination of different methods for side-lobe suppression and reduction of out-of-band radiation described in [**69**] and [**75**].

The second part of the problem is to design the inlay system robust against interference from existing systems. This is a non-trivial task as many deployed legacy systems have sub-optimal interference characteristics according to modern standards. Most inlay designs therefore try to mitigate the interference of the existing system using sophisticated signal processing and error correcting codes. This is also the approach taken by B-AMC.

The two parts of the co-existence problem cannot be seen in isolation. Any approach to one of both problems has consequences for the other. Therefore it is necessary to find an integrated solution. Depending on the efficiency of the mutual interference suppression two types of inlay systems are possible: The first type is an inlay system that can be deployed completely independent of existing systems. This is an ideal case that can seldom be achieved. The second type of inlay system requires a certain level of coordination. In the case of B-AMC the assessment of the interference between B-AMC and DME has shown that both systems cannot operate reliably in directly adjacent channels [**74**]. Therefore their use has to be coordinated.

Close inspection of L-band spectrum usage reveals that the range form 962 MHz to 1025 MHz and 1150 MHz to 1213 MHz is used only for DME reply channels i.e. only the DME transponder sites will use these frequencies for transmissions. Therefore it can be assumed that a B-AMC ground-station transmitting in the same region will most likely not disturb a nearby (in terms of frequency and distance) airborne DME receiver. Consequently, as a first measure to reduce interference between both systems, B-AMC was designed as a Frequency Division Duplex ***FDD*** system[54]. The B-AMC Forward Link (***FL*** i.e. ground to air) is transmitted in the same region of spectrum as the DME reply (i.e. ground to air) channels, from 985 MHz to 1009 MHz. This respects safety margins for UAT, SSR and GNSS (cf. Figure 6-11).

Finding an appropriate spectrum allocation for the B-AMC Reverse Link (***RL*** i.e. air to ground) is less obvious as there is no region exclusively in use by DME interrogation channels. Respecting safety margins for the critical systems, two candidate intervals remain: 1048 MHz to 1072 MHz and 1111 MHz to 1135 MHz. As the first option is currently less used by DME, the B-AMC RL has been allocated in this region (1048 MHz to 1072 MHz). The second region is considered as optional extension for now. Thus 24 FL and RL channels are available for the operation of B-AMC[55].

---

[54] Another reason for the use of FDD was to avoid the large guard interval required between the FL and RL section of TDD.

[55] This document cites the original B-AMC spectrum allocation as proposed in [**66**] and [**68**]. However, in the course of further research several proposals for the extension of the spectrum have been made. In addition it was considered to reduce the channel spacing from 1 MHz to 500 KHz for more flexible frequency planning. (The extended radio spectrum is less crowded by DME.) See for instance [**52**] and [**18**].

The RL spectrum has to be shared by airborne DME and B-AMC transmitters. Therefore its usage has to be coordinated. Each DME site uses only one channel. As there are much more DME sites[56] than DME channels, DME requires a lot of internal coordination itself. The 126 DME channels have to be assigned in a sophisticated internal frequency planning process. This process tries to minimize the interference between adjacent DME transponder sites and to maximize the overall DME channel reuse.

It is an important consequence of this procedure that not all DME channels are used locally: At any given point in space only a subset of all possible channels is actually used. In order to allow both systems to operate reliably, B-AMC frequency planning tries to take advantage of this by making sure that active DME and B-AMC channels are sufficiently separated.

Frequency planning is a complex task and shall not be discussed in further detail here. A comprehensive overview of the B-AMC frequency planning approach and a draft frequency plan on the basis of DME channel allocations from 2008 can be found in [**52**].

Another problem caused by the sharing of the RL spectrum is co-site interference. It results from the fact that the RL spectrum is used by DME both for transmitting and receiving. Co-site interference is caused when the (airborne) B-AMC radio is transmitting on the RL while the airborne DME unit has tuned its receiver to a nearby DME channel. Although B-AMC has been designed to produce very little out-of-band interference, it cannot be completely avoided. In addition, as the B-AMC signal originates from the same aircraft, there is almost no attenuation, resulting in the unimpeded reception of strong interference by the DME receiver. All DME signals received in this period would be completely destroyed.

Note that co-site interference is not such a big problem if DME is sending while a B-AMC ground-station is receiving the RL as B-AMC has been designed to cope with this type of interference. However, an aircraft-station receiving the FL is also affected by co-site interference from a transmitting on-board DME. The co-location of airborne equipment and the sharing of the RL frequency space cannot be avoided; the only possible approach to mitigate co-site interference is therefore to use error correcting codes (DME interference towards B-AMC) and to avoid operating both radios at the same time (B-AMC interference towards DME).

On a historical note co-site interference is not a new problem. It has already been an issue during the development of UAT and VDL3. VDL3 was never deployed. In the

---

[56] The area around the airport Paris Charles de Gaulle has the highest density of DME stations in Europe. Within a radius of 261 nautical miles it contains 675 DME and TACAN sites as of 2008 [**52**].

case of UAT the selected solution was to introduce a suppression bus to indicate to one system that the other is transmitting. The victim system can then turn off its receiver (or take any other measure it finds appropriate) to react to the sudden increase in interference. Obviously this concept can only work if transmissions are infrequent. In the case of B-AMC a similar approach has been taken. The situation is however asymmetric as the suppression bus has to "mute" only the DME receiver while B-AMC is transmitting on the RL. Suppression in the other direction (DME to B-AMC) is not envisaged as B-AMC tries to mitigate interference from DME with error correcting codes. It should be noted though, that a low duty cycle of the B-AMC RL transmitter is a requirement for the unimpeded operation of DME. As this is not strictly a physical layer problem we will return to the discussion of the B-AMC duty cycle later.

6.2.2.3 Modulation

B-AMC is a multi-carrier system based on Orthogonal Frequency Division Multiplexing *OFDM* i.e. the B-AMC radio signal is spread over several simultaneously transmitted sub-carriers. The frequencies of these sub-carriers are chosen to be orthogonal (in the sense of functional analysis) as this eliminates inter-carrier interference without the need for guard bands. Each sub-carrier is then modulated with a conventional modulation scheme like Quadrature Phase-Shift Keying *QPSK* or Quadrature Amplitude Modulation *QAM*.

The spacing of the sub-carriers has been chosen according to the propagation properties of the L-band. In addition, carrier spacing was influenced by two further design goals: First the sub-carrier spacing has been chosen such as to assist in interference suppression: Small sub-carrier spacing results in reduced out-of-band radiation. Secondly it has been decided to use Orthogonal Frequency-Division Multiple Access *OFDMA* on the RL. OFDMA is a method of multiple-access, where each user transmits on a different OFDM sub-carrier (or several sub-carriers given that the sets are disjoint). It can therefore be seen as a distributed variant of OFDM and a special case of FDMA. The more sub-carriers are available, the more users can simultaneously access the link. Thus it was desirable to arrange for a sufficiently large number of carriers.

Under the motivation of these design goals the number of OFDM sub-carriers for B-AMC has been chosen to be 64 with a sub-carrier spacing of 10.4167 KHz. The 500 KHz wide B-AMC channel is only covered by the central 48 sub-carriers. The remaining 16 carriers are located above and below the used spectrum. Of the eight sub-carriers at each side two are used as cancelation carriers for side-lobe suppression (see [**75**] for details) and six are used as empty guard carriers. Data is transmitted as a series of OFDM symbols on the 48 data sub-carriers.

The symbol duration has been set to 120 microseconds. Of these 120 microseconds 96 are used for the actual OFDM symbol, while the remaining 24 microseconds are guard time to avoid inter-symbol interference. The large guard time is also required for transmit windowing to further reduce the interference towards other L-band systems.

Each OFDM symbol is constituted by the 48 modulation symbols of the sub-carriers. With QPSK modulation[57] two bits can be encoded per symbol and sub-carrier. Thus B-AMC offers a raw per channel data rate of 800 kbit/s at 400 kbaud. Note however, that this does not take any overhead into account. The real usable data rate is lower, as some of the symbols have to be used for synchronization and channel estimation. In addition the interference from DME requires strong error correcting codes reducing the net data rate further.

6.2.2.4 *Synchronization and Framing*
In order for an airborne radio to be able to correctly receive and transmit OFDM symbols it has to synchronize its clock with the ground station. For this purpose synchronization symbols are inserted into the FL channel every 54 symbols (6.48 milliseconds). At this rate synchronization symbols are inserted more often than necessary [**69**]. However, this allows the radio to keep synchronized even if it missed a synchronization symbol (e.g. due to interference).

Data symbols between two instances of synchronization symbols comprise one FL data OFDM frame. An FL OFDM frame has therefore a length of 54 symbols or 6.48 milliseconds and is 48 sub-carriers wide. For consistency the RL data OFDM frame is defined to have the same length, although it is not delimited by synchronization symbols. See Figure 6-13 and Figure 6-14.

It should be noted that the OFDM frame is a logical unit and has no impact on the physical layer design beyond the placing of synchronization symbols. However, OFDM frames play a role in the application of the Forward Error Correction *FEC* as frames are always encoded en-block (by convention). This is discussed in the next section.

Another challenge the B-AMC physical layer has to address is channel fading. Fading is a distortion of the radio channel caused by multi-path reception and Doppler spread. Multi-path reception is not always an issue for B-AMC, as aircraft cruising in high altitudes communicate under nearly line-of-sight conditions. However, during take-off and landing multi-path induced fading commonly occurs due to reflections of the signal on the airport buildings and the ground.

In order to reduce the effects of fading, well-known symbols (pilot symbols) are periodically inserted into the transmission for channel estimation and equalization. The

---

[57] All published assessments of the original B-AMC system have been conducted assuming QPSK modulation as this modulation is very robust under heavy interference. Other modulation schemes have been investigated in the course of further research to provide higher data rates. However it should be noted that increasingly complex modulation schemes are more susceptible to interference.

distance between pilot symbols is chosen according to the worst expected change rate of the channel in time and frequency [**69**]. In the case of B-AMC the FL pilot symbol spacing has been chosen to be 12 symbols (1.44 milliseconds) with a pilot symbol on every sub-carrier [**69**]. As the RL has no synchronization symbols, additional pilot symbols can be inserted in the RL channel. Therefore the RL symbol spacing is slightly shorter with 9 and 10 symbols (1.08 and 1.2 milliseconds). For the placement of synchronization and pilot symbols in the OFDM frames see Figure 6-13 and Figure 6-14[58].

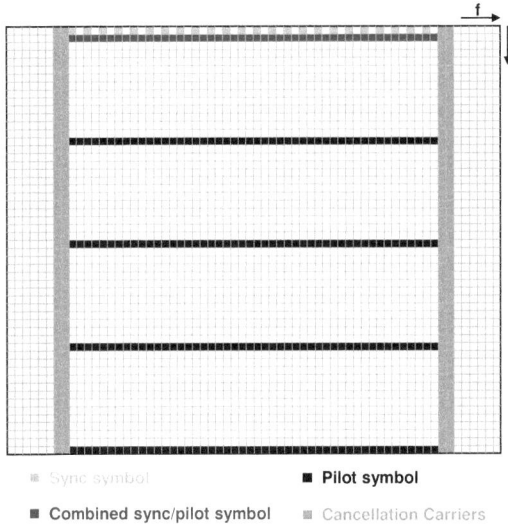

■ Sync symbol ■ **Pilot symbol**
■ **Combined sync/pilot symbol** ■ Cancellation Carriers

Figure 6-13: FL B-AMC data OFDM frame [69].

The layout of the FL and RL OFDM frames discussed and displayed above has been designed to allow airborne radios to stay synchronized over time. It does however not provide any means to acquire an initial synchronization. Thus, in addition to regular OFDM frames (also referred to as Data OFDM frames) the B-AMC physical layer offers two further frame types to acquire synchronization during cell-entry and handover.

Before an airborne radio can log into a B-AMC cell it needs to collect some configuration information of the cell it wishes to join. This information is broadcast in broadcast *BC* frames periodically inserted into the FL. If the radio has not been logged

---

[58] An alternative layout has been proposed in [**68**]. It does not change the number and spacing of symbols of a single sub-carrier, however, the relative positions of pilot and synchronization symbols on different sub-carriers have been changed to be more robust against DME interference. Figure 6-13 and Figure 6-14 display the original version.

into a B-AMC cell it will use this information to perform cell-entry to a B-AMC network. If an aircraft radio has already joined the B-AMC network in another cell, it ignores the BC frames of this cell and uses the BC frames of adjacent cells to measure their signal quality and to collect configuration information. (BC frames of one B-AMC network are synchronized in time.) This information is then used to determine the need for a handover.

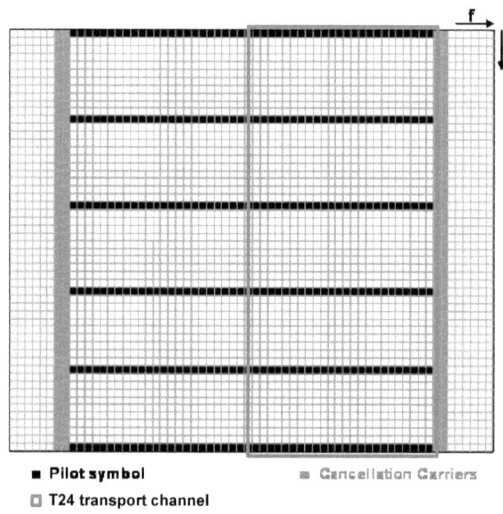

- Pilot symbol
- Cancellation Carriers
- T24 transport channel

Figure 6-14: RL B-AMC data OFDM frame [69].

While the usage of BC frames for cell-entry does not impose any additional constraints on the frame layout beyond the provisions for initial synchronization, the usage of BC frames during handover does imply some constraints. If an aircraft has already joined one B-AMC cell it needs to retune its radio to be able to receive BC frames from an adjacent cell. Reconfiguring the radio hardware takes a short amount of time, thus an airborne radio is not able to receive the complete BC frame of another cell. Consequently the BC frame is split into three parts. The first and last parts of the broadcast frame (sub-frame 1 and sub-frame 3) convey only information relevant to aircraft preparing to perform cell-entry in the local cell. This time is therefore available for non-local aircraft to retune their radios. The middle part of the frame (sub-frame 2) is used for the transmission of handover-related information for non-local aircraft.

The total length of the BC frame is 56 symbols (6.72 milliseconds). It is therefore larger than the 54 symbol data OFDM frame. Sub-frame 1 and sub-frame 2 each have a length of 15 symbols (1.8 milliseconds). This is slightly longer than the propagation delay of the nominal 200 nautical miles maximum range of B-AMC (1.26 milliseconds) giving even very distant aircraft enough time to retune their radios. The remaining 26 symbols in the middle are used by sub-frame 2. Figure 6-15 illustrates the layout of the BC sub-frames 1 and 2 including the placement of synchronization and pilot symbols. BC sub-frame 3 is identical to BC sub-frame 1.

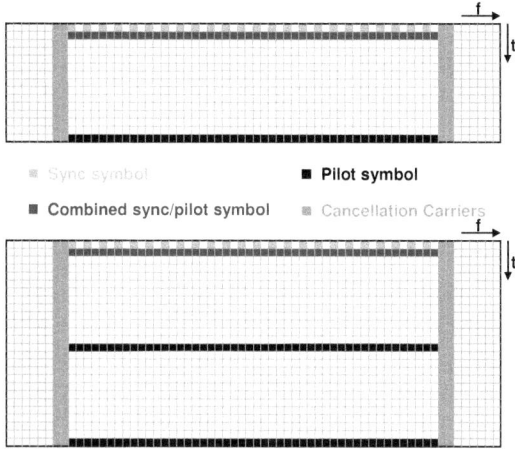

Figure 6-15: B-AMC broadcast OFDM sub-frames 1 and 2 [69].

Complementary to the FL BC frames a RL equivalent is required for an airborne radio to announce its presence to a ground-station. This equivalent is provided by random access frames *RA* frames. RA frames and BC frames are inserted into the FL and RL at the same time therefore both frames have an identical length of 6.72 milliseconds. The RA frame is split into two sub-frames of 3.36 milliseconds length to offer two random access opportunities. As the airborne radio cannot yet know its time-advance (the propagation delay to the ground-station) the layout of the RA sub-frames has to include guard intervals with the length of the maximum propagation delay (1.26 milliseconds). Taking away the guard interval at the beginning and end of each sub-frame, 840 microseconds (7 symbols) remain for the transmission of a net-entry request.

Just as the airborne radio cannot know its time-advance, it cannot know the required transmission power. RA frames are therefore sent with maximum power. Thus, unlike all other B-AMC frames the RA frame uses only the central 18 sub-carriers for transmission to reduce the out-of-band radiation caused by the high power signal.

Note that the guard intervals at both ends of the RA sub-frame cannot be expressed in integral numbers of OFDM symbols (1.26 milliseconds = 10.5 symbols). The reason for this lies in the fact that an airborne radio logging into a cell is not synchronized and cannot adhere to symbol boundaries therefore. Consequently the RA frame has to contain synchronization symbols in order to allow the ground-station to synchronize to the aircraft. The RA frame is the only RL frame containing synchronization symbols.

The layout of the RA frame including the positions of synchronization and pilot symbols is illustrated in Figure 6-16.

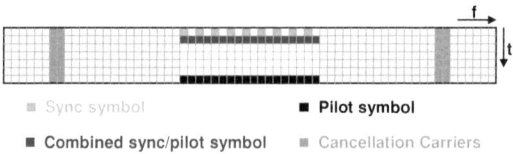

Figure 6-16: B-AMC random access OFDM frame [69].

Cell-entry to a B-AMC cell is performed by the exchange of BC and RA frames. When the aircraft-station enters the B-AMC cell it scans the forward link for BC frames to acquire FL synchronization and the ground-station parameters via the broadcast control channel **BCCH** transmitted in this frame. Now the aircraft-station transmits a RA frame to inform the ground-station of its presence. The ground-station responds with the correct time-advance and power settings for the aircraft in the common control channel **CCCH** on the forward link. The airborne radio can now be configured correctly for reverse link transmissions.

6.2.2.5 Frame Structure

In addition to being separated by frequency division duplex the B-AMC RL and FL channels are also structured in time. This time structure is a hierarchical frame structure built upon OFDM frames.

The largest element of the frame structure is the super-frame **SF**. A super-frame has a length of 240 milliseconds (2000 OFDM symbols). Super frames are constructed by the concatenation of 37 OFDM-frames: 1 BC/RA frame and 36 DATA frames. A sequence of 9 DATA frames is called a multi-frame **MF**. Thus a super frame can alternatively be described as one BC/RA frame followed by 4 multi-frames. A multi-frame has a length of 58.32 milliseconds. Multi-frames have no specific meaning for the physical layer. Their use by the data link layer will be discussed in the next sections. The B-AMC frame structure is illustrated in Figure 6-17.

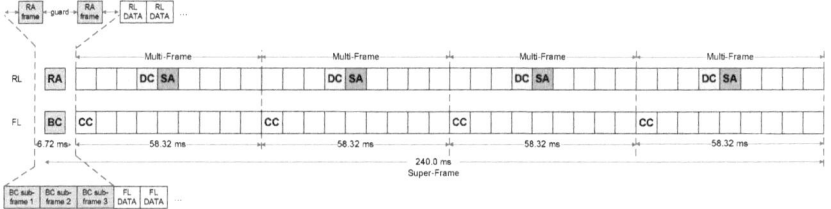

Figure 6-17: B-AMC super-frame structure.

The B-AMC control channels are mapped to recurring frames in each super-frame and multi-frame. The BC frame and RA frame at the beginning of each super-frame are used to convey the logical random access channel **RACH** and the logical broadcast control channel **BCCH** required for the cell-entry procedure. Within each multi-frame three data frames are reserved for control channels. On the forward link the first data frame is reserved for the common control channel **CCCH**. In the reverse link direction two data frames are reserved for the dedicated control channel **DCCH** and for the synchronized access channel **SACH**. The remaining data frames are used for the FL and RL data channel **DCH** and voice channel **VCH**, respectively.

Note that the length of the super-frame and the length of the multi-frame have been chosen to be compatible with the framing of the AMBE ATC10B vocoder. Currently this is the only digital vocoder certified for operational use in the aeronautical environment. It produces voice samples every 20 milliseconds, which are transmitted in bursts of 60 milliseconds (i.e. 3 samples per burst). Therefore the length of the super-frame has been chosen to be a multiple of 60 milliseconds.

6.2.2.6 Transport Channels and Coding

B-AMC employs Orthogonal Frequency Division Multiple Access **OFDMA** to allow simultaneous access to disjoint subsets of the 48 OFDM sub-carriers of an OFDM frame. These subsets are called transport channels. Using OFMDA different types of transport channels with different transmission bandwidths can be realized by selecting an appropriate number of *n* distinct OFDM sub-carriers in a particular frame. This is denoted as a transport channel of type *Tn* where *n* ranges from 1 to the maximum number of useable subcarriers, which is 48. This concept is illustrated for a T24 transport channel in Figure 6-14.

In order to protect the transmitted data from interference it was decided to use error correcting codes for Forward Error Correction **FEC**. These (block-)codes are applied to each transport channel separately. The protocol simulations in [**50**] and section 6.2.4.7 indicated that maximum tolerable transport channel error rate (probability for one or more bit errors in a transport channel) is 10^{-2}, thus the coding algorithms were selected according to this requirement.

It was proposed to use code catenation based on an inner convolutional code and an outer Reed-Solomon block code with rates $R_{CC}=0.5$ and $R_{BC}=0.9$, respectively [**69**]. The payload sizes and coding rates[59] for the transport channels defined in [**69**] are displayed in Table 6-1. Default QPSK modulation is assumed. Note that the transport channels conveyed in BC and RA frames have slightly different parameters (not displayed in the

---

[59] The coding rate is the ratio of the uncoded payload to the coded data (i.e. payload/FEC(payload)).

table) and that the coding of the T1 transport channel was not defined during the B-AMC project.

Table 6-1: B-AMC transport channel properties.

Traffic channel type	T48	T24	T12	T6	T3
Used subcarriers	48	24	12	6	3
QPSK data symbols	2304	1152	576	288	144
Coding rate	0.44	0.44	0.44	0.43	0.42
Traffic channel capacity (bit)	2048	1024	512	248	120

The displayed coding was chosen considering the worst case interference of DME: A DME station transmitting 3600 pulse pairs per second (which is the maximum allowed duty cycle of DME) would result in 15 to 20 destroyed symbols per OFDM frame. However, in the presence of less interference the coding could be relaxed and more powerful modulations than QPSK could be used. Table 6-2 cites the user data rates from [**69**] (taking the overhead of the RA, BC, CC, DC, and SA control channels into account, but no LLC overhead) that can be achieved on the FL using other coding and modulation schemes.

Table 6-2: B-AMC FL user data rates with alternative coding and modulation configurations [69].

Convolutional Code	$R_{CC} = 1/2$		$R_{CC} = 2/3$		$R_{CC} = 3/4$	
RS Code	$R_{BC}=0.9$	-	$R_{BC}=0.9$	-	$R_{BC}=0.9$	-
QPSK	273.07 kbit/s	302.4 kbit/s	362.88 kbit/s	403.2 kbit/s	408.24 kbit/s	453.6 kbit/s
8-PSK		453.6 kbit/s		604.8 kbit/s		680.4 kbit/s
16-QAM		604.8 kbit/s		809.4 kbit/s		907.2 kbit/s
64-QAM		907.2 kbit/s		1209.6 kbit/s		1360.8 kbit/s

Alternative coding and modulation schemes were, however, not investigated in detail as the proposed inlay deployment made the necessary favorable interference conditions unlikely. The B-AMC research concentrated therefore on the highlighted default coding and modulation.

In the B-AMC evaluation it was assumed that the FEC achieves an error rate of 10^{-2} for T24 transport channels. This was the design goal of the physical layer. If other transport channels were used, equivalent error rates were assumed i.e. if a T48 transport channel was used it was presumed that it would not perform better or worse than two T24 transport channels.

The development of the FEC is extremely complex as it depends strongly on the assumed interference conditions [72] [73]. Several optimizations not taken into account during the B-AMC project were later proposed during further research towards the L-DACS 1 system [28][29].

6.2.3 Medium Access-Sub Layer

The author's major contribution to the B-AMC research was the analysis and design of the medium access approach presented in this and the following sections. The author devised a protocol design providing dependable medium access to a high number of users without any dependency of the access latency on the data traffic pattern as opposed to the B-VHF approach. This was realized by the introduction of a dedicated and periodic control channel for each aircraft-station. This decouples the medium access algorithm from the data traffic pattern and makes medium access contention-free.

The data link layer has no knowledge of physical layer OFDM frames. In fact, it does not even use them, as all data is transmitted in transport channels protected by FEC. Therefore the medium access sub-layer has to provide an abstraction for the physical layer frame structure. OFDM frames are presented to the data link layer as time slots that can be used for the transmission of transport channels.

A B-AMC super-frame comprises four multi-frames and a Random Access *RA* slot on the RL and a Broadcast *BC* slot on the FL. The RA slot conveys the logical Random Access Channel *RACH* in a transport channel using the complete RA frame. Similarly, on the FL the BC slot conveys the logical Broadcast Control Channel *BCCH* in three transport channels mapped to the three sub-frames of the BC frame. The super-frame is illustrated in Figure 6-17.

Figure 6-18 and Figure 6-19 display the B-AMC transport channel configuration within multi-frames: Splitting the RL data OFDM frames into two T24 transport channels, allows for the simultaneous access of two aircraft-stations to the data channel *DCH*. The RL data OFDM frames used for the DC and SA channels are split into forty-eight T1 transport channels to offer the maximum number of control channels[60]. As the ground-station is the only user of the FL, only T48 transport channels are used in this direction.

On the FL, the first slot (Common Control *CC* slot) of each multi-frame is used for a T48 transport channel carrying the logical Common Control Channel *CCCH*. The remaining 8 slots of the FL multi-frame are used for the transmission of up to eight *T48* transport channels conveying the logical channels of the user plane in ground-to-air

---

[60] The assumption that all 48 OFDMA sub-carriers could be accessed simultaneously by different aircraft stations was a working hypothesis taken in the B-AMC project. A more realistic physical layer implementation was later proposed during the L-DACS 1 development.

direction. The maximum achievable data rate for the user plane channels (DCH and VCH) is thus 273.07 kbit/s assuming default QPSK modulation and coding.

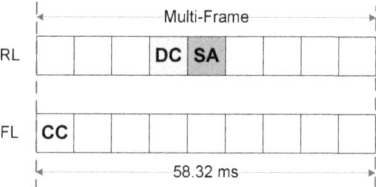

Figure 6-18: B-AMC multi-frame structure.

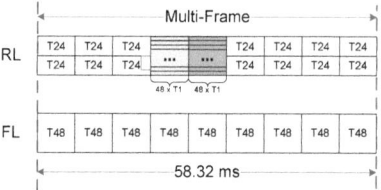

Figure 6-19: B-AMC transport channel configuration.

On the RL, there are seven data slots and two special purpose slots per multi-frame. The data slots provide a maximum shared data rate of 238.93 kbit/s for the air-to-ground user plane channels (DCH and VCH) under the same assumptions as above.

Transport channels are assigned to individual aircraft-stations on demand. The available bandwidth per user may therefore vary. The Synchronized Access *SA* slot is used for the logical Synchronized Access Channel SACH. In this slot only *T1* transport channels are used (48 per slot). Each aircraft-station is assigned one *T1* transport channel (i.e. a single RL OFDMA sub-carrier), so that the system provides one dedicated low bit-rate transport channel per multi-frame for the SACH of 48 aircraft-stations. If the number of aircraft-stations is not equal to 48, the SACH assignments are distributed over the SA slots of several multi-frames in round-robin.

The Dedicated Control *DC* slot has the same structure as the SA slot and uses the same assignment policy. It is used to provide each aircraft-station with dedicated low bit-rate transport channels for its logical Dedicated Control Channel *DCCH*.

The positions of the CC, SA, and DC slots within the multi-frame were chosen to give the radio equipment enough processing time (2-4 slot lengths ~ 12 – 25 ms) between incoming and outgoing messages.

The mapping of logical channels to transport channels and physical channels is illustrated in Figure 6-20 from the perspective of the aircraft station. Note that all control plane channels are statically assigned to time slots and transport channels as described above. This is not the case for user plane channels. These channels require a medium access procedure for the dynamic assignment of resources.

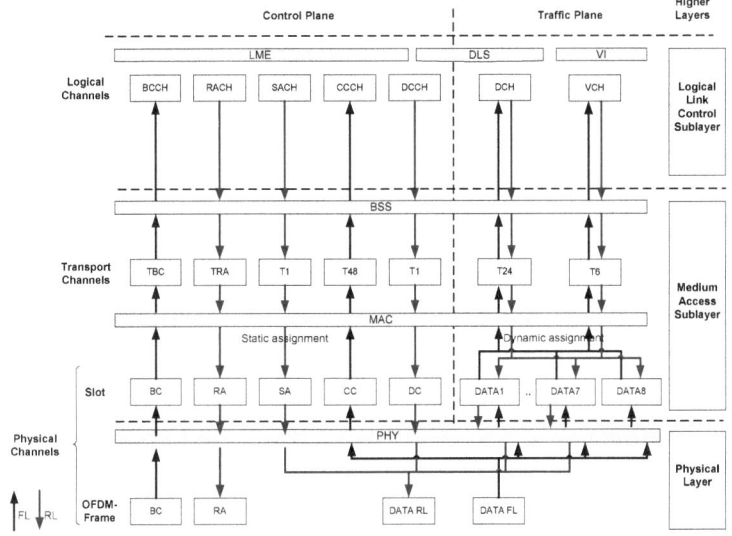

Figure 6-20: B-AMC logical channel mapping (aircraft-station perspective).

6.2.3.1 Forward Link Medium Access Sub-Layer

B-AMC uses FDD with separated FL and RL channels to provide full-duplex communication. The FL and RL medium access procedures can therefore be discussed separately. Since the FL is exclusively used by the ground-station, no sophisticated multiple access scheme is required in this direction. The ground-station directly allocates FL transport channels and manages access priorities. Nevertheless it is interesting analyze the FL medium access performance.

The performance of the B-AMC medium access sub-layer can be analyzed using a Markovian data traffic model: The logical link control layer is assumed to behave like a Poisson process generating packets of constant size 1024 bit (cf. section 5.3) with rate λ.

6.2.3.2 Forward Link Medium Access Sub-Layer Analysis

The user plane FL medium access is a comparatively simple process. Whenever a FL DLS fragment (DLS-PDU) is generated by the logical link control sub-layer it is put into the FL transmission queue in the BSS. At the beginning of each FL data slot the full transport capacity (one T48 transport channel, 2048 Bit) is taken from the transmission queue and placed on the channel. By this the B-AMC FL medium access becomes essentially an M/D/1 queuing system: Packets arrive according to a Poisson process (i.e. exponentially distributed inter-arrival times), the service time is deterministic (i.e. fixed packet size), and there is one server (i.e. physical channel). This is illustrated in Figure 6-21. M/D/1 queuing systems can be treated analytically.

Note that this model does not take the active queue management of the BSS into account. Active queue management is extremely difficult to treat analytically therefore only covered by simulation. The presented results apply thus to B-AMC with a single class of service or the average performance of all classes of service (assuming work conserving active queue management). Modeling the logical link control layer as a Poisson process does not take the data link service protocol into account. The details of the DLS protocol are only covered by simulation for the same reasons as indicated above.

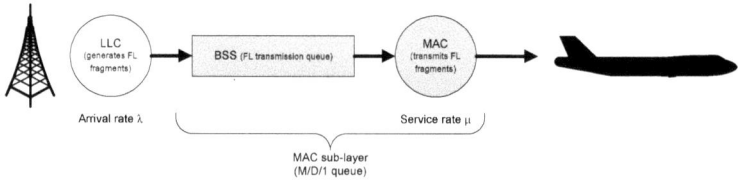

Figure 6-21: FL MAC sub-layer transmission.

For a given average offered load L the average packet arrival rate λ is

$$\lambda = \frac{L}{p}.$$

The average service time $E(X)$ for the transmission of the packet in a FL slot of length s is determined by the ratio of the packet size p to the size of the $T48$ transport channel. Thus the average service rate μ of the FL is:

$$\mu = E(X)^{-1} = \left(\frac{p\,s}{T48}\right)^{-1} = \left(\frac{p\,6.48\,ms}{2048\,bit}\right)^{-1}.$$

The average time in system (i.e. latency) $E(T)$ for an M/D/1 queue is

$$E(T) = \frac{2-\rho}{2\mu(1-\rho)}$$

where $\rho = \lambda X$.

In our case $E(T)$ corresponds to the average latency of the FL MAC sub-layer transmission. Note that the basic M/D/1 model does not take the slotted structure of the B-AMC FL into account, thus we have to increase it by one average slot length (i.e. you always miss the current slot)

$$E(T') = \frac{2-\rho}{2\mu(1-\rho)} + \frac{1}{\mu}.$$

In order to compute the variance of the MAC sub-layer transmission latency we need one further definition: The n-th moment of the residual service time R of an M/G/1 queue (of which the M/D/1 queue is just a special case) is given by

$$E(R^n) = \frac{E(X^{n+1})}{(n+1)E(X)}.$$

The variance of the waiting time W of a M/G/1 queue can then be calculated from the residual service time and the second moment of the residual service time as

$$\sigma^2(W) = \frac{\rho}{(1-\rho)^2}\left(\rho E(R)^2 + (1-\rho)E(R^2)\right)$$

Thus if the first three moments of the service time X are known the variance of the average waiting time can be calculated. Since the service time X of our queue is constant we immediately get

$$E(X^n) = X^n \text{ and}$$

$$\sigma^2(X) = 0.$$

The constant service time X and the waiting time W are obviously uncorrelated, thus the variance of the time in system (i.e. latency) T is

$$\sigma^2(T) = \sigma^2(W) + \sigma^2(X) = \sigma^2(W).$$

Using Chebyshev's inequality we can now estimate the 95% percentile of the FL MAC sub-layer transmission latency T^{95} by

$$T^{95} \leq E(T') + 4\sigma(T).$$

Note that the variance of T and T' are equal. Simulation results indicate that the less conservative estimation

$$T^{95} \cong E(T') + 3\sigma(T)$$

provides a very good approximation of the measured 95% percentile.

A comparison of this formal model with simulation results is displayed in Figure 6-22. Dots denote measurements of the average and 95% percentile of the FL MAC performance, lines indicate the theoretical results T' and T^{95}. Note that the simulation results below do not include the simulation of the LLC sub-layer protocols (i.e. DLS transport service). MAC-SDUs are directly generated by a Poisson process on top of the MAC sub-layer.

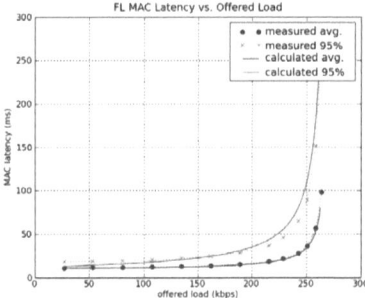

Figure 6-22: B-AMC FL MAC sub-layer transmission latency (simulation and analytical model).

6.2.3.3 *Reverse Link Medium Access Sub-Layer*

The B-AMC RL uses a bandwidth on demand scheme. Medium access is arbitrated by a contention free resource reservation cycle and granted by the ground-station. In order to acquire RL communications resources, each aircraft-station has to report its resource needs to the ground-station. On the basis of these reports, the ground-station will then allocate RL transport channels according to the configured allocation policy.

Aircraft-stations transmit their resource requests over the logical SACH channel in the SA slot. Each of the 48 *T1* transport channels is used by one aircraft in round-robin. If there are less than 48 aircraft-stations each will therefore have multiple channels per SA slot. However, this is currently not used.

The time needed to process the resource request of all aircraft within a cell defines the request cycle. The average length of the request cycle grows linearly with the number of users. Each aircraft-station has exactly one SACH transport channel per request cycle.

The ground-station maintains a table of requested resources. Whenever it receives a new resource request, it updates the table accordingly. By this, it has always a complete picture of the resource demand in the cell. Note that either the aircraft-station or the ground-station has to account for resource grants that have already been issued, but not been used yet to avoid duplicate requests.

The resource request and assignment procedure is illustrated in Figure 6-23 assuming 96 (i.e. 2 x 48) airborne users. For more (or less) than 96 users, the cycle extends over an appropriate number of multi-frames. Note that the boundaries of the reservation and allocation cycles need not coincide with the SA and CC slot borders if the number of aircraft per cell is not a multiple of 48. The logical boundary may lie within the slots in this case.

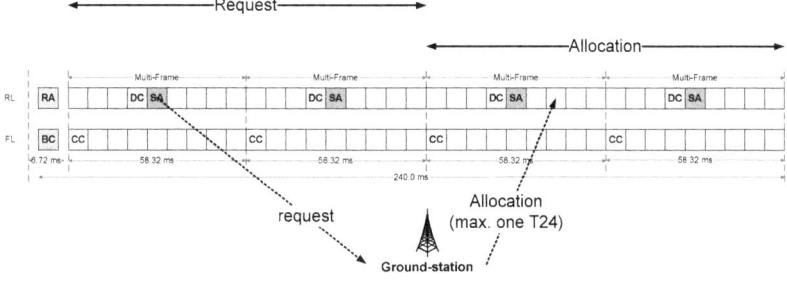

Figure 6-23: RL resource request and assignment procedure.

6.2.3.3.1 RL Resource Allocation

Although the structure of the resource request cycle is fixed, the modus of the RL resource allocation may be freely configured. For the purpose of the current system performance investigations, the resource allocation algorithm was chosen by the author such as to provide a low airborne duty cycle to reduce co-site interference towards other airborne systems and to behave in a very stable and predictable way.

In the time between each SA slot and CC slot the ground-station recalculates the resource allocation table according to the updated resource request table. According to [**69**] all allocations are *T24* transport channels (1024 bit; 128 Byte) i.e. each aircraft is assigned the smallest number of *T24* channels sufficient to satisfy its resource request. If the amount of requested resources is not equivalent to an integral number of transport channels, the transmitted data has to be padded accordingly.

Note however, that no aircraft-station is assigned more than one *T24* transport channel. This restriction has been introduced to guarantee for an extremely low duty cycle to avoid co-site interference.

In the following CC slot the computed resource allocations are granted to aircraft-stations in round-robin manner. Resource grants are only issued to the 48 aircraft-stations scheduled to transmit their resource requests in the next SA slot. If the sum of all allocations is greater than the channel capacity, some aircraft-stations have to get empty allocations. Using only *T24* transport channels this corresponds to a maximum of 14 allocations per multi-frame.

The author's rationale for linking resource allocations and resource requests was twofold: The first reason is that this approach allows for increased signaling efficiency, as the 48 aircraft included in the resource allocation are the same as in the next resource request. This information can therefore be transmitted in the same table together with other signaling information in the CC slot (i.e. the CC contains a signaling table for 48 aircraft). The second reason for this arrangement was that it guarantees the reservation cycle on the RL and the allocation cycle on the FL to be logically non-overlapping (although they partially overlap in time in the first/last multi-frame; note that Figure 6-23 displays the logical view). This ensures that the ground-station has complete knowledge of the resource demand before making an assignment.

6.2.3.3.2 Transmission Queues

Analogue to the FL case the B-AMC Special Services **BSS** entity provides the management of the MAC transmission queues of the voice channel **VCH**, data channel **DCH**, and dedicated control channel **DCCH** on the RL. The most demanding part of this task is the multiplexing and de-multiplexing of DLS fragments (DLS-PDUs) of multiple DLS entities with different classes of service to and from the data channel DCH queue.

In the protocol specification [**69**] a weighted fair queuing algorithm was proposed to handle different classes of services. However, in the course of further research the author found priority queue to be more suitable, as priority levels of aeronautical communication are hard (inelastic) priorities and fairness can also be provided by the resource allocation algorithm.

The transmission queue of the voice channel **VCH** provides a buffer for the synchronization of the voice samples produced by the AMBE ATC10B vocoder and the B-AMC frame structure. As the average multi-frame length (60 milliseconds) and the frame length of the vocoder (three 20 millisecond samples transmitted in 60 milliseconds) are equal, long term synchronization is assured. However, as the actual multi-frame length within one super-frame is slightly smaller than the sample size with only 58.32 milliseconds (due to the BC/RA slot), a cumulative offset of 16.8 milliseconds has to be buffered. If the vocoder is not synchronized to the super-frame structure, an additional buffer of up to one vocoder frame length is required. The required capacity of the VCH transmission queue is therefore 76.8 milliseconds. Greater buffer sizes should be avoided, not to increase the voice latency unnecessary.

The transmission queues of the other logical channels (RACH, BCCH, CCCH, and SACH) are directly managed by their users (the LME and the MAC). None of these queues may have a queue length greater than one as all control messages have to be sent immediately. Therefore they require only minimal management which can be performed locally.

6.2.3.4 Reverse Link Medium Access Sub-Layer Analysis

RL medium access performance is determined by two major factors: The resource reservation/allocation process and the queuing delay in the BSS transmit queues. The latency of the resource allocation process depends on the length of the request cycle. As indicated in the previous section 48 aircraft can issue a resource request per multi-frame (remember that the average length of the multi-frame is 60 milliseconds). The average time required to collect the resource request of all registered aircraft is the average length of the request cycle l_{rc}. It is determined by

$$l_{rc} = \begin{cases} \dfrac{n}{N_{c,used}} 60\,ms & for\ n \geq 48 \\ 60\,ms & for\ n < 48 \end{cases}$$

where the number of registered aircraft is denoted with n. $N_{c,used}$ is the number of usable subcarriers (i.e. 48). Note that the average length of the request cycle can never be less than the average length of the multi-frame.

Assuming that resource requests are uniformly distributed within a request cycle, an aircraft will, on average, have to wait for half a cycle until its request is collected. Once the request has been received, it takes exactly one cycle until the resource is assigned. The average length of the resource allocation process l is thus 1.5 l_{rc}. However, as beginning and end of the allocation cycle partially overlap in time we have to subtract one multi-frame length.

$$\boxed{l = 1.5 l_{rc} - 60\,ms}$$

The other functions of the B-AMC RL medium access sub-layer can be described as a system of two concatenated queuing systems.

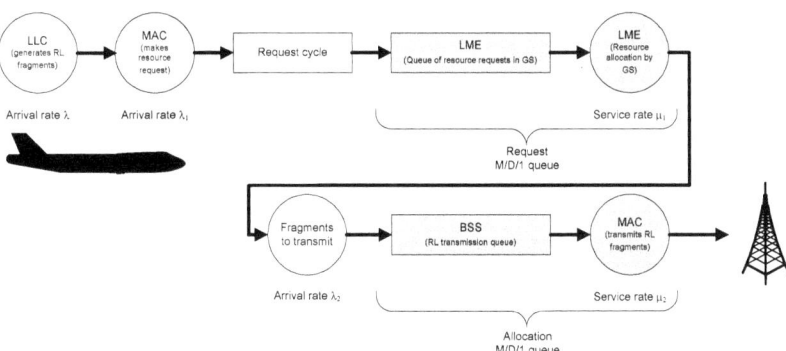

Figure 6-24: RL MAC sub-layer transmission.

The first queue is the queue of resource allocations in the ground-station. Assuming that this M/D/1 queue can process r allocations of size A per multi-frame (regardless of the allocation scheme) the "arrival rate per allocation" is thus λ/r using the same definition of λ as in the FL case. However, as the resource allocation algorithm considers only r

grants per multi-frame, by definition only r of n aircraft-stations are effectively taken into account per multi-frame. The arrival rate at the request queue is therefore

$$\lambda_1 = \frac{\lambda}{r}\frac{r}{n} = \frac{\lambda}{n}$$

independently of the allocation scheme.

The service rate of the allocation queue is r allocations per multi-frame. At a maximum user data rate of $C=238.93\ kbit/s$ it is

$$\mu_1 = \frac{C}{rA}.$$

In our case $A=p=1024\ bit$ (one T24 transport channel) and therefore $r=14$.

The transmit queues in the aircraft are the second queuing system. On average only 48 of n aircraft are "active" per multi-frame (i.e. request or receive resources). Therefore, on average only the $48/n$–the fraction of the total load arrives at the aircraft transmit queues per multi-frame:

$$\lambda_2 = \frac{48\,\lambda}{n}.$$

Assuming that the resource allocation process is fair[61] the transmit queues are processed with the same fraction of the total RL capacity:

$$\mu_2 = \frac{48\,C}{n\,p}.$$

Using constant size transport channels the airborne transmit queues are obviously M/D/1 queues.

The average RL MAC sub-layer transmission latency T is the sum of the average length of the request cycle, the average time in the allocation queue, and the average time in the transmit queue:

$$\boxed{E(T) = 1 + E(T_1) + E(T_2)}$$

where T_1 and T_2 are calculated analogue to the FL case. The same applies for the estimation of the 95% percentile

$$\boxed{T^{95} \cong E(T) + 3\sigma(T)}.$$

---

[61] The B-AMC simulations used round-robin resource allocation. There is a formal prove for the fairness of round-robin.

The calculated RL performance is compared to one selected case in Figure 6-25. Although not displayed it is noteworthy that the accuracy of the author's analytical model is the same in other cases. Note that the average performance of the system degrades only linearly with an increasing number of aircraft per cell. B-AMC therefore exhibits a form of built in graceful degradation.

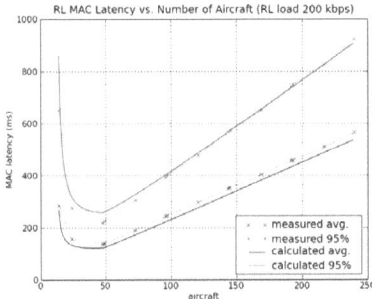

Figure 6-25: RL MAC sub-layer transmission latency at 200 kbit/s.

Note: At the left of the graphs in Figure 6-25 an increase of the latency is indicated. The reason for this is that constant bit rate traffic for the complete cell causes more traffic at individual aircraft-stations if cell population is low, hence transmission queues get longer. This is reflected in the graph.

6.2.3.5 Revised Reverse Link Medium Access Sub-Layer

In the course of further research towards the L-DACS 1 system the B-AMC system was critically analyzed by the author. This analysis indicated a number of shortcomings in the original protocol specification. This resulted in a revised protocol specification by the author [22] that was later used as input for the L-DACS 1 development. Within the MAC sub-layer the protocol revision resulted in a revised RL resource allocation approach. LLC changes also introduced with this revision are discussed in section 6.2.4.

The protocol enhancements for the RL resource allocation cycle comprise two crucial elements, namely the resource allocation and the cycle itself. First we discuss the resource allocation.

In the original protocol configuration all allocations were made on the basis of *T24* transport channels (1024 bit; 128 Byte) i.e. each aircraft was assigned the smallest number of *T24* channels sufficient to satisfy its resource request. Note that no aircraft may be assigned more than one transport channel per cycle. This restriction was introduced to guarantee a low duty cycle for co-site interference mitigation. In the revised protocol specification the maximum grant size is increased to one *T48* transport channel (2048 bit; 256 Byte). Note that this does not increase the duty cycle as one *T48* transport channel can still be conveyed in a single slot. The revised transport channel layout is illustrated in Figure 6-26.

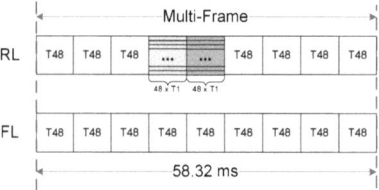

Figure 6-26: Revised B-AMC transport channel configuration.

In the following CC slot the computed resource allocations are granted to aircraft in round-robin manner. If the sum of all allocations is greater than the channel capacity, some aircraft get empty allocations. In the revised protocol specification (using *T48* transport channels) this corresponds to a maximum of 7 allocations per multi-frame.

In the original description resource grants were issued to the 48 aircraft scheduled to transmit their resource requests in the next SA slot. However, this approach had a significant drawback: It proved problematic that the request cycle and the allocation cycle were synchronized in time; after issuing a request the aircraft had to wait for one complete cycle until the resource grant could be issued (cf. Figure 6-23).

In the author's enhanced specification the allocation cycle has an offset of one multi-frame with respect to the request cycle to ensure that resource grants can be issued immediately. Although the difference might seem subtle, the combination of both enhancements is a simple and efficient improvement that has a significant impact on the system. As we will see in the next section, the overall RL performance is almost doubled. The revised request cycle is illustrated in Figure 6-27.

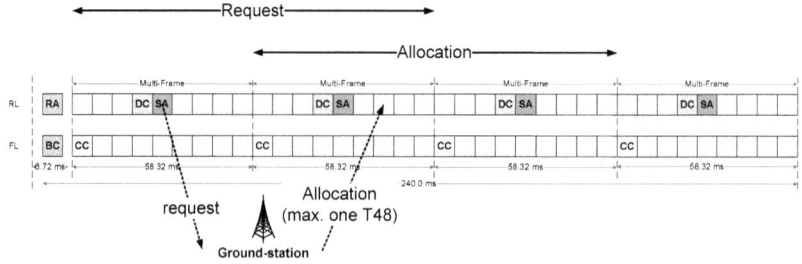

Figure 6-27: Revised RL resource request and assignment procedure.

It should, however, be noted that the revised request cycle may come at the price of reduces signaling efficiency as allocations and requests have to be announced separately now. In addition, the overlapping of the request and allocation cycle seems to increase the variance of the latency slightly.

6.2.3.6 *Revised Medium Access Sub-Layer Performance Analysis*

Assuming that resource requests are uniformly distributed within a request cycle, an aircraft will, on average, have to wait for half the request cycle until its request is collected. The average length of the resource allocation process l is thus $0.5\ l_{rc}$.

$$\boxed{l = 0.5\,l_{rc}}$$

Note that

$$l = 1.5\,l_{rc} - 60ms$$

in the original resource allocation scheme is longer for high numbers of aircraft-stations

The calculation of the revised RL MAC sub-layer transmission latency is analogue to the calculations in section 6.2.3.4 and therefore omitted here. The resulting RL MAC sub-layer performance of the revised approach is compared to one selected result of the original specification in Figure 6-25. The dashed black lines indicate the performance of the original medium access scheme. It can be identified clearly, that the new approach offers significant performance gains for large numbers of users.

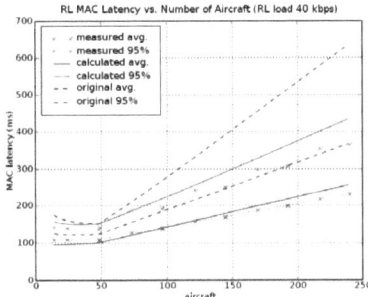

Figure 6-28: Revised B-AMC RL MAC sub-layer transmission latency at 40 kbit/s for p=2048 bit (packet size).

6.2.3.7 *Physical Layer and Medium Access Sub- Layer Performance*

The author's analytical treatment of the B-AMC medium access sub-layer yielded two results: The first result was the formal analysis of the B-AMC medium access sub-layer providing a first estimate of the performance of the complete B-AMC system. The protocols of the LLC sub-layer cannot improve the system performance beyond the performance of the MAC sub-layer in terms of latency and throughput (although reliability may be improved) i.e. the MAC sub-layer analysis indicates the performance boundaries of an optimal system implementation.

The theoretical FL performance is plotted in Figure 6-29 for the default coding and modulation. Under the requirements defined in Table 5-16 (A-EXEC requirement indicated by the horizontal dashed line) B-AMC can support up to approximately 260 kbit/s offered load on the FL, which excludes some of the defined use cases. ENR.250 and "ENR Large ATS+AOC with A-EXEC" could only be supported with higher coding and modulation schemes not sufficiently defined during the B-AMC study. In the RL direction the system performance depends on the offered load and the number of registered aircraft-stations. For typical scenarios with an average offered load of up to 50 kbit/s (A-EXEC requirement indicated by the vertical dashed line) the B-AMC system can therefore support up to 280 users, which is sufficient for all investigate use cases.

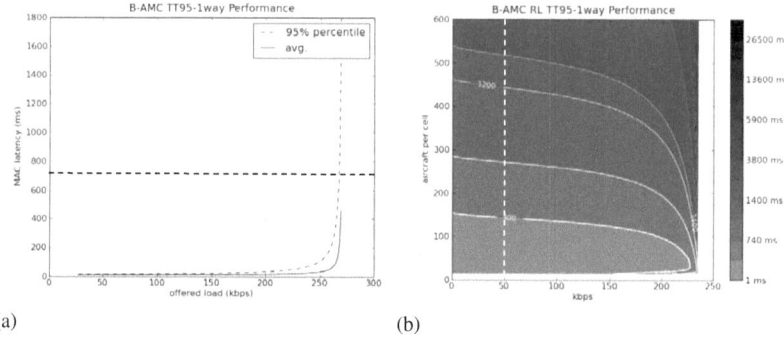

(a)   (b)

Figure 6-29: B-AMC MAC sub-layer transmission latency (a) FL and (b) RL.

The second result was that the formal analysis defined the range of expected results. An implementation or simulation of the B-AMC protocol can therefore be validated against the theoretical results i.e. the correlation of theoretical results and simulation results (Figure 6-22, Figure 6-25, and Figure 6-28) indicates the correct implementation of the author's medium access sub-layer simulation used to derive further properties of the system.

In summary the formal analysis of the B-AMC medium access approach confirmed the adequacy of the author's design for the stated requirements and the correctness of his computer simulation implementation.

6.2.4 Logical Link Control Sub Layer
The original specification of B-AMC [69] contained only rudimentary information on the protocols of the logical link control sub-layer. The performance evaluations [50] used only high level abstractions of these protocols (DLS and LME) as the focus of the B-AMC study was on the MAC design.

This section discusses the user data transmission protocol of the Data Link Service DLS introduced by the author during later research. It is important to note that the DLS protocol specification was added together with the MAC revision [22] by the author in preparation of the L-DACS 1 development i.e. the architecture of the B-AMC protocol stack was already given and could not be changed in the design of the DLS protocols. The link management protocols of the LME and the voice transmission protocols of the VI are not discussed here.

The purpose of the DLS protocol is to provide the higher layers with virtually error free transmission of user data. The first design goal of the DLS protocol development was therefore to improve the continuity (i.e. reliability) of the wireless B-AMC link. This is formally discussed in section 6.2.4.2.

The second design goal was to provide link adaption making the usage of the B-AMC link transparent. Higher layer protocols may use packet sizes not supported by the B-AMC data link (i.e. too small or too large for a transport channel). The DLS protocol shall therefore be able to fragment higher layer packets for transmission and reassemble them after reception. The order of higher layer packets shall be preserved and the duplication of packets shall be avoided as this would trigger the congestion avoidance mechanisms of the transport protocols.

6.2.4.1 Data Link Service Architecture
The logical link control sub-layer provides bearer services with different classes of service to the upper layers. Each class and priority is realized with a dedicated Data Link Service *DLS* entity (cf. Figure 6-32). B-AMC supports two transmission modes: Reliable point-to-point transport and unreliable multicast transport. Each of these modes is offered in several priority levels covering the latency requirements specified in Table 5-12.

The implementation of the unreliable multicast transport service is straightforward and simple. Messages received from the upper layers are fragmented into DLS-PDUs and injected into the data channel *DCH* transmission queue of the BSS. Priorities are managed by the BSS using a priority queue. Note that point-to-multipoint communication is only possible on the forward link due to the star shaped B-AMC network topology (cf. Figure 6-8). If desired, aircraft-station and ground-station could use the unreliable transport service for point-to-point transmissions, too. This option was however not used in the results discussed in this thesis.

The implementation of the reliable transport service is more complex. Messages received from the higher layers are segmented into DLS fragments (DLS-PDUs) suitable for the transmission over the medium access sub-layer. In order to correct transmission errors the reliable transport service employs an Automatic Repeat reQuest *ARQ* protocol. The ARQ control information is carried in the headers of the DLS-PDUs (sequence numbers) and dedicated control messages (positive and negative acknowledgements). When the DLS receiver accepts a DLS-PDU is will acknowledge the received data with the sequence number of the received fragment. In the general case acknowledgements for received PDUs may either be piggybacked on PDUs carrying user data (e.g. DLS-PDUs) or transmitted separately. In the case of B-AMC acknowledgements are transmitted separately as control messages over the dedicated control channel *DCCH*. If the transmitter does not receive an acknowledgement within a specified time it will assume that the fragment was lost and retransmit it.

Based on this architecture the main functions of the reliable DLS protocol can be identified. On the transmitter side we have two major functions. The first function is the segmentation of higher layer messages into DLS-PDUs and the corresponding header management to facilitate reassembly in the receiver. The second function is the management of sending buffers and retransmissions. Transmitted DLS-PDUs have to be stored in sending buffers for possible retransmissions and need to be removed from the buffer when they are acknowledged. This includes the management of the retransmission timers to ensure recovery from lost acknowledgements and flow management adjusting the number of transmission buffers.

On the receiver side we find two equivalent main functions. The first function is the reassembly of received fragments into higher layer messages. The second function is the management of the receive buffers. Received DLS-PDUs are not immediately forwarded to the reassembly function to enforce in-order delivery of data (retransmissions may change the order) but stored in buffers until the correct order can been established. A fragment may only be buffered if it was receive correctly, that is, receive buffer management includes error detection (e.g. using frame check sequences). Correctly receive DLS-PDUs need to be acknowledged by the transmission of an according control message.

The author's justification and implementation of this protocol architecture is discussed in the remainder of this section.

6.2.4.2 Data Link Service ARQ Analysis
The design of the reliable DLS protocol has to be carried out taking two main requirements into consideration: Reliability and responsiveness. Reliability is formalized by the notion of continuity i.e. it is linked with the detection and recovery of lost and duplicated packets. The analysis below indicates under which conditions ARQ is required to ensure the stated continuity requirements and justifies the use of ARQ in B-AMC.

High levels of continuity can either be achieved by the application of error correcting codes (Forward Error Correction *FEC*), the retransmission of erroneous packets (Automatic Repeat reQuest *ARQ*; sometimes also called backward error correction), or a combination of both approaches (Hybrid ARQ *HARQ*). The continuity c that can be achieved using these approaches can be calculated by

$$c(p, R) = \sum_{n=0}^{R} (1-p)p^n$$

if the higher layer message is small enough to be conveyed in a single packet. p is the effective packet error rate after FEC (if forward error correction is applied). R is the maximum number of retransmissions supported by the ARQ protocol. Note that $R=0$ is equivalent to not using ARQ.

For large higher layer messages that need to be transmitted in m fragments continuity is given by

$$c(p, R, m) = c(p, R)^m$$

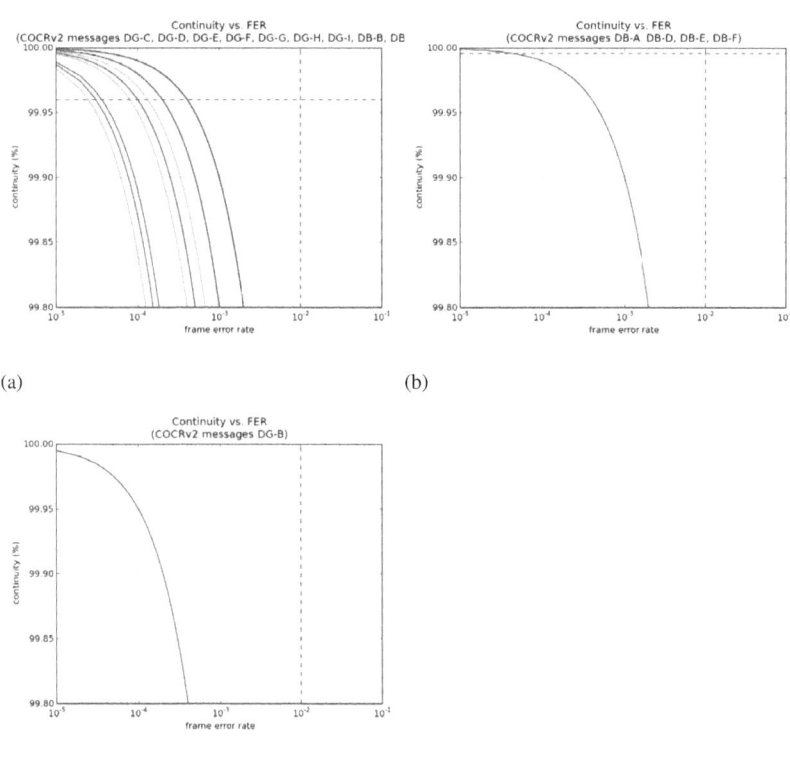

Figure 6-30: Continuity of COCRv2 messages (no ARQ).

Figure 6-30 plots the achievable continuity for the COCRv2 services according to the message sizes of section 5.4.2 without using ARQ. The expected frame error rate[62] of

---

[62] The frame error rate refers to the T24 transport channel error rate (cf. section 6.2.2.6).

B-AMC after FEC is 10^{-2}. This is indicated with vertical dotted lines. The required level of continuity is marked by the horizontal dotted line. Note that different service classes have differing requirements. The calculations show clearly that the required continuity cannot be achieved with the current FEC and without ARQ. Not allowing retransmissions the effective frame error rate would have to be increased by three orders of magnitude. The usage of strong error correcting codes in B-AMC cannot be avoided in any case due to the unfavorable interference conditions of the radio channel. Using the default coding and modulation (cf. section 6.2.2.6) a frame error rate of 10^{-2} can be achieved using FEC. However, in this case the coding rate is 1/2, that is, for each bit of information two bits have to be transmitted on the channel (i.e. 100% overhead). Lower frame error rates would come at the cost of over-proportionally increasing the coding overhead even more, thus any remaining errors have to be recovered by retransmissions i.e. B-AMC has to apply HARQ[63].

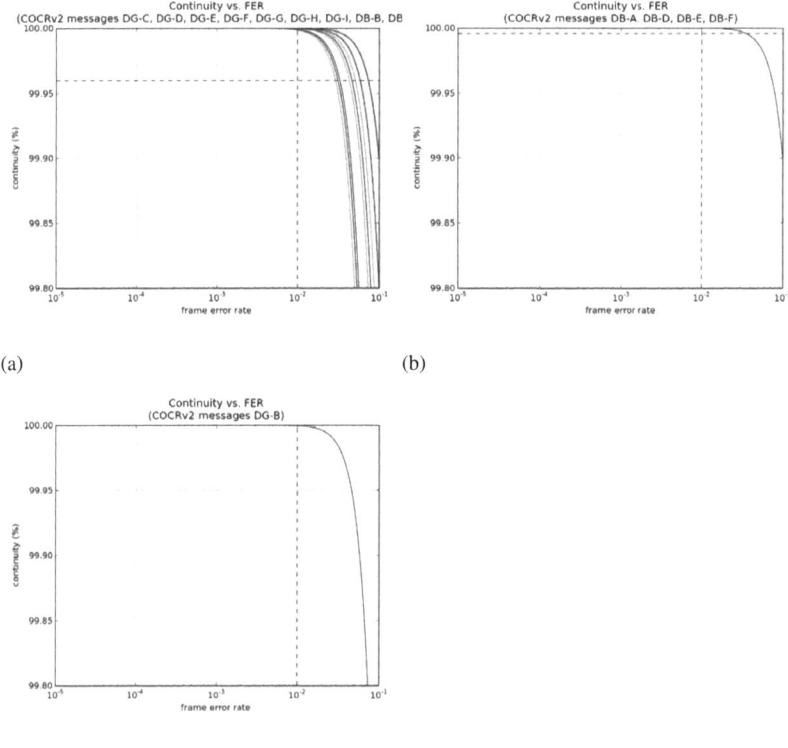

(a)   (b)

(c)

Figure 6-31: Continuity of COCRv2 messages (ARQ up to 2 retransmissions).

---

[63] The precise term is Type 1 HARQ. The more advanced Type 2 HARQ (with progressively increasing FEC) is not used in B-AMC.

Figure 6-31 displays the levels of continuity that can be achieve by allowing up to two ARQ retransmissions ($R=2$). The results indicate that the requirements can now be fulfilled for the expected frame error rate of B-AMC and for all service classes in this case.

An additional benefit of ARQ is that the non-duplication of messages is enforced by the protocol. Thus the main focus of the author's DLS ARQ design was on the efficient recovery from packet losses through retransmissions. The efficiency of the retransmission mechanism is determined by the ability to retransmit lost fragments of a message such that the expiration time of the message is not violated i.e. the protocol had to be designed to provide quick retransmissions in order to be effective.

6.2.4.3 Data Link Service ARQ Functional Model

The original B-AMC specification stated that the reliable point-to-point transport service shall be implemented as a selective repeat ARQ protocol. It was proposed to use the HDLC [59] protocol. However, further research by the author indicated that HDLC is not an adequate protocol for B-AMC; the special characteristics of the medium access required adaptations to improve its operation over the wireless channel. This resulted in the author's specification of the new protocol described below [22].

The new reliable DLS protocol is realized by a selective repeat sliding window ARQ protocol with positive and negative acknowledgements (*ACKs* and *NAKs*). It uses different logical channels in the aircraft-station and the ground-station.

In the aircraft-station (i.e. RL direction) separate channels are used for the transmission of user and control data (acknowledgements). DLS-PDUs containing user data are transmitted over the logical data channel DCH. DLS-PDUs conveying control data are transmitted over the dedicated control channel DCCH. This separation was introduced by the author to facilitate the expedited transmission of acknowledgements. The DCCH provides a low bit-rate channel with regularly scheduled dedicated resources that need not be requested by the MAC sub-layer i.e. the delay introduced by the request-allocation cycle can be avoided for control data.

Expedited delivery of DLS acknowledgements is important to ensure the fast retransmissions of destroyed packets. Retransmitting lost packets in the data link layer is only useful if this retransmission is carried out significantly faster than a transport layer retransmission. If the data link layer retransmission introduced a delay in the order of magnitude of the end-to-end delay, the transport layer protocol would also detect the lost packet and perform a wasteful duplicate retransmission (in addition to the unnecessarily triggering the congestion avoidance mechanism).

In the ground-station (i.e. FL direction) all packets (user and control data) are transmitted via the data channel DCH. A dedicated control channel is not necessary, as the ground-station can manage the access to the DCH locally i.e. multiplexing user and control data on same channel is possible without suffering from the request-allocation delay.

The protocol flow of a RL DLS transmission is as follows: When an aircraft-station receives a higher layer packet this packet is fragmented into DLS-PDUs which are forwarded to the DCH queue of the BSS according to the size of the ARQ sending window. The BSS will now request transmission resources from the ground-station via the SACH as described in section 6.2.3. When the BSS receives a resource allocation on the CCCH it takes the granted amount of data (one or more transport channels worth of data) from the transmission queue of the DCH and forwards it to the MAC and PHY layer. The BSS selects the data to send according to its priority. This is repeated until the BSS queue is empty.

The peer BSS in the ground-station stores received data in a buffer. When a complete DLS-PDU can be reassembled, it is forwarded to the logical link control sub-layer. The peer DLS protocol instance in the ground-station generates an acknowledgement for the received DLS-PDU and forwards it back to the BSS for transmission to the aircraft-station on the DCH. This is repeated until all fragments (DLS-PDUs) of the higher layer packet have been received and acknowledged.

The protocol flow in the FL direction is analogue with the notable exception, that the aircraft-station transmits acknowledgement over the DCCH. This is illustrated in Figure 6-32. Note that one DLS protocol instance is required for each class of service and aircraft-station in the AS and the GS.

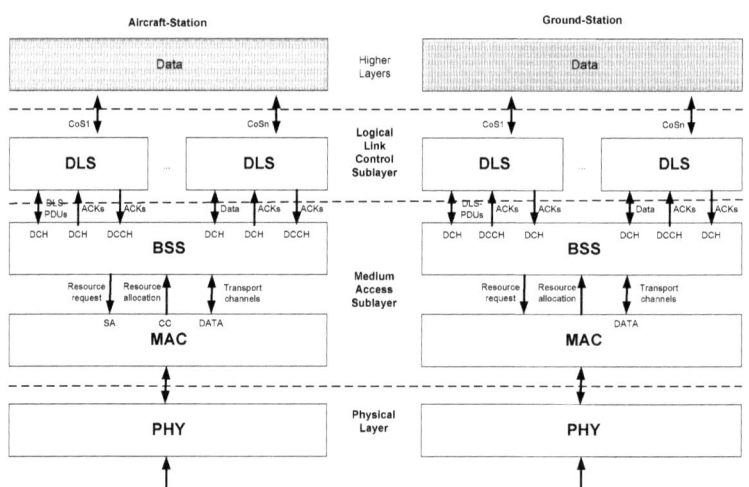

Figure 6-32: B-AMC DLS Protocol flow.

A challenge introduced by the sharing of the BSS transmission queues by multiple DLS protocol instances is that ACKs of all RL connections have to use the same dedicated control channel **DCCH**. The DCCH is a very low bit-rate channel that offers only the capacity to transmit one control packet per request-allocation cycle. In order not to delay the transmission of low priority ACKs and NAKs excessively, multiple airborne DLS instances may multiplex their control information into one DCCH control message. Note however, that the maximum size of this message (which was not defined in the B-AMC project) limits the number of service classes. It was assumed in the author's simulations that three ACKs can be conveyed in one control message (i.e. three classes of service).

In the FL direction ACKs are multiplexed onto the data channel DCH with the priority of their connection's service class.

6.2.4.4 Data Link Service Segmentation and Reassembly
Each DLS protocol instance splits higher layer packets (DLS-SDUs) into fragments (DLS-PDUs) suitable for the transmission over the B-AMC channel. Each higher layer packet may be split into several fragments. However, each fragment may contain only data from a single higher layer packet.

The default DLS fragment size is set to the size of the T48 transport channel (2024 bit) to achieve a packet error rate equivalent to the transport channel error rate. Larger fragment sizes would result in higher error probabilities p (cf. section 6.2.4.2) reducing the effectiveness of the protocol. The generated DLS-PDUs are forwarded to the BSS according to the size of the DLS ARQ sending window.

The BSS interprets the queued DLS fragments as a byte stream (ignoring fragment boundaries) and fragments it into a series of constantly sized transport channels. The BSS can now perform active queue management on a queue of equally sized objects. The functional model of the DLS and BSS fragmentation is illustrated in Figure 6-33.

The original B-AMC protocol proposed to use weighted fair queuing; however, in the author's revised B-AMC specification [**22**] this was changed to priority queuing taking the strict priority requirements of the COCR traffic pattern into account.

The peer BSS has to reassemble DLS-PDUs from the received transport channels before it can forward them to the DLS in the logical link control layer. Received transport channels are therefore stored in the BSS receive buffer for this purpose.

Note, that DLS fragments may be smaller than transport channels if the packet size is not a multiple of the transport channel size. This is illustrated for packet 1 and packet 2 in Figure 6-34. If the transport channels are not transmitted successively, as is the case on the RL (cf. Figure 6-51) and may be the case for low priority FL transport channels, the transmission latency of the conveyed DLS-PDUs may therefore vary strongly.

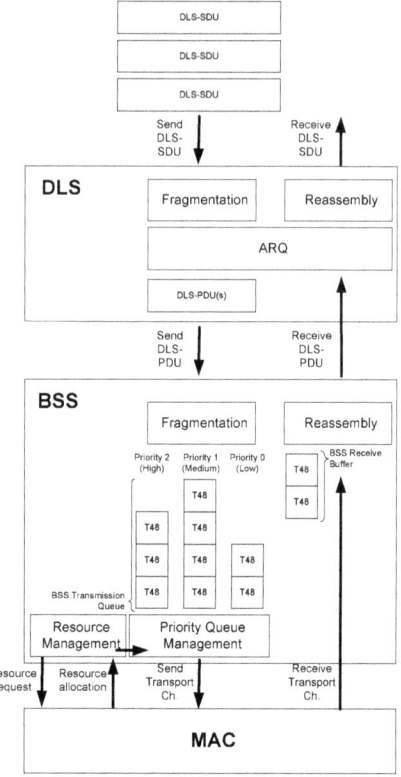

Figure 6-33: B-AMC DLS and BSS fragmentation.

The implementation of segmentation and reassembly was not studied in detail in B-AMC. Consequently no exact header formats were defined. The overhead introduced by the DLS and BSS headers is therefore approximated by 10% of the packet size in the author's simulations. The fragmentation and reassembly mechanism applies to the reliable and the unreliable DLS transport services in the same way with the exception of the ARQ buffer management.

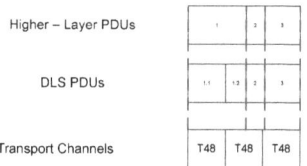

Figure 6-34: B-AMC DLS and BSS fragmentation.

6.2.4.5 Data Link Service ARQ Buffer Management for Retransmissions

The sending DLS protocol instance is informed about a successful transmission by the reception of a positive acknowledgement ACK. If the receiving DLS has identified a lost packet by a gap in the received DLS-PDU sequence numbers[64] it may inform the sending DLS with a negative acknowledgement NAK. However, if the NAK is lost or the lost DLS-PDU is not immediately followed by another DLS-PDU[65] the sending DLS can only resort to retransmission timers.

A retransmission timer is started for each transmission buffer of a DLS-PDU. If now acknowledgement is received, the retransmission timer will eventually go off and trigger the retransmission of the packet.

The minimum value for the retransmission timer is obviously one round-trip time. However, the real round-trip time is not a-priori known in the B-AMC protocol. It depends on the queuing delay in the BSS, the fragmentation into transport channels the MAC request-allocation cycle, and the number of concurrent DLS connections competing for the same channel resources. It has therefore to be estimated from measurements. The correct estimation of the medium-access sub-layer round-trip time is crucial for the efficient operation of the DLS ARQ protocol as the retransmission timer is set on the basis of this estimation.

The current MAC transmission latency is not known to the DLS, but it can be assumed to change only slowly over time as it is dominated by the length of the request-allocation cycle (i.e. the number of registered aircraft-stations). The queue length in the BSS and the availability of channel resources are, however, highly volatile. This is due to the combination of multiple classes of service with high numbers of users making the amount of point-to-point connections competing for the same resources unusually high. For a typical en-route cell with approximately 150 registered aircraft and a conservative setting of three priority levels the number of connections exceeds already 450 (multicast not included). The revised B-AMC MAC can, however, make only 7 RL allocations per multi-frame. Note that these allocations are not predictable for the airborne station, as they depend on the unknown resource requests of other users. The sharing of limited RL resources by a large number of connections can therefore cause high variance in the round-trip time of DLS connections.

The DLS round-trip time is estimated using van Jacobson's algorithm [**76**]. This algorithm is known to be robust against high variations of delay. New estimates are

---

[64] Note that corrupted packets can be detected using a CRC or similar frame check sequence. However, a failed CRC check is not suitable to identify a lost packet. A failed CRC check indicates that the packet has been altered during transmission i.e. the sequence number field of the received packet is not reliable anymore and should not be used to request a retransmission.

[65] This is often the case in the COCR traffic pattern due to the high frequency of small packets that can be transmitted in one DLS-PDU (cf. section 5.4.2).

derived from the measured round-trip time *rtt* of correctly received packets and the standard deviation of their latency *dev* using a low pass filter. The retransmission timer is then set according to the algorithm to

$$timeout \leftarrow rtt + 4\,dev\,.$$

This is an estimate for the 95% percentile of the round-trip time. Extensive documentation for this well-known algorithm can be found in the literature. Each retransmission that is caused by a timeout invokes a slightly modified variant of Karn's algorithm: First the timeout value is multiplied by four to provide an adequate backoff:

$$timeout \leftarrow 4 \cdot timeout\,.$$

In the second step, the estimation of the round-trip time, mean, and standard deviation are multiplied by four, too. This causes a backoff of the complete connection and ensures that single senders do not behave too aggressively (this is a deviation from Karn's algorithm):

$$\begin{aligned}rtt &\leftarrow 4 \cdot rtt \\ dev &\leftarrow 4 \cdot dev\end{aligned}.$$

If no round-trip timer estimator is available (e.g. at connection set-up), the timeout is set to a default value (3 seconds).

6.2.4.6 Data Link Service ARQ Buffer Management for Flow Control

In addition to providing increased reliability the DLS protocol shall also ensure the efficient operation of the data link service i.e. the DLS protocol shall provide a mechanism for flow control to avoid congestion within the BSS and allocation queue.

The data channel DCH transmission queue of the BSS is shared by all connections in the aircraft and the ground-station. Higher priority connections conveying bursty traffic may therefore surprisingly consume bandwidth that lower priority connection assumed to be available. In addition, the arrival and departure of new aircraft at the cell boundary increases and decreases the number of connections frequently. This makes it very hard for a single DLS instance to estimate the available channel resources and to set its sending window accordingly[66].

A well-known approach to this problem is to employ an additive-increase/multiplicative-decrease approach. If there are no timeouts, the DLS increases the sending window by *a* packets per round-trip time.

---

[66] Note that changing the ARQ sending window size *W* is equivalent to changing the sending rate *r* as

$$r = \frac{W}{RTT}.$$

$$window \leftarrow window + a$$

In the case of a timeout the sending window is reduce by the factor $m<1$.

$$window \leftarrow m \cdot window$$

The values of $a=1$ and $m=0.75$ are known to work well with B-AMC [22].

TP4 and TCP use the same approach for flow control and congestion avoidance with significantly less aggressive settings ($a=0.5$ and $m=0.5$ in case of TCP). Note that it is not necessary to decrease the window size on the receipt of a negative acknowledgement (NAK) as NAKs can only be caused by interference which is unrelated to flow control.

6.2.4.7 Data Link Service ARQ Protocol Performance

The performance of the reliable data link service was investigated by the author under varying frame (i.e. transport channel[67]) error rates from 10^{-5} to $8 * 10^{-1}$. The simulation scenario comprised 100 aircraft-stations, each transmitting 1 kbit/s in the FL and RL direction. This load is well below the capacity limits of B-AMC. The B-AMC SDU size was set to 125B (cf. section 5.3).

Figure 6-35 shows that DLL offered load increases as expected with increasing frame error rate. The 95% confidence intervals of the measurements are indicated with error bars in the graph. The increase of the data link layer offered load is caused by retransmissions of corrupted DLS-PDUs. Note that the RL data link layer offered load drops below the higher layer offered load for frame error rates greater than $4 * 10^{-1}$. This is not a serious problem since the operation of B-AMC under such bad channel conditions is not envisaged, however, it indicates a principle problem of the B-AMC ARQ protocol.

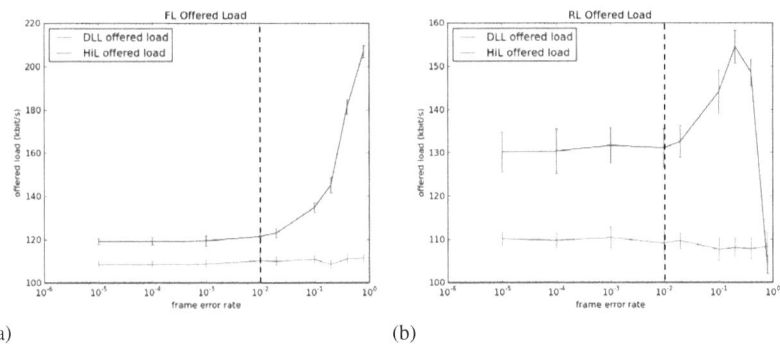

Figure 6-35: Offered load; 100 AS, 100 kbit/s FL, 100 kbit/s RL, varying FER.

---

[67] It was assumed that a T48 resource allocation would be encoded as two T24 transport channels within the same slot as this approach offers increased FEC performance.

Together with the increasing rate of frame errors and retransmissions a rise of the 95% percentile of the one-way latency can be observed in Figure 6-36. The latency starts to grow significantly for frame error rates above 10^{-1}. The most stringent latency requirement (740 milliseconds) is indicated by the horizontal dashed line.

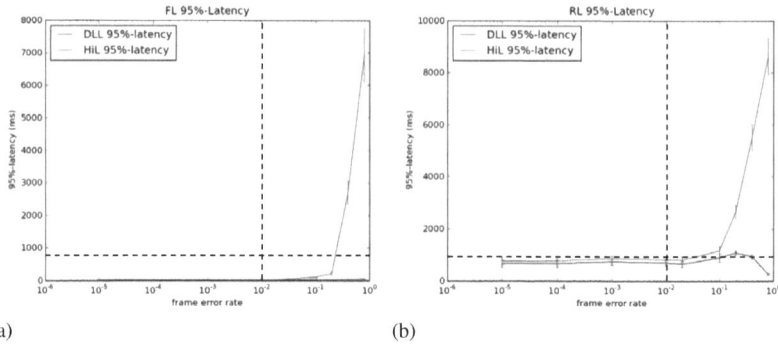

Figure 6-36: 95% percentile of latency; 100 AS, 100 kbit/s FL, 100 kbit/s RL, varying FER.

In the FL direction the increase of the latency can be explained with the growing size of the BSS queue (see Figure 6-37). Although the B-AMC interface queue above the DLS remains stable, the BSS queue builds up rapidly at frame error rates above 10^{-2}. This behavior is caused by the BSS queue between the DLS entity and the MAC entity. The queue virtually increases the bandwidth delay product of the B-AMC FL link by its capacity (unbound in the simulation). When the number of retransmissions increases under higher frame error rates the DLS timer management correctly estimates the increasing round-trip time caused by the BSS queuing delay. However, if the estimate of the round-trip time grows slower than the delay incurred by the BSS queue the DLS protocol will incorrectly trigger retransmissions. Fortunately, the bounded 95% percentile of the FL BSS queue indicates that this effect is only temporary until the DLS timer management has adjusted. However, the qualitative behavior of the BSS queue shows that the DLS timer management may fail under these circumstances.

On the RL this effect cannot be observed. This can be explained by the fact that the RL round-trip time is generally much more stable than the FL round-trip time. The FL round-trip time is defined by the interval between the transmission of a DLS-PDU and the reception of the ACK. As ACKs can only be transmitted in the DC slot by aircraft-station the FL round-trip time may vary by one request cycle. An ACK for a RL transmission can, however, be scheduled by the ground-station immediately after the reception of the DLS-PDU. This makes the RL round-trip time much more predictable for the AS and results in more accurate round-trip time estimates. This is reflected by the correct behavior of the RL DLS protocol which does not inflate the BSS queue. However, due to the fact each RL retransmission increases the RL round-trip time by one complete request cycle the RL transmission rate (which is W/RTT) drops rapidly under high frame error rates to the point where not all higher layer packets can be delivered anymore although the B-AMC capacity limit is never reached.

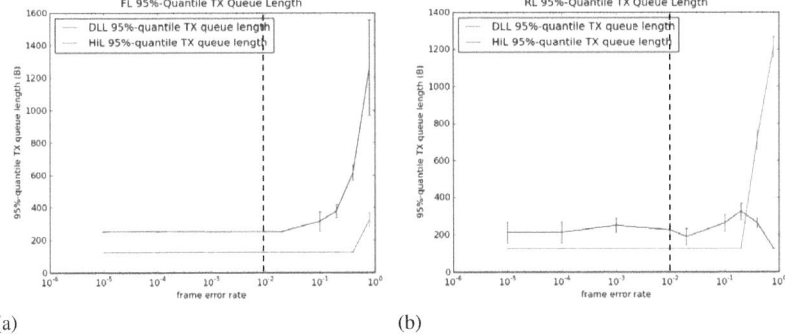

Figure 6-37: 95% percentile of queue length; 100 AS, 100 kbit/s FL, 100 kbit/s RL, varying FER.

In summary the author's simulation results indicate that the working point of the B-AMC DLS protocol should lie below a frame error rate of 1% (esp. Figure 6-36. (b).). This was taken into account in the physical layer design process. The eventual physical layer transport channel error rate is marked with a doted vertical line in Figure 6-35, Figure 6-36, and Figure 6-37.

6.2.5 Performance Evaluation

The performance evaluation of the compete B-AMC protocol was carried out by the author in a computer simulation implementing the medium access sub-layer and the logical link control sub-layer according to the methodology described in section 5.5. In total 672 B-AMC simulations and evaluations were carried out. This section presents the discussion of selected simulation results according to the evaluation criteria stated in section 5.6.

6.2.5.1 Simulation Parameters

The B-AMC computer simulation implemented the author's revised B-AMC protocol discussed in the previous sections.

The simplified scenarios were simulated using a higher layer packet size of 125 Byte (cf. section 5.3) with a single class of service. The B-AMC project did not define exact header formats. Thus, in order to account for the expected header overhead, the offered load was increased by 10%. The simulation duration was set to 500 seconds plus 5 additional seconds of follow up time. Each scenario was simulated ten times with different random seeds.

The detailed scenarios were simulated using TMA.x and ENR.x simulation session traces as input. The service classes defined in [46] were mapped to three B-AMC priorities according to their TD95-FRS latency requirements: Services with a latency requirement below two seconds, services with a latency requirement below ten seconds, and the remaining services. Table 6-3 displays this mapping. Note that 2 is the highest priority and 0 is the lowest priority.

The broadcast service classes of the FL use the unreliable multicast DLS transport service. The addressed service classes use the reliable DLS transport protocol (i.e. ARQ).

Table 6-3: B-AMC mapping of COCRv2 service classes to priorities.

Class of Service (CoS)	Expiration Time (ET) (s)	95% percentile (TD95-FRS) (s)	Priority	ARQ
DG-A	-	9.8	1	Yes
DG-B	1.6	0.74	2	Yes
DG-C	5.0	1.4	2	Yes
DG-D	7.8	2.4	1	Yes
DG-E	8.0	3.8	1	Yes
DG-F	12.0	4.7	1	Yes
DG-G	24.0	9.2	1	Yes
DG-H	32.0	13.6	0	Yes
DG-I	57.6	26.5	0	Yes
DG-J	-	13.6	0	Yes
DG-K	-	26.5	0	Yes
DG-L	-	51.7	0	Yes
DB-A	3.2	0.4	2	No
DB-B	4.8	1.2	2	No
DB-C	8.0	1.2	2	No
DB-D	3.2	1.2	2	No
DB-E	8.0	1.2	2	No
DB-F	16.0	1.2	2	No

The "ENR Large ATS + AOC with A-EXEC", ENR.225 and ENR.250 scenarios were not simulated as B-AMC does not provide sufficient bandwidth for them. More powerful coding and modulation schemes could be used for these scenarios, however, the according physical layer parameters have not been defined in the B-AMC project as the focus lay on the most robust coding and modulation schemes. In addition, the characteristics of the inlay channel made it doubtful that more aggressive coding and modulation schemes could provide the required performance (i.e. transport channel error rate).

The B-AMC protocol overhead was taken into account analogue to the simplified scenarios with and 10% increase of the offered load. The simulation duration was 3600 seconds plus 100 seconds of follow up time.

Both types of simulation scenarios used the same physical layer settings. The T24 transport channel error rate was set to 10^{-2}. This is equivalent to a bit error rate of 10^{-5} if other transport channel types are used. The control channels were assumed to be error free.

6.2.5.2 Responsiveness

- Ground-to-air (FL) one-way latency of user-data.
- Air-to-ground (RL) one-way latency of user-data.
- Do the 95%-percentile values of the one-way latency satisfy the requirements of Table 5-12 and Table 5-13: yes/**no**?

The responsiveness of the B-AMC system was evaluated using the detailed evaluation scenarios of section 5.4. Table 6-4 presents the evaluation results for the TMA.x scenarios. The TD95-FRS requirements are fulfilled in all cases and for all service classes.

Table 6-4: B-AMC responsiveness TMA.x scenarios (TD95-FRS in ms).

Scenario	TMA.15		TMA.30		TMA.45		TMA.60		TMA.75	
	FL	RL	FL	RL	FL	RL	FL	RL	FL	RL
all	22	512	22	567	22	606	22	706	22	752
DB-D	17	-	17	-	17	-	17	-	17	-
DB-E	18	-	18	-	18	-	18	-	18	-
DG-A	18	216	19	238	20	189	18	245	21	241
DG-C	25	218	25	238	25	190	25	240	23	238
DG-D	75	980	76	1,064	77	1,161	77	1,325	78	1,437
DG-F	84	217	77	247	88	195	88	248	69	241
DG-J	3,732	220	3,885	242	4,255	214	4,894	249	5,268	247
DG-K	310	293	417	362	365	381	363	470	395	516

Table 6-5 and Table 6-6 present the evaluation of the B-AMC responsiveness in the ENR.x scenarios. With the exception of the ENR.200 scenario the requirements of the COCRv2 service classes are always fulfilled. However, if the results are inspected per service (not displayed in the tables) it becomes apparent that some service requirements are not fulfilled although the requirement of the service class is fulfilled. In the ENR.150 and the ENR.175 scenarios the latency requirement of the FLIPINT service (service class DG-D, 2400 milliseconds) is not fulfilled. In the ENR.200 scenario the TD95-FRS requirement of the WXGRAPH service (service class DG-J; 13600 milliseconds) is also failed. The according results are marked red in Table 6-6.

Table 6-5: B-AMC responsiveness ENR.x scenarios (TD95-FRS in ms).

Scenario	ENR.25		ENR.50		ENR.75		ENR.100		ENR.125	
	FL	RL	FL	RL	FL	RL	FL	RL	FL	RL
all	23	423	24	424	25	424	43	540	51	791
DB-B	16	-	17	-	19	-	19	-	18	-
DB-E	18	-	18	-	18	-	18	-	17	-
DG-A	52	131	19	129	17	131	19	191	19	277
DG-C	20	129	19	133	19	134	20	187	19	245
DG-D	78	469	87	458	81	438	87	601	96	900
DG-J	1,682	128	2,797	135	2,842	139	3,897	192	5,619	258
DG-K	20	187	28	219	62	202	155	274	331	435

Table 6-6: B-AMC responsiveness ENR.x scenarios (TD95-FRS in ms).

Scenario	ENR.150		ENR.175		ENR.200		ENR.225		ENR.250	
	FL	RL	FL	RL	FL	RL	FL	RL	FL	RL
all	59	1,003	63	1,448	70	1,855	-	-	-	-
DB-B	17	-	17	-	13	-	-	-	-	-
DB-E	17	-	15	-	13	-	-	-	-	-
DG-A	23	284	24	544	31	670	-	-	-	-
DG-C	18	246	18	420	17	490	-	-	-	-
DG-D	113	1,127	114	1,665	126	2,129	-	-	-	-
DG-J	7,939	288	10,959	494	20,764	602	-	-	-	-
DG-K	480	493	668	868	1,340	1,066	-	-	-	-

Figure 6-38 and Figure 6-39 display the results in graphical form. The results show clearly that the B-AMC priority management in the BSS is able to provide differing levels of quality of service for different service classes. The effects of the strict priority queuing of in the BSS queue can be clearly identified in Figure 6-39 (a). As all users share the same BSS queue the priority of the highest service classes can be enforced over all other service classes (e.g. DG-C). Only the lower service classes show a significant degradation of responsiveness with the increasing load of the channel (e.g. DG-K). Note that the y axis uses a logarithmic scale.

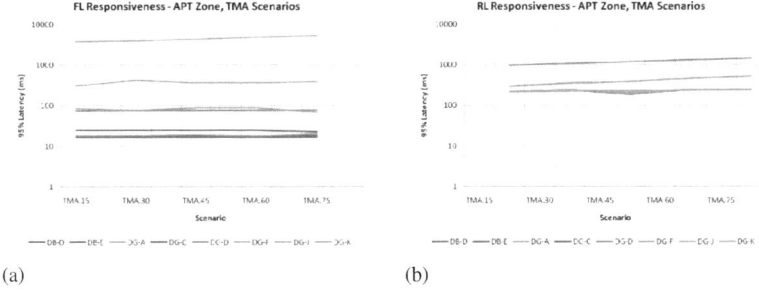

(a)   (b)

Figure 6-38: B-AMC responsiveness TMA.x scenarios (TD95-FRS in ms).

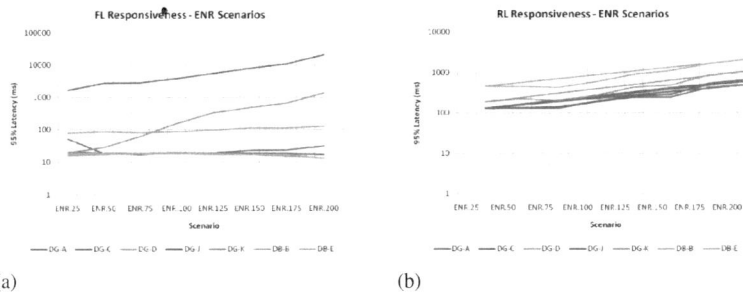

(a)   (b)

Figure 6-39: B-AMC responsiveness ENR.x scenarios (TD95-FRS in ms).

Figure 6-40 displays the measured forward link responsiveness of the ENR.200 scenario. Figure 6-40 (a) is a scatter plot of the measurements (simulation time vs. measured higher layer latency). Figure 6-40 (b) presents the distribution histogram of the measured values. The average and the 95% percentile of the measurements are indicated by green and red lines in both graphs. Note that the bulk of the latency measurements is very low as it was assumed that the physical layer would be able to decode individual transport channels separately. Most of the measurements correspond therefore to small higher layer packets that can be conveyed in a single transport channel. The smaller number of high measurement values corresponds to larger higher layer packets[68].

---

[68] For the distribution of packet sizes cf. section 5.4.2.

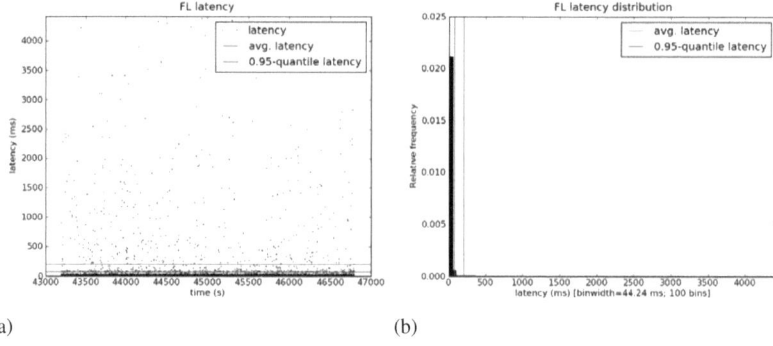

Figure 6-40: B-AMC FL responsiveness ENR.200 (TD95-FRS in ms).

Figure 6-41 (a) and (b) display the scatter plot of the measured reverse link latencies and the distribution histogram of the measurements. In addition to the influence of the higher layer packet size we can now also clearly identify the effects of the medium access request cycle. The maximum number of aircraft-stations in the ENR.200 scenario is 229. The average request cycle is thus 286.25 milliseconds (cf. section 6.2.3.4). In the lower part of Figure 6-41 (a) we can recognize the three stages of a reliable transmission of small higher layer packets: Request of resources (1), transmission (2), and retransmission in the case of error (3). Each of these steps takes up to one request cycle.

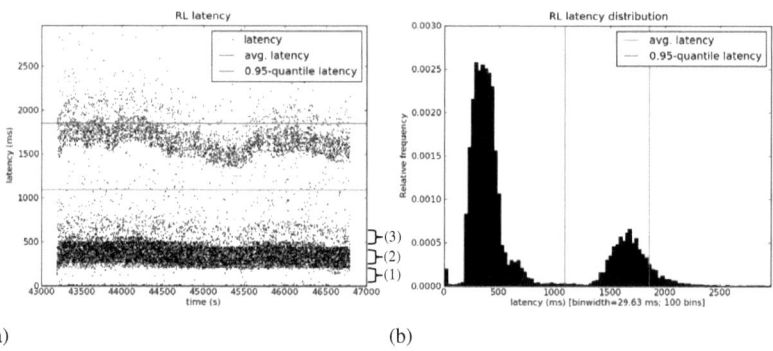

Figure 6-41: B-AMC RL responsiveness ENR.200 (TD95-FRS in ms).

The second cluster of measurement in the interval from 1500 to 2000 milliseconds is caused by large higher layer packets requiring multiple allocations. In this case the influence of the DLS flow control becomes visible. The flow control mechanism transmits one window size's worth of data per round-trip time i.e. the variations of the latency measurement in this interval are equivalent to the fluctuations of the estimated round-trip time and the current sending window size. The flow control algorithm remains stable over the complete simulation time (note the Gaussian distribution of the latency in the discussed interval) providing sufficient performance in most cases. However, the large gap between the two clusters of measurements indicates that the B-AMC timer management is could be improved.

6.2.5.3 Reliability
- Continuity of addressed user-data.
- Continuity of broadcast user-data.
- Does the system continuity satisfy the requirements of Table 5-14 and Table 5-15: yes/**no**?

The evaluation of the B-AMC reliability was also carried out using the detailed simulation scenarios. Table 6-7 displays the continuity achieved by B-AMC in the TMA.x scenarios. The broadcast service classes DB-D and DB-E use the unreliable DLS transport service. The unreliable transport service relies only on the physical layer forward error correction and cannot correct errors by retransmissions. The analysis of section 6.2.4.2 indicated that the required level of continuity cannot be achieved by the B-AMC FEC alone. It is therefore not surprising that the continuity requirements of the DB-D and DB-D service classes are not met. The fulfillment of this requirement would require the use of stronger FEC schemes for the broadcast services.

In the case of the addressed service classes B-AMC achieves a very high level of continuity, but cannot fulfill the requirements for all service classes. Especially the service classes with the lowest priorities (who experience the highest level of round-trip time variance due to the BSS queue management) suffer from expired packets caused by the DLS timer management.

Table 6-7: B-AMC reliability (continuity in %); TMA.x scenarios.

Scenario	TMA.15		TMA.30		TMA.45		TMA.60		TMA.75	
	FL	RL	FL	RL	FL	RL	FL	RL	FL	RL
all	99.35	99.99	98.80	99.05	99.03	99.94	99.25	99.86	99.78	99.40
DB-D	98.99	100.0	98.98	100.0	98.93	100.0	98.98	100.0	99.01	100.0
DB-E	99.01	100.0	99.15	100.0	99.05	100.0	98.94	100.0	98.97	100.0
DG-A	100.0	100.0	100.0	100.0	100.0	100.0	100.0	100.0	100.0	100.0
DG-C	100.0	100.0	100.0	100.0	100.0	100.0	100.0	100.0	100.0	100.0
DG-D	100.0	100.0	100.0	98.56	99.77	99.91	99.87	99.79	99.91	99.09
DG-F	100.0	100.0	100.0	100.0	100.0	100.0	100.0	100.0	100.0	100.0
DG-J	99.78	99.95	98.78	100.0	98.97	99.98	99.32	99.98	99.99	100.0
DG-K	98.37	100.0	98.17	100.0	98.84	100.0	98.95	100.0	99.90	100.0

Table 6-8 and Table 6-9 present the continuity achieved in the ENR.x scenarios. The pattern of the results is the same as in the TMA.x case. Although the level of continuity is very high the evaluation criteria cannot be fulfilled in all cases.

Table 6-8: B-AMC reliability (continuity in %); ENR.x scenarios.

Scenario	ENR.25		ENR.50		ENR.75		ENR.100		ENR.125	
	FL	RL	FL	RL	FL	RL	FL	RL	FL	RL
all	99.89	100.0	99.24	100.0	99.07	100.0	99.06	99.95	99.24	99.93
DB-B	98.58	100.0	99.14	100.0	99.02	100.0	99.04	100.0	99.01	100.0
DB-E	98.82	100.0	98.81	100.0	98.93	100.0	99.05	100.0	98.98	100.0
DG-A	100.0	100.0	100.0	100.0	100.0	100.0	100.0	100.0	100.0	100.0
DG-C	100.0	100.0	100.0	100.0	100.0	100.0	100.0	100.0	100.0	100.0
DG-D	100.0	100.0	100.0	100.0	99.86	100.0	99.77	99.94	99.74	99.92
DG-J	100.0	100.0	99.17	100.0	98.96	100.0	98.96	99.96	99.19	99.98
DG-K	100.0	100.0	100.0	100.0	100.0	100.0	99.80	100.0	99.80	99.96

Table 6-9: B-AMC reliability (continuity in %); ENR.x scenarios.

Scenario	ENR.150		ENR.175		ENR.200		ENR.225		ENR.250	
	FL	RL	FL	RL	FL	RL	FL	RL	FL	RL
all	98.86	99.99	97.42	99.90	98.18	99.81	-	-	-	-
DB-B	99.00	100.0	99.01	100.0	99.04	100.0	-	-	-	-
DB-E	99.01	100.0	99.04	100.0	99.00	100.0	-	-	-	-
DG-A	100.0	99.73	100.0	99.69	99.86	100.0	-	-	-	-
DG-C	100.0	100.0	100.0	100.0	100.0	100.0	-	-	-	-
DG-D	99.91	100.0	99.78	99.90	99.25	99.78	-	-	-	-
DG-J	98.69	99.97	96.92	99.98	97.93	100.0	-	-	-	-
DG-K	99.92	99.94	99.79	99.88	99.61	99.79	-	-	-	-

6.2.5.4 Efficiency

- Ground-to-air (FL) channel utilization.
- Air-to-ground (RL) channel utilization.
- Ground-to-air (FL) channel efficiency.
- Air-to-ground (RL) channel efficiency.

Channel efficiency is the ratio of the successfully delivered user data to the amount of data sent on the physical channel including all control overhead i.e. it gives a measure of the total protocol overhead. In the calculation of efficiency the 10% header overhead of the user data is taken into account. Further it is assumed that the DC, SA, and CC slot are always completely used by the according control channels. These assumptions had to be taken as the B-AMC project concentrated on the analysis and design of the protocol. The exact packet and header formats were out of the scope of this design study.

Channel utilization is the percentage of the physical layer capacity that is actually used by the protocol. In the calculation of utilization the same assumptions on the DC, SA, and CC slot usage are made as above.

Table 6-10 displays the channel efficiency and channel utilization values of the TMA.x scenarios. Table 6-11 and Table 6-12 present the same measurements for the ENR.x scenarios.

Table 6-10: B-AMC channel efficiency and utilization; TMA.x scenarios.

Scenario	TMA.15		TMA.30		TMA.45		TMA.60		TMA.75		
	FL	RL	FL	RL	FL	RL	FL	RL	FL	RL	
Ch. efficiency	45%	5%	46%	6%	46%	7%	47%	8%	48%	9%	%
Ch. utilization	28%	24%	28%	24%	28%	25%	29%	25%	29%	25%	%

Table 6-11: B-AMC channel efficiency and utilization; ENR.x scenarios.

Scenario	ENR.25		ENR.50		ENR.75		ENR.100		ENR.125		
	FL	RL	FL	RL	FL	RL	FL	RL	FL	RL	
Ch.efficiency	10%	1%	24%	2%	37%	4%	48%	8%	56%	10%	%
Ch.utilization	13%	22%	17%	23%	22%	24%	30%	25%	41%	13%	%

Table 6-12: B-AMC channel efficiency and utilization; ENR.x scenarios.

Scenario	ENR.150		ENR.175		ENR.200		ENR.225		ENR.250		
	FL	RL	FL	RL	FL	RL	FL	RL	FL	RL	
Ch. efficiency	61%	15%	64%	19%	67%	24%	-	-	-	-	%
Ch. utilization	54%	28%	68%	30%	86%	33%	-	-	-	-	%

Figure 6-42 displays the TMA.x results in graphical form. It can be seen clearly that the TMA.x scenarios utilize the B-AMC channel only lightly. On the forward link the physical channel is only used up to 29% and on the reverse link up to 25%.

The channel efficiency is very low in both link directions. The forward link efficiency is never greater than 50% and the reverse link efficiency is even below 10%. These values can be explained by the assumption that the DC, SA, and CC slots are always fully used. The full usage of the CC slot on the forward link contributes 33.33 kbit/s of control overhead. This is equivalent to approximately 11% of the channel capacity. On the reverser link the full usage of the DC and SA slot produce an aggregate data rate of 66.67 kbit/s for the control channels. This is equivalent to 22% of the channel capacity. It may be assumed that the control channel would not always be fully used in a real system. Thus, the presented values should be interpreted as an estimate for the lower boundary of the B-AMC efficiency.

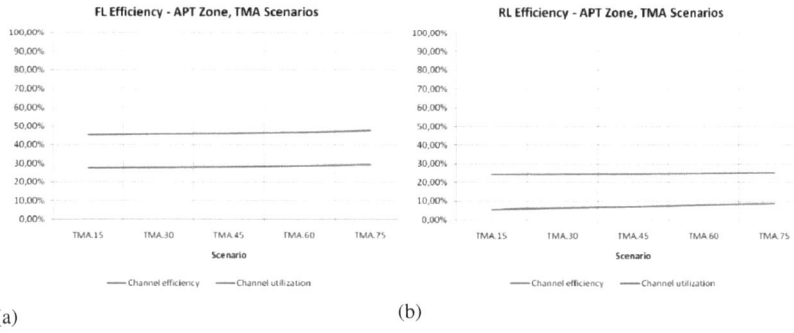

Figure 6-42: B-AMC efficiency; TMA.x scenarios.

Figure 6-43 (a) and (b) display the B-AMC efficiency for the ENR.x scenarios. Unlike the TMA.x scenarios the forward link load is much higher in this case. In the ENR.200 scenario the FL physical channel is utilized up to 86%. The reverse link is, however, still only lightly loaded at a channel utilization of less than 33%.

The efficiency of both link directions is again dominated by the assumptions on the control channel usage. The upper boundary of the forward link efficiency under assumption of a fully used CC slot is 89%. In the investigated scenarios B-AMC achieves up to 67% efficiency on the forward link. The degradation of the efficiency gain with increasing load is caused by the growing amount of retransmissions versus the constant load of the control channels. On the reverse link the achieved efficiency is comparable to the TMA.x scenarios as the ENR.x RL traffic is not much higher.

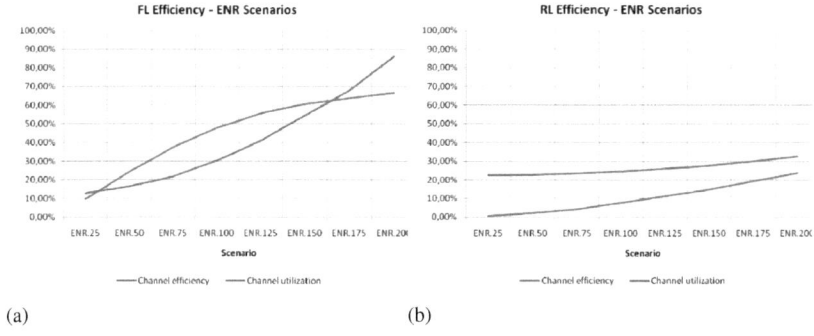

Figure 6-43: B-AMC efficiency; ENR.x scenarios.

It is important to note that the discussion of the B-AMC channel efficiency is only valid within the context of the assumptions on the CC, DC, and SA slot usage. A different duty cycle of the control channels would also result in differing results.

- Interface queue length.

Table 6-13, Table 6-14, and Table 6-15 present the measurements of the B-AMC queue lengths. The length of the BSS queue and the DLS queues have been measured separately.

Table 6-13: B-AMC queue length; TMA.x scenarios.

Scenario	TMA.15		TMA.30		TMA.45		TMA.60		TMA.75		
	FL	RL	FL	RL	FL	RL	FL	RL	FL	RL	
Avg. q. len. (BSS)	2,246	181	2,356	198	2,271	213	2,136	217	2,088	230	B
95% q. len. (BSS)	14,592	1,262	14,850	1,280	14,336	1,280	14,080	1,280	13,824	1,280	B
Avg. q. len. (DLS)	3,438	98	3,167	117	2,952	102	3,034	107	2,833	116	B
95% q. len. (DLS)	18,176	256	17,664	256	17,152	256	17,296	256	16,640	256	B

Table 6-14: B-AMC queue length; ENR.x scenarios.

Scenario	ENR.25		ENR.50		ENR.75		ENR.100		ENR.125		
	FL	RL	FL	RL	FL	RL	FL	RL	FL	RL	
Avg.q.len.(BSS)	3,402	192	3,412	171	3,214	178	3,801	187	4,726	208	B
95%q.len.(BSS)	14,848	1,024	15,360	1,024	14,848	1,024	15,616	1,024	17,213	1,262	B
Avg.q.len.(DLS)	3,703	106	4,655	105	4,816	107	4,952	109	5,368	111	B
95%q.len.(DLS)	15,104	256	17,296	256	17,552	256	17,808	256	18,064	256	B

Table 6-15: B-AMC queue length; ENR.x scenarios.

Scenario	ENR.150		ENR.175		ENR.200		ENR.225		ENR.250		
	FL	RL	FL	RL	FL	RL	FL	RL	FL	RL	
Avg. q. len. (BSS)	5,783	211	6,935	214	13,359	207	-	-	-	-	B
95% q. len. (BSS)	21,365	1,262	24,064	1,262	45,553	1,262	-	-	-	-	B
Avg. q. len. (DLS)	5,225	113	6,130	110	6,579	113	-	-	-	-	B
95% q. len. (DLS)	18,432	256	19,344	256	19,600	256	-	-	-	-	B

Figure 6-44 displays the results of the TMA.x scenarios in graphical form. The forward link measurements show that the DLS and BSS queue grow to significant lengths (in total more than 30,000 Bytes) although the offered load of the TMA.x scenarios is well below the B-AMC capacity limits. This is an indication that the DLS flow control under-estimates the forward link bandwidth-delay product.

In the reverse link direction the opposite situation can be observed. The DLS queue length is short, while the BSS queue length is comparatively high. This indicates that the DLS flow control over-estimates the reverse link bandwidth-delay product and fills the BSS queue with excessive traffic.

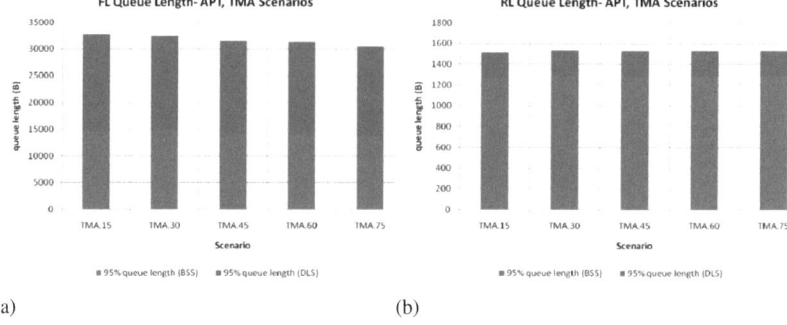

Figure 6-44: B-AMC queue length; TMA.x scenarios.

Figure 6-45 show a similar behavior for the ENR.x scenarios. The forward link is slightly under-utilized (the physical channel is used only up to 80% cf. section 6.2.5.4) which leads to growing DLS and BSS queues. On the reverse link the high BSS queue lengths indicate the over-estimation of the link capacity by the DLS flow management.

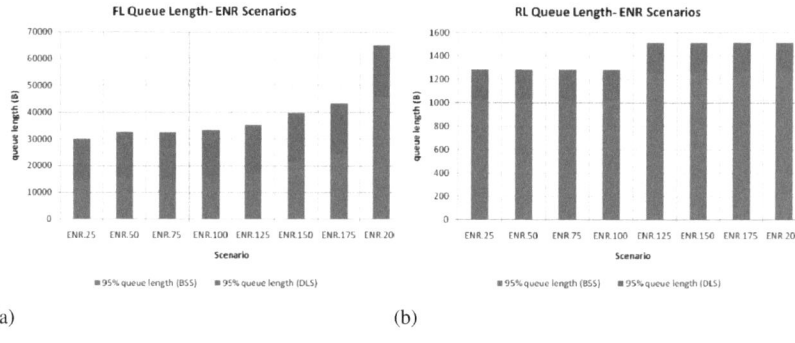

Figure 6-45: B-AMC queue length; ENR.x scenarios.

- Resource distribution fairness.

Table 6-16, Table 6-17, and Table 6-18 display the measured fairness of the reverse link latency. The 95% percentile of the reverse link latency has been selected as indicator, as it is sufficient to fully characterize the resource distribution fairness in the absence of significant packet loss. The results indicate that B-AMC achieves near-optimal fairness between different users[69]. This is due to the MAC resource allocation cycle which enforces round-robin scheduling.

---

[69] Note that there is only one user of the forward link (the ground-station). The evaluation of forward link fairness is therefore not meaningful. Note also that only the fairness between different users is measured. Due to the BSS priority management fairness is not given within one user's data traffic.

Table 6-16: B-AMC RL fairness TD95-FRS; TMA.x scenarios.

Scenario	TMA.15	TMA.30	TMA.45	TMA.60	TMA.75	
RL Fairness (TD95-FRS)	99.93	99.94	99.93	99.93	99.93	%

Table 6-17: B-AMC RL fairness TD95-FRS; ENR.x scenarios.

Scenario	ENR.25	ENR.50	ENR.75	ENR.100	ENR.125	
RL Fairness(TD95-FRS)	99.96	99.94	99.93	99.93	99.93	%

Table 6-18: B-AMC RL fairness TD95-FRS; ENR.x scenarios.

Scenario	ENR.150	ENR.175	ENR.200	ENR.225	ENR.250	
RL Fairness (TD95-FRS)	99.93	99.93	99.93	-	-	%

6.2.5.5 Scalability
- Does the system fulfill the latency requirements of Table 5-16 in all applicable scenarios: **yes**/no?

Scalability was evaluated using the simplified evaluation scenarios. The results of Table 6-19 show that B-AMC fulfils the simplified requirements to the 95% percentile of the one-way latency in all applicable scenarios.

Table 6-19: B-AMC scalability (TD95-FRS).

Scenario	PIAC	95% percentile of latency (TD95-FRS)						
		ATS Only, with A-EXEC		ATS+AOC, with A-EXEC		ATS Only, without A-EXEC		ATS+AOC, without A-EXEC	
		FL	RL	FL	RL	FL	RL	FL	RL
APT Zone	26	-	-	-	-	19	410	26	409
APT Surface	264	-	-	-	-	19	134	18	135
TMA Small	44	19	141	19	141	19	141	19	141
TMA Large	53	19	169	19	169	19	169	19	169
ENR Small	45	19	141	26	141	19	141	20	141
ENR Medium	62	19	185	26	185	19	185	21	185
ENR Large	204	19	337	-	-	19	337	47	338
ENR Super Large	522	19	718	-	-	19	718	-	-

Note that the extremely short FL latencies are caused by the assumption that the B-AMC physical layer is able to decode each received transport channel individually and immediately. It is also notable that the most stringent latency requirement (740 milliseconds), which are only required in the scenarios supporting the A-EXEC service, is fulfilled in all cases. This indicates an over-engineering of the dedicated control channel capacity, which could be reduced in some scenarios.

- Does the system provide the required level of continuity in all applicable scenarios: yes/**no**?

The evaluation of the B-AMC continuity in the simplified scenarios indicates that the achieved continuity is generally very high, but not high enough to fulfill the requirements of Table 5-16 in all scenarios. The results of section 6.2.5.6 indicate that the reason for this behavior lies in the high variance of the one-way latency which causes the occasional expiration of higher layer packets.

Table 6-20: B-AMC scalability (continuity).

Scenario	PIAC	Continuity in %							
		ATS Only, with A-EXEC		ATS+AOC, with A-EXEC		ATS Only, without A-EXEC		ATS+AOC, without A-EXEC	
		FL	RL	FL	RL	FL	RL	FL	RL
APT Zone	26	-	-	-	-	99.98	99.95	99.88	99.94
APT Surface	264	-	-	-	-	99.99	99.92	100.0	99.87
TMA Small	44	99.96	99.9	99.96	99.9	99.96	99.9	99.96	99.9
TMA Large	53	99.96	99.88	99.96	99.88	99.96	99.88	99.96	99.88
ENR Small	45	99.96	99.87	99.8	99.89	99.96	99.87	99.89	99.88
ENR Medium	62	99.96	99.89	99.82	99.9	99.96	99.89	99.87	99.89
ENR Large	204	99.98	99.94	-	-	99.98	99.94	99.8	99.94
ENR Super Large	522	99.97	99.93	-	-	99.97	99.93	-	-

6.2.5.6 Resilience

- How does the system performance change with rising numbers of users?

The performance of the B-AMC protocol under rising numbers of users was evaluated using similar simulation settings as used in the simplified evaluation scenarios. The higher layer packet size was set to 125 Bytes. The total offered load of user data was set to 100 kbit/s on the forward link and to 100 kbit/s on the reverse link distributed uniformly over the aircraft-station population. The size of the AS population varied from 14 to 240 users.

Figure 6-46 (a) displays the behavior of the 95% percentile of the one-way latency in the forward link direction. The 95% confidence intervals of the measurements are indicated by error bars in the graph. As expected, the latency of the transmission is independent of the number of users, although it is notable that the values show some variance caused by retransmissions. This variance is, however, well within the 95% percent confidence intervals of the measurement. It may therefore be interpreted insignificant within the desired measurement confidence.

Figure 6-46 (b) shows the behavior of the reverse link 95% percentile of the one-way latency. It is interesting to compare the results below to the MAC sub-layer results of Figure 6-25 and Figure 6-28 of section 6.2.3.4 and section 6.2.3.6[70]. Both results have been produced by the same computer simulation, however, the results of this section include the DLS ARQ protocol of the logical link control sub-layer (i.e. the complete B-AMC protocol stack) which was not included in the previous sections (which considered only the B-AMC protocol stack up to the MAC sub-layer).

The linear increase of the latency with the number of users is still clearly visible. However, the comparison of the results indicates that the DLS protocol introduces significant variance[71] into the reverse link latency. The increased variance can only be caused by the retransmission and flow control mechanisms of the DLS which have no knowledge of the MAC sub-layer state.

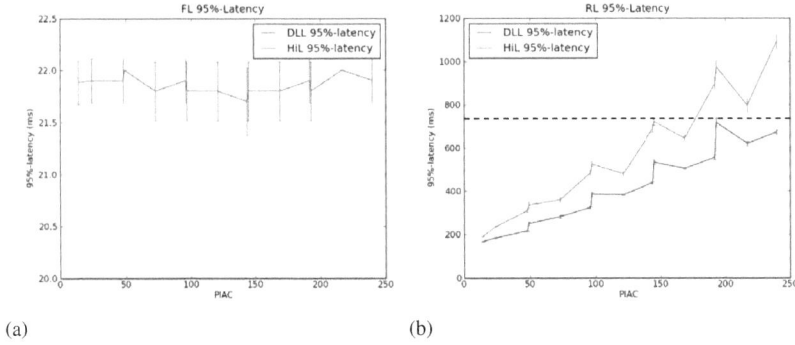

(a) (b)

Figure 6-46: B-AMC resilience under varying AS population; 95% percentile of latency. Note the fluctuations caused by the variance of the DLS retransmissions.

The evaluation of B-AMC under rising user data load will provide further evidence for this. Note that the variance of the DLS retransmissions is highest if the PIAC is near a multiple of the DC slot size (i.e. near 48, 96, 144, and 192). In this case the DLS round-trip time will experience the highest variance. This is caused by the relatively frequent shifting of acknowledgement opportunities into the next DC slot by the round-robin assignment in the DC. The higher variance of the DLS round-trip time results in an increased DLS retransmission timeout as the timeout value is set to the estimate of the

---

[70] Note that the results of the previous sections assumed a different offered load than this section.

[71] Note that the 95% percentile reflects the impact of increasing variance very strongly.

95% percentile[72] of the round-trip time. If the PIAC is between two multiples of the DC slot size (i.e. between 48 and 96, 96 and 144, etc.) the variance of the DLS round-trip time is lowest and the impact on the DLS timer management is significantly reduced. The comparison with the A-EXEC latency requirement (740 milliseconds) indicates that B-AMC can only support up to 200 aircraft-stations under this requirement. This is clearly below the theoretical maximum of the MAC sub-layer performance of 300 users (cf. section 6.2.3.7) and another indication for a sub-optimal DLS approach.

- How does the system performance change under rising user data load?

The behavior of B-AMC under rising user data load was evaluated in a similar scenario as used above. The higher layer packet size was set to 125 Bytes. The number of aircraft-stations logged into the ground-station was set to 100 AS. The offered load of the produced by the higher layers was varied from 29 kbit/s to 297 kbit/s on the forward link and 26 kbit/s to 260 kbit/s on the reverse link. The offered load was uniformly distributed among the 100 registered aircraft-stations.

The simulation results for the forward link direction are displayed in Figure 6-47 (a) and Figure 6-48 (a). The maximum achievable FL goodput is approximately 225 kbit/s. Note that the overhead of the B-AMC DLS and MAC headers was approximated by a 10% increase of the offered load reducing the net throughput to 202.5 kbit/s. This is approximately 75% of the channel capacity (273.07 kbit/s) user plane capacity and below the theoretical maximum of 260 kbit/s (cf. section 6.2.3.7). The B-AMC forward link starts to experience losses for offered loads above 200 kbit/s. Above the capacity threshold of 225 kbit/s losses are caused by excessive load which is also indicated by the build-up of the B-AMC interface queue in Figure 6-49 (a). The losses experienced in the range from 200 kbit/s to 225 kbit/s need a more detailed explanation.

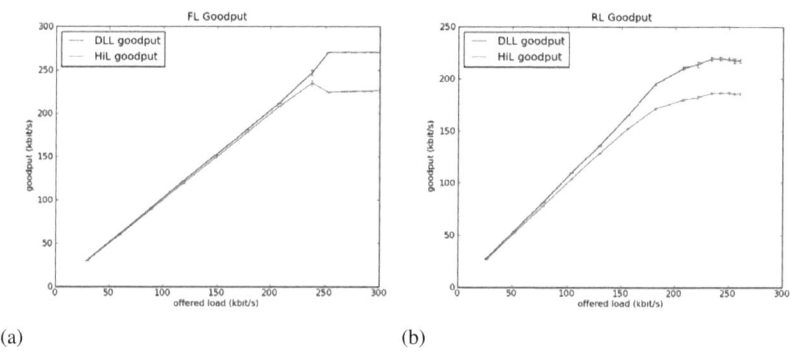

(a)   (b)

Figure 6-47: B-AMC resilience under varying load; goodput.

---

[72] Note that the 95% percentile reflects the impact of increasing variance very strongly.

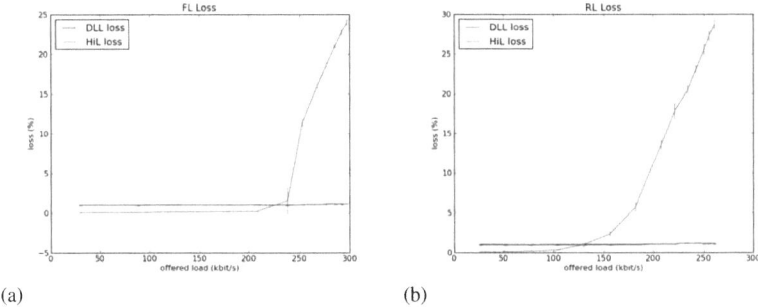

Figure 6-48: B-AMC resilience under varying load; loss.

Figure 6-49 (a) shows that the BSS queue starts to grow for offered loads beyond 200 kbit/s. This indicates that the DLS round-trip time estimation begins to underestimate the MAC sub-layer delay after this point leading to unnecessary retransmissions. These retransmissions increase the BSS queue length recursively amplifying the effect. The growing length of the BSS queue for offered loads beyond 200 kbit/s significantly increases the latency leading to increasing losses through expiration i.e. forward link packets are "lost" in the BSS queue due to imperfect timer management.

The simulation results of the B-AMC reverse link shows a different behavior. The maximum achievable goodput is approximately 185 kbit/s. Subtracting 10% overhead this is equivalent to 166.5 kbit/s net goodput or 70% of the reverse link user plane capacity. Unlike the forward link the reverse link experiences small amounts of losses very early. The percentage of lost packets increases, however, slowly. This and the fact that the BSS queue length remains stable (Figure 6-49 (b)) is an indication that the DLS timer-management over-estimates the round-trip time of the MAC sub-layer. The lost packets expire therefore in the DLS sending window while they are queued for retransmission.

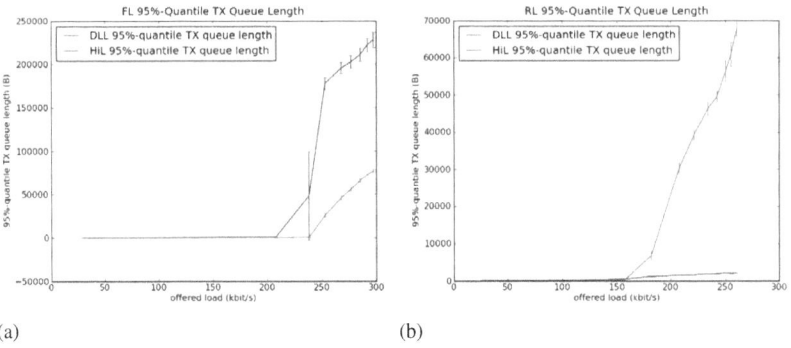

Figure 6-49: B-AMC resilience under varying load; queue length.

6.2.6 Discussion of B-AMC

This section summarizes and discusses the findings of the author's B-AMC evaluation. It is important to note that B-AMC was a design study. It was not the objective of the project to develop a system specification ready for implementation. Consequently some aspects of the system were analyzed in detail while others were left aside i.e. the results of this section were produced to identify potential design deficiencies in the B-AMC protocol and to estimate the expected performance.

The focus of the author in the B-AMC study was on the design and analysis of a medium access approach suitable for safety related systems. After the end of the B-AMC project this work was continued by the author in preparation of L-DACS 1. The focus of this research was, however, on the analysis and design of suitable user plane protocols in the logical link control sub-layer.

Figure 6-50 displays the B-AMC protocol entities and protocol functions. The mapping of protocol functions to the different entities is shown in brackets[73]. The following sections follow this functional model loosely in the discussion of the design issues indentified in the B-AMC protocol evaluation.

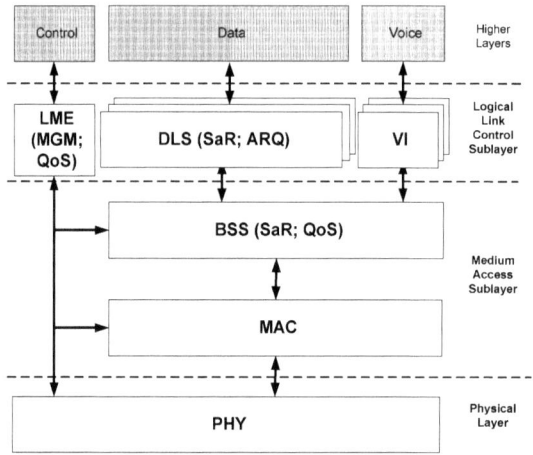

Figure 6-50: B-AMC protocol entities and functions.

6.2.6.1 Physical Layer

During the further development of the physical layer it became apparent that the use of OFDMA as it was proposed in B-AMC (parallel access of aircraft-stations to single sub-carriers) may be problematic to implement in existing hardware. The number of parallel

---

[73] The abbreviations are as follows: Management (MGM), Segmentation and Reassembly (SaR), Automatic Repeat Request (ARQ), Quality of Service (QoS), Medium Access (MAC), and Physical layer (PHY).

OFDMA accesses to the physical channel had therefore to be reduced. A typical approach to this problem would be the use of OFDMA tiles spanning several symbols in frequency and time direction (cf. section 6.3.2.1).

B-AMC used fixed size MAC-PDUs (i.e. T48 transport channels). Implementing a tile-based approach on the physical layer would provide the opportunity to implement variable sized MAC-PDUs by concatenating appropriate number of tiles. This approach would provide increased flexibility for resource allocation (e.g. the desired duty cycle can be taken into account by the resource allocation algorithm) and would result in less overhead (i.e. reduced need for padding).

Another benefit of supporting variable sized MAC-PDUs would lie in better support for adaptive coding and modulation - a topic that was touched only briefly in the B-AMC design. More advanced ACM could also provide the possibility to user stronger forward error correction for broadcast messages and to support the ENR.225 and ENR.250 scenarios.

However, changes on the physical layer like reducing the number of parallel OFDMA accesses on the reverse link, or changing the size of the MAC-PDUs would require modifications at the medium access sub-layer, with possible impact upon the logical link control sub-layer.

6.2.6.2 *Medium Access Sub-Layer*
The first focus of the author during the B-AMC study was on the analysis and design of a medium access protocol suitable for safety-related communication. Medium access to the forward link poses no specific challenges as it is under the sole control of the ground-station. Reliability and fairness can therefore be ensured by resource scheduling. However, the medium access to the reverse link raises challenges specific to the aeronautical environment: Due to the high radio range of the system an unusually high number of users (i.e. aircraft-stations) has to be supported. In addition, medium access should be swift and dependable to allow safety related communication.

6.2.6.2.1 Deterministic Medium Access
The author's design of the B-AMC medium access approach builds on the lessons learnt from his analysis of the B-VHF medium access. The B-VHF approach was based on resource requests sent in random access slots. However, in order to cope with significant numbers of users B-VHF required high numbers of random access slots. But even so the MAC latency would rise sharply under high load.

In addition to the poor performance the second problem of the random access based B-VHF approach was that it was essentially non-deterministic, which posed a major problem for a safety-related system. The medium access latency depended on the number of medium access attempts of the aircraft-stations i.e. the system performance was determined by the application's data traffic pattern, which is neither predictable nor under the control of the system.

B-AMC medium access was therefore based on a new approach devised by the author to solve these problems. It was designed to provide dependable medium access to a high number of users without any dependency of the access latency on the data traffic pattern. This was realized by the introduction of a dedicated and periodic control channel for each aircraft-station. The aircraft-stations use this channel to provide the ground-station with periodic updates on their resource needs. This decouples the medium access algorithm from the data traffic pattern.

Providing dedicated resources for each control channel makes medium access contention-free. The medium access latency is therefore only coupled to the number of aircraft-stations served by the ground-station. The medium access performance degrades thus only linearly with the number of users and not exponentially as in the case of random access.

The B-AMC medium access approach was analyzed by the author using formal analysis and simulation. Both approaches yield the same results and confirm that the stated design goals have been achieved.

6.2.6.2.2 Control Channel Overhead

Deterministic contention free medium access comes at the price of the overhead introduced by the dedicated control channels. In the case of a safety related communication a higher level of overhead is certainly acceptable if it makes the system more dependable, however, it would nevertheless be desirable to minimize this overhead as far as possible.

The efficiency (i.e. 100% minus overhead) of the B-AMC protocol is dominated by the fixed size control channels. Under the worst case assumption of fully used control channels B-AMC can achieve high levels of efficiency only when the user load is high in comparison to the control channel load. However, suffering from low efficiency under low load is not a real problem as the channel capacity is not needed in this case anyway.

Medium access to the B-AMC reverse link control channels in the SA and DC slots is based on the access to individual sub-carriers. If this approach would be changed to a tile-based method the structure of the synchronized access channel and dedicated control channel had to be adapted. Tiles would offer more payload capacity than a single sub-carrier. The efficiency of the reverse link control channels could be therefore increased if the B-AMC SA and DC slots were merged into a single dedicated control slot hosting the combined functionality.

A tile-based approach would also offer the opportunity to dynamically change the size of the control channels on forward link and reverse link (i.e. the number of tiles used for the control channel's slot) according to the current demand. In that case sufficient bandwidth for all control messages could be guaranteed and the overhead could be reduced.

6.2.6.2.3 Prioritized Medium Access in the BSS

The logical link control sub-layer and the medium access sub-layer are not directly connected. The access of the DLS to the logical channels provided by the MAC is governed by the BSS entity. The B-AMC DLS is completely decoupled from the MAC by the BSS. The BSS accepts packets from the DLS and resource allocations from the MAC. It fragments variable sized DLS packets to fixed size MAC-PDUs before transmitting them over the logical channels provided by the MAC according to their priority.

The purpose of the BSS entity in the B-AMC design was to ensure prioritized medium access of competing service classes by active queue management. B-AMC proposed to use class-based weighted fair queuing in the BSS. However, the evaluation of the B-AMC performance indicated that such sophisticated queuing disciplines are not necessary to provide fair and prioritized medium access.

6.2.6.2.4 Segmentation and Reassembly in the BSS

The priority management of the BSS operates on fixed sized MAC-PDUs (i.e. transport channels). This generates a need for a second level of segmentation and reassembly in addition to the segmentation and reassembly in the DLS. It would be desirable to avoid this second level of fragmentation to reduce the system complexity and overhead.

If a tile-based approach would be used, variable sized MAC-PDUs would become possible. Variable sized MAC-PDUs would provide significantly more flexibility and less overhead. However, providing quality of service by active queue management is only feasible with small, fixed-sized MAC-PDUs (i.e. resource grants). Thus, in the case of variable sized MAC-PDUs a different approach to prioritized medium access would be needed.

6.2.6.3   Logical Link Control Sub-Layer

The second focus of the author's work on B-AMC was the analysis and design of suitable user plane transport protocols for the logical link control sub-layer. The main challenge in fulfilling this objective is to ensure the correct interaction of the DLS, BSS and the MAC. The priority of DLS PDUs is managed by the BSS, however, the sending rates of the different protocol instances providing different classes of service have to be coordinated as they compete for the same channel resources. As the DLS cannot directly interact with the lower layers (MAC and PHY) this coordination is a non-trivial task.

6.2.6.3.1   Segmentation and Reassembly

The DLS fragments higher layer packets to DLS-PDUs. As the size of the resource allocation is fixed, the variable sized DLS-PDUs cannot be aligned with the allocation boundaries i.e. DLS –PDUs may be split over several allocations (i.e. transport channels). This design may lead to sub-optimal fragmentation of DLS packets[74]. In addition, the second level of fragmentation performed by the BSS can significantly increase the variance of the transmission time of DLS packets if a single DLS-PDU is transmitted in several transport channels as illustrated for DLS-PDU 1.1 in Figure 6-51. This increases the estimated round-trip time and thus the retransmission timer setting unnecessarily.

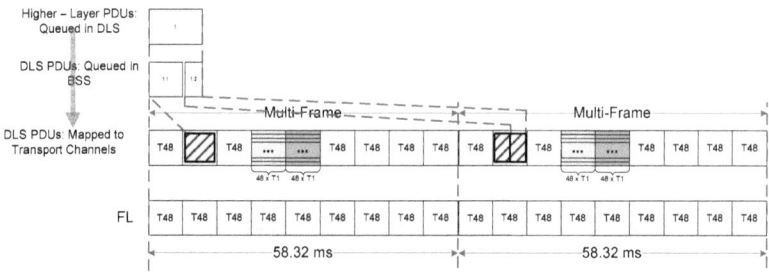

Figure 6-51: Sub-optimal mapping of RL packets to transport channels.

The packet fragmentation could be significantly improved if there was only one level of fragmentation based on feedback from the MAC sub-layer and variable sized MAC-PDUs (i.e. resource allocations). If the BSS were removed from the protocol stack and the DLS were made aware of MAC sub-layer resource allocation size, DLS packets could be fragmented directly to the appropriate size.

The system design would be significantly simplified by removing one additional level of fragmentation. However, a consequence of removing the BSS would be that the DLS has to manage quality of service by itself.

6.2.6.3.2 Flow Control

An additional benefit of removing the BSS would be that only one queue remains in the system: The interface queue of the DLS. With the BSS present, there are two queues in the system, increasing the overall system complexity as the storage capacity of the BSS queue leads to a further decoupling of DLS and MAC. This made DLS flow control and timer management difficult in the B-AMC design.

The B-AMC DLS requires flow control to regulate the amount of data passed to the BSS entity in the MAC sub-layer. If the DLS data rate is not controlled, the DLS may produce congestion in the BSS queue. As the BSS entity has no means to report the

---

[74] It has been reported that this scheme works best if the size of the DLS packets and the size of the BSS fragments is equal, effectively eliminating the BSS fragmentation from the protocol stack [**19**].

available bandwidth (which is only known by the ground-station MAC entity), the B-AMC DLS has to estimate the network load from measurements of (un)successful packet transmissions. Then, the DLS can set the transmission window accordingly. DLS flow control could be significantly simplified if the airborne DLS were made aware of the resource allocations issued by the ground-station.

The ground-station has a complete view of all resource needs in the system as it collects the resource requests of all stations (including its own). This knowledge is used to compute the resource allocations for all airborne DLS entities. Therefore, the resource allocations that are periodically transmitted by the ground-station contain already the complete knowledge of the available transmission resources. Consequently the size of the resource allocation is also the optimal DLS transmission window size. This is known as credit based flow management

However, a credit-based approach is complex to implement if the logical link control sub-layer comprises multiple DLS entities or DLS queues without common state. Hence, a common quality of service function assigning allocated resources to different DLS instances would be needed.

6.2.6.3.3 Timer Management

The B-AMC timer management is relatively complex as the DLS has no information about the medium access sub-layer status. The retransmission timer depends on relatively complex measurements and estimations of the observed data link round trip time. The DLS uses algorithms usually implemented in higher layer protocols (i.e. van Jacobson's and Karn's algorithms in TCP) to accomplish this task. Although it has been shown that these algorithms can provide good performance in the data link layer too, they are difficult to optimize and require careful fine-tuning.

Operating several DLS instances (i.e. classes of service) within the same B-AMC stack efficiently has proven to be particularly difficult as the DLS instances share no state with the MAC sub-layer. The DLS timer management could be simplified significantly if the logical link control sub-layer was made aware of the MAC state: Acknowledgements and data packets are sent in specific time slots occurring at well-known instants i.e. if the DLS were made aware of the MAC frame structure it would be possible to achieve near optimal timer management by counting transmission opportunities of data packets and acknowledgements. This approach would offer much greater algorithmic robustness than the fine-tuning of the current approach.

6.2.6.4 Summary

The main achievement accomplished by the author in the B-AMC study was the development of a dependable medium access approach suitable for safety related communication. The development was based on the careful analysis of the B-VHF results, formal analysis, and computer simulations. The new MAC algorithm is deterministic, fair, contention free, and provides linear graceful degradation. After the

B-AMC project the author's scheme was used in the L-DACS 1 and L-DACS 2 protocol developments.

The main issue that has been identified by the author in the B-AMC evaluation is the sub-optimal performance of the logical link control sub-layer user plane protocols due to the weak coupling of the MAC and LLC sub-layers. B-AMC could therefore not fulfill all requirements. The analysis of the results indicates that the tight coupling of DLS and MAC – by omitting the BSS entity - would provide more simplicity and better performance than the loose coupling implemented in the B-AMC design. The author's proposed protocol changes were therefore:

- Tight coupling between DLS and MAC
  - Signal MAC state to DLS for timer management and window management
- Remove BSS
  - Let the DLS fragment packets directly into MAC-PDUs
  - The problems introduced by the weak coupling of DLS and MAC outweigh the benefits of simple priority management in the BSS.
- Implement variable sized MAC-PDUs
  - Increase flexibility of resource allocation
  - Decrease fragmentation
- Implement variable sized control channels
  - Control channel capacity can be increased on demand
  - Better isolation of control and data traffic

Figure 6-52 displays the proposed simplified protocol stack. The BSS has been removed and its functionality was moved into the DLS.

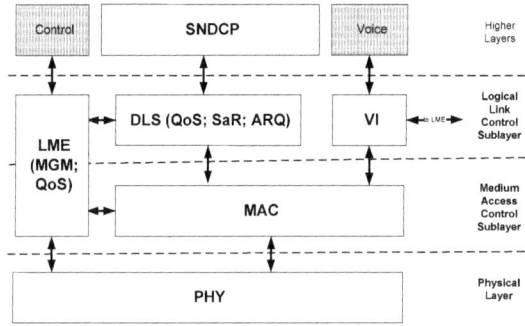

Figure 6-52: Proposed protocol stack.

6.3 L-DACS 1

Action plan 17 ended after the B-AMC study. The outcome of EUROCONTROL's and FAA's activities was that no single future radio system candidate could be fully recommended yet. However, the AP17 activities identified several desirable features the future L-band system should provide. Thus EUROCONTROL funded the initial specification of two independent L-band Digital Communication System L-DACS proposals: L-DACS 1 and L-DACS 2. These draft specifications should enable prototyping activities to clarify system compatibility issues that could not be covered analytically or via modeling (e.g. spectrum compatibility issues) and are out of the scope of this thesis [3].

B-AMC was identified as the most promising L-DACS 1 candidate by EUROCONTROL. Together with the other L-DACS 1 candidate TIA-902 P34 [25] and IEEE 802.16e WiMAX [26] it was therefore selected to provide the technological basis for the development of an L-DACS 1 system. The specification of L-DACS 1 [1] was based on input from these standards and the author's critical examination of the B-AMC results.

After the end of the EUROCONTROL funded specification effort the development of L-DACS 1 was continued in the "Consolidated L-DACS 1 based on B-AMC" CoLB project of the Austrian research promotion agency FFG. This project produced an updated specification and extensive guidance material [32]. Further information can be found in the relevant publications [27][28][29][30]. If not stated otherwise the discussion of L-DACS 1 in this thesis is based on the revised protocol specification [32].

While the author concentrated on the medium-access development in the B-AMC study, he concentrated on the design of the logical link control layer and the simplification of the system architecture during the L-DACS 1 project. Merging B-AMC with other candidate technology's features and protocols led to significant changes and modifications relative of the original B-AMC system design. The author's major innovation of the L-DACS 1 research was the complete re-design of the user plane LLC protocols. The HDLC based sliding window protocol of B-AMC was replaced by a two-layer credit-based ARQ protocol. These changes led to a significantly simplified and algorithmically much more robust LLC design.

6.3.1 System Architecture
In spite of multiple modifications the L-DACS 1 design preserved the main B-AMC system characteristics. It was designed to provide an air-ground and an air-air data link with optional support for digital air-ground voice. Like B-AMC, the L-DACS 1 air-ground mode is optimized for data communication and designed to simultaneously

support Air Traffic Services *ATS* and Aeronautical Operational Control *AOC* communications services. The air-air mode is not discussed in this thesis [75].

The L-DACS 1 air-ground mode system architecture was derived from the B-AMC system architecture. It is a cellular point-to-multipoint system with a star-topology where aircraft-stations are connected to a ground-station via a full duplex radio link. The ground-station is the centralized instance controlling the air-ground communications within a certain volume of space called an L-DACS 1 cell.

The L-DACS 1 protocol stack is based on the author's analysis of the B-AMC functional architecture and his proposed revised protocol stack layout in Figure 6-52. It defines two layers, physical layer and data link layer as illustrated in Figure 6-53.

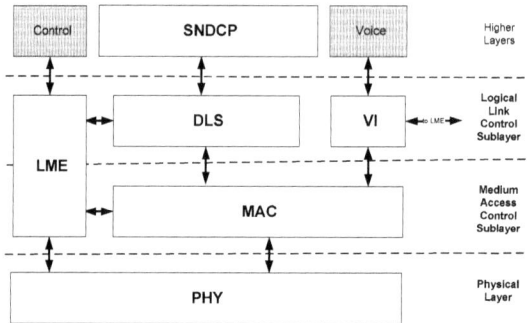

Figure 6-53: L-DACS 1 protocol stack.

The physical layer provides the means to transfer data over the radio channel. The L-DACS 1 ground-station simultaneously supports bi-directional links to multiple aircraft-stations under its control. The forward link direction and the reverse link direction are separated by frequency division duplex *FDD*. In the RL direction different aircraft-stations are separated in time (using time division multiple access *TDMA*) and frequency (using orthogonal frequency division multiple access OFDMA).

The ground-station transmits a continuously stream of OFDM symbols on the forward link. Aircraft-stations transmit, however, discontinuous on the RL with radio bursts sent in precisely defined transmission opportunities using resources allocated by the ground-station LME. An aircraft-station accesses the RL channel autonomously only during cell-entry. All other reverse link transmissions, including control and user data, are scheduled and controlled by the ground-station.

---

[75] An overview of the L-DACS 1 air-air protocols designed by the author is provided in [**30**] and [**37**].

The data link layer provides the necessary protocols to facilitate concurrent and reliable data transfer for multiple users. The functional blocks of the L-DACS 1 data link layer architecture are organized in two sub-layers: The medium access sub-layer and the logical link control sub-layer. The logical link control sub-layer manages the radio link and offers a bearer service with different classes of service to the higher layers. It comprises the Data Link Services *DLS*, and the Voice Interface *VI*. The medium access sub-layer contains only the Medium Access *MAC* entity. Cross-layer management is provided by the Link Management Entity *LME*. The Sub-Network Dependent Convergence Protocol *SNDCP* provides the interface to the higher layers.

The *MAC* entity of the medium access sub-layer manages the access of the LLC entities to the resources of the physical layer. It provides the logical link control sub-layer with the ability to transmit user and control data over logical channels. The peer LLC entities communicate only over logical channels and have no concept of the underlying physical layer.

Prior to fully utilizing the system, an aircraft-station has to register at the controlling ground-station in order to get a statically assigned dedicated control channel for the exchange of control data with the ground-station. The ground-station dynamically allocates the resources for user data channels according to the current demand as signalled by the aircraft-stations.

Except for the initial cell-entry procedure all communication between the aircraft-stations and the controlling ground-station (including procedures for requesting and allocating resources for user data transmission and retransmission timer management), is fully deterministic and managed by the ground-station. Under constant load, the system performance depends only on the number of aircraft-stations serviced by the particular ground-station and linearly decreases with increasing number of aircraft.

Bidirectional exchange of user data between the ground-station and the aircraft-station is performed by the Data Link Service DLS entity using the logical data channel *DCH* for user plane transmissions[76]. Control plane transmissions from the aircraft-station to the ground-station are performed over the logical dedicated control channel *DCCH*. Ground-to-air control information is transmitted in the common control channel. The random access channel *RACH* and the broadcast control channel *BCCH* are used for cell-entry, cell-exit, and handover. The relation of the logical channels to the functional blocks of the L-DACS 1 logical link control layer is illustrated in Figure 6-54.

---

[76] Note that the VI also uses the DCH for its transmissions. The dedicated voice channel VCH was removed in the revised specification [**29**].

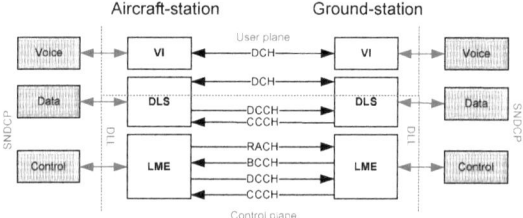

Figure 6-54: L- DACS 1 logical channel structure.

The Data Link Service **DLS** provides the acknowledged and unacknowledged exchange of user data over the point-to-point reverse link or point-to-multipoint forward link. There is one DLS in the aircraft-station and one peer DLS for each AS in the ground-station.

The ground-station Link Management Entity **LME** provides centralized resource management for L-DACS 1. It assigns transmission resources, provides mobility management and link maintenance. It assigns forward link and reverse link resources taking channel occupancy limitations (e.g. limiting the AS duty cycle) into account. In addition, LME provides dynamic link maintenance service (power, frequency and time adjustments) and supports Adaptive Coding and Modulation ACM.

The Voice Interface **VI** provides support for virtual voice circuits. The voice interface provides only the transmission and reception services, while LME performs creation and selection of voice circuits. Voice circuits may either be set-up permanently by the ground-station LME to emulate party-line voice or may be created on demand.

L-DACS 1 shall become a sub-network of the Aeronautical Telecommunications Network ATN. The Subnetwork Dependent Convergence Protocol **SNDCP** provides the L-DACS 1 interface to the network layer and a network layer adaptation service required for transparent transfer of Network layer Protocol Data Units N-PDUs of possibly different network protocols (ATN/IPS and ATN/OSI). The SNDCP should also provide compression and encryption services required for improving and securing the wireless channel.

6.3.1.1 Input from Other Systems

Most features of the L-DACS 1 data link layer design are based on the author's experience gained from B-AMC. The most important protocol element adopted from B-AMC is the medium access approach. The protocol stack architecture and the data link service protocol were redesigned by the author on the basis of the lessons learnt from B-AMC.

However, a considerable amount of input was also received from other AP17 candidate systems. Probably the most influential external input[77] to the L-DACS1 design came from the TIA-902 P34 standard [25]. The message formats of the medium access layer and the addressing scheme were directly derived from this system.

The concept of tiles and FL and RL allocation maps was adopted from the WiMAX standard [26]. Additional input from WiMAX has gone into the design of the physical layer, which is not discussed in depth within this thesis.

6.3.2 Physical Layer Overview

The specific L-band interference situation has influenced the design of both B-AMC and L-DACS 1. Both systems were designed to minimize interference to and from other L-band systems as well as to other systems operating close to the aeronautical L-band (e.g. GSM, UMTS). As was already the case with B-AMC the air-ground mode of L-DACS 1 works in the aeronautical L-band (960 –1164 MHz). It is intended to operate as a Frequency Division Duplex *FDD* system with separate radio channels for the forward link and reverse link according to the analysis of section 6.2.2.2.

The preferred L-DACS 1 deployment option is an inlay system. The system radio bandwidth (approximately 0.5 MHz) enables an inlay deployment analogue to B-AMC, where L DACS 1 channels, nominally separated by 1 MHz, are placed at 0.5 MHz offset from DME channels. However, L-DACS 1 can also be deployed as non-inlay system with FL and RL channels placed within contiguous blocks of spectrum not occupied by the DME system. As a third option L-DACS 1 can be deployed in parallel to the DME system by re-using a set of non-contiguous DME channels vacated for that purpose. Different combinations of these scenarios are possible as well. A generic approach for allocating L-DACS 1 FL and RL channels is shown in Figure 6-55. This approach is applicable to all deployment options and uses the same frequency allocations as proposed for B-AMC.

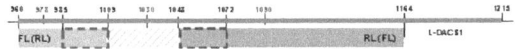

Figure 6-55: L-band usage for L-DACS 1 air-ground communications.

The L-DACS 1 OFDM parameters were chosen according to the characteristics of the aeronautical mobile L-band channel [28][29]. The forward link and reverse link channels have an effective bandwidth of 498.05 kHz each. Within that bandwidth, 50 OFDM sub-carriers are placed, separated by 9.765625 kHz. Each sub-carrier is separately modulated with a symbol duration of T_s = 120 µs.

---

[77] Kindly supported by FAA, NASA, MITRE, and ITT.

The physical layer design includes propagation guard times sufficient for a maximum range of 200 nautical miles. In real deployments the L-DACS 1 maximum transmission power may, however, have to be limited in order to protect receivers of other L-band systems.

In the case of an inlay deployment the maximum range may have to be reduced due to strong the interference constraints. However, the maximum range is also limited by other factors: The evaluation of B-AMC indicated that the forward link cannot provide the necessary capacity for very large cells in the European core area: The "ENR Large ATS + AOC with A-EXEC", ENR.225 and ENR.250 scenarios could not be supported. This is equivalent to a maximum operational range of approximately 140 nautical miles. Long-range capability is, however, still desired. It is required for off-shore coverage or remote sectors with large communications distances and low numbers of aircraft.

6.3.2.1 Synchronization and Framing

L-DACS 1 employs a physical layer frame structure derived from B-AMC. Each forward-link super-frame has a length of 240 milliseconds and starts with a leading 6.72 milliseconds broadcast *BC frame* internally divided into three OFDM sub-frames BC1, BC2 and BC3. The BC OFDM frame is followed by four multi-frames of each 58.32 milliseconds length. Each forward link multi-frame is divided into nine *Data frames* with the same internal structure.

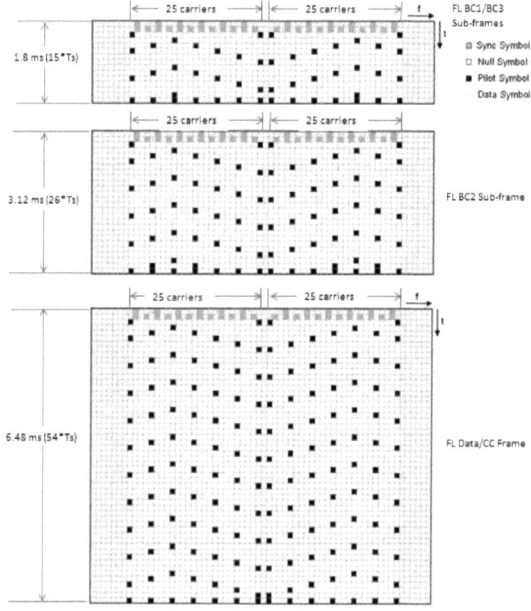

Figure 6-56: L-DACS 1 FL OFDM frame structure [31].

The physical layer structure of the forward link OFDM frames is shown in Figure 6-56. The use of OFDM symbols is indicated in the legend on the right side of the diagram. The OFDM frame duration is indicated on the left side in milliseconds and numbers of symbols.

On reverse link each super-frame comprises two opportunities for random-access RA OFDM sub-frames and four multi-frames. The time allocated for the two random access opportunities corresponds to the duration of the forward link BC OFDM frame (6.72 milliseconds). Reverse link multi-frames have the same duration as the forward link multi-frames (58.32 ms) and are divided into a synchronization section and up to 160 data tiles.

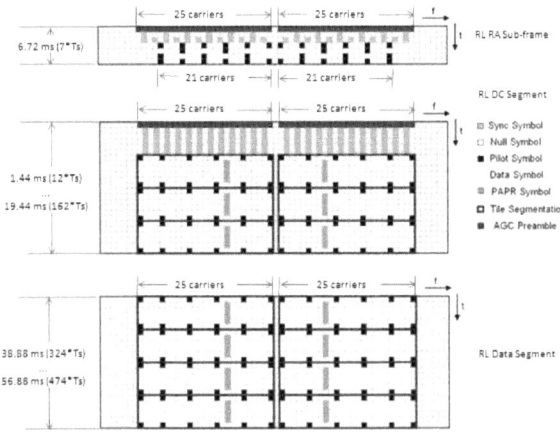

Figure 6-57: L-DACS 1 RL OFDM frame structure [31].

A reverse link *RA sub-frame* starts with a preamble followed by two synchronisation symbols and four OFDM symbols comprising 34 pilot symbols and 134 modulated data symbols. Each reverse link multi-frame starts with a preamble (one symbol in Figure 6-57) followed by a number of synchronisation symbols (five in Figure 6-57; this is the minimum) and a variable number of OFDM tiles depending on the number of synchronization symbols[78].

One *tile* spans 6 successive OFDM symbols and 25 consecutive OFDM sub-carriers. Each tile comprises 12 modulated pilot tones, 4 symbols for Peak to Average Power Ratio PAPR reduction and 134 modulated data symbols for payload data. Tiles are

---

[78] The synchronization section may be increased reducing the number of available data tiles. In this document the minimal synchronization section size (five symbols) is always assumed which leaves space for 160 data tiles on the reverse link.

indicated by brown rectangles in Figure 6-57. The physical layer structure of the reverse link frames is illustrated in the same figure.

6.3.2.2 Frame Structure

L-DACS 1 structures the physical layer on the basis of OFDM frames and OFDM segments. OFDM frames are used on the forward link and on the reverse link. OFDM segments are only used on the reverse link. Frames and segments are combined into multi-frames and super-frames as in B-AMC.

An OFDM frame represents the fixed-length sequence of contiguous OFDM symbols as defined in section 6.3.2.1. An OFDM segment represents the variable-length sequence of contiguous tiles on the reverse link.

The L-DACS 1 super-frame is the highest element of the physical layer framing hierarchy. The super-frame duration is 240 milliseconds or 2000 OFDM symbols. This is a multiple of the voice sample length (20 milliseconds) produced by the AMBE ATC10B vocoder. A forward link super-frame comprises a broadcast frame BC sub-divided into the BC1, BC2, and BC3 sub-frames and four multi-frames. A reverse link super-frame comprises two random-access opportunities in the RA frame and four multi-frames. The super-frame layout is illustrated in Figure 6-58.

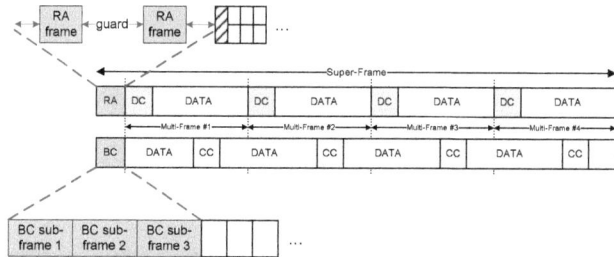

Figure 6-58: L-DACS 1 super-frame structure.

The length of the forward link and reverse link multi-frames is 58.32 milliseconds or 486 symbols. Each forward link multi-frame comprises 9 Data OFDM frames. A variable number of these frames, starting with the fifth data frame, use a different channel coding and are designated as CC frames.

Each RL MF comprises one DC segment and one Data segment. These segments are sub-divided into tiles. The reverse link DC segment starts with the RL synchronization symbols and the first two reverse link tiles. Its length is variable between two tiles and fifty-two tiles. The remaining RL tiles create the reverse link data segment.

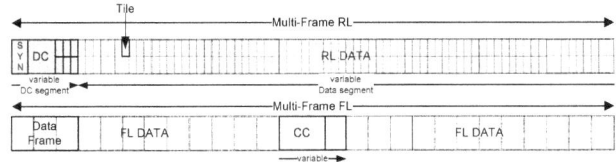

Figure 6-59: L-DACS 1 multi-frame structure.

Note that the L-DACS 1 frame structure is more flexible than the B-AMC frame structure. The sizes of the control and data channels can now be adjusted. Note also that the DC and the SA slot have been merged.

6.3.2.3 Modulation and Coding

All forward link and reverse link control and user data is transmitted in PHYsical layer Service Data Units *PHY-SDU*s protected by forward error correction FEC. The transmitting PHY layer receives PHY-SDUs from the medium access sub-layer, applies error correcting coding, and performs other physical layer tasks like interleaving and modulation. The result is then mapped onto a constellation of data symbols within an OFDM frame or OFDM tile (i.e. a PHY-PDU).

The PHY-SDU size depends on the number of coded and modulated data symbols and on the used modulation and coding scheme. It is defined by considering only modulated data symbols. The MAC sub-layer is only aware of the position and size of the PHY-SDU. Thus the physical layer overhead of the particular frame, like pilot symbols, synchronization symbols, preamble symbols or PAPR symbols, is transparent to the medium access sub-layer.

There are several types of forward link PHY-SDUs intended for different purposes. BC1, BC2, and BC3 PHY-SDUs convey the logical broadcast control channel BCH. They are mapped to the BC1, BC2, and BC3 OFDM frames on the forward link. Within each forward link multi-frame three PHY-SDUs are mapped to each OFDM frame i.e. a forward link multi-frame comprises twenty-seven PHY-SDUs. The logical common control channel *CCH* is conveyed in the thirteenth PHY-SDU and up to eleven following PHY-SDUs (i.e. up to twelve PHY-SDUs in total). The remaining forward link PHY-SDUs are used for the logical data channel *DCH*. Note that CC PHY-SDUs and Data PHY-SDUs use different forward error correction schemes. The FL multi-frame is illustrated in Figure 6-60.

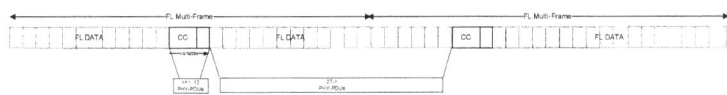

Figure 6-60: FL multi-frame.

Similarly, there are several types of reverse link PHY-SDUs dedicated to different purposes. RA PHY-SDUs convey the logical random access channel **RACH** and are mapped to RA OFDM frames. Within each reverse link multi-frame each tile corresponds to one reverse link PHY-SDU. The tiles of the DC segment convey the logical dedicated control channel **DCCH**. The tiles of the data segment convey the logical data channel **DCH**. The RL multi-frame is illustrated in Figure 6-61 assuming the minimum number of synchronization symbols.

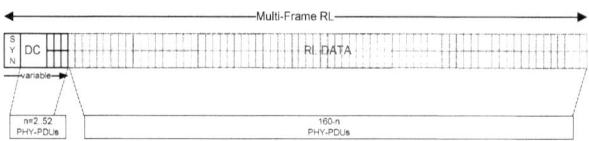

Figure 6-61: RL multi-frame.

L-DACS 1 employs a concatenated block coding **CC** and Reed-Solomon **RS** coding scheme implemented in the physical layer. The receiving physical layer performs the channel decoding and error correction over each received PHY-SDU[79], but it cannot determine whether the received data is error-free or not. Error detection is therefore performed in the logical link control sub-layer using Cyclic Redundancy Checks CRCs.

PHY-SDUs used for the transmission of control channels (BC, RA, CC, and DC PHY-SDUs) use the most robust forward error correction scheme. The coding of the Data PHY-SDUs may be changed according to the radio channel conditions by means of Adaptive Coding and Modulation **ACM**. If the L-DACS 1 cell is configured to use the same ACM scheme for all user data transmissions this is called cell-specific coding. Alternatively, the ground-station may specify and adjust ACM settings individually for each aircraft-station. This is called user-specific ACM. The original specification [1] defined different forward link PHY-SDU layouts for cell-specific and user-specific coding. In the course of later research this was, however, removed[80]. Cell-specific and user-specific ACM use the same frame layout now.

The reverse link and forward link PHY-PDUs comprise the same number of modulated symbols for any given ACM setting, only the PHY-SDU capacity (i.e. number of payload bits) changes dependent on the overhead of the ACM scheme.

Table 6-21 summarizes the L-DACS 1 coding and modulation schemes. The table gives the modulation of the OFDM sub-carriers, the rate of the convolutional code, the total

---

[79] It was proposed to extent the FEC over several consecutive PHY-SDUs for increased performance. Meeting of the author with DLR on July 27th 2010 in Oberpfaffenhofen. These results were not published at the time of this writing.

[80] Meeting of the author with DLR on July 27th 2010 in Oberpfaffenhofen. These results were not published at the time of this writing.

coding rate including the RS code, and the available forward link data rate assuming two CC PHY-SDUs per multi-frame. The parameters of the Reed-Solomon code can be found in [1].

Table 6-21: L-DACS 1 adaptive coding and modulation schemes [1].

ACM Type	Modulation	CC rate	Total coding rate with RS	FL data rate kbit/s
1 (default)	QPSK	1/2	0.45	303.3
2	QPSK	2/3	0.60	400.0
3	QPSK	3/4	0.67	450.0
4	16QAM	1/2	0.45	606.7
5	16QAM	2/3	0.60	806.7
6	64QAM	1/2	0.45	906.7
7	64QAM	2/3	0.60	1220.0
8	64QAM	3/4	0.68	1373.3

Note that the development of forward error correction coding is extremely complex. Several optimizations of the presented specification have been proposed in the course of further research by DLR and Frequentis AG, but have not been published at the time of this writing.

Table 6-22 and Table 6-23 show the size and data capacity of forward link and reverse link PHY-SDUs. The tables indicate the OFDM (sub-)frames in which the PHY-SDUs are transmitted and the number of PHY-SDUs within a (sub-)frame, multi-frame and super-frame. Note that the "PHY-PDU Size" columns in Table 6-22 and Table 6-23 denote the number of modulated data symbols at the physical layer. The "PHY-SDU Size" columns indicate the maximum size of the corresponding PHY-SDU in payload bits.

Table 6-22: Number, Size and Capacity of FL PHY-PDUs and PHY-SDUs

OFDM (sub-) Frame Type	PHY-PDU Type	Nr. of PHY-PDUs per OFDM (sub-) Frame	Nr. of PHY-PDUs per MF	Nr. of PHY-PDUs per SF
BC1 Sub-Frame	BC1	1	N/A	1
BC2 Sub-Frame	BC2	1	N/A	1
BC3 Sub-Frame	BC3	1	N/A	1
Data/CC Frame	CC	3	n=1...12	m=1...48
Data/CC Frame	Data	3	27-n	(27*4)-m

OFDM (sub-) Frame Type	PHY-PDU Type	PHY-PDU Coding	PHY-PDU Size (Data Symbols)	PHY-PDU Modulation (ACM Type)	PHY-SDU Size (Uncoded Bits)
BC1 Sub-Frame	BC1	½ CC + RS(74,66,4)	602	1	528
BC2 Sub-Frame	BC2	½ CC + RS(139,125,7)	1120	1	1000
BC3 Sub-Frame	BC3	½ CC + RS(74,66,4)	602	1	528
Data/CC Frame	CC	½ CC + RS(101,90,5)	814	1	720
Data/CC Frame	Data	Variable	814	1-8	728 - 3296

Table 6-23: Number, Size and Capacity of RL PHY-PDUs and PHY-SDUs

OFDM (sub-) Frame/Segment Type	PHY-PDU Type	Nr. of PHY-PDUs per OFDM (sub-) Frame/Segment	Nr. of PHY-PDUs per MF	Nr. of PHY-PDUs per SF
RA Sub-Frame	RA	0-1	N/A	0-2
DC Segment	DC	n=2...52	n=2...52	m=8...208
Data Segment	Data	160-n	160-n	640-m

OFDM (sub-) Frame/Segment Type	PHY-PDU Type	PHY-PDU Coding	PHY-PDU Size (Data Symbols)	PHY-PDU Modulation (ACM Type)	PHY-SDU Size (Uncoded Bits)
RA Sub-Frame	RA	½ CC + RS(16,14,1)	134	1	112
DC Segment	DC	½ CC + RS(16,14,1)	134	1	112
Data Segment	Data	Variable	134	1-8	112 - 528

6.3.3 Medium Access Sub-Layer

The MAC entity of the medium access sub-layer manages the access of the LLC entities to the resources of the physical layer. Its design is based on the medium access concepts devised by the author for the B-AMC protocol. The medium access sub-layer provides the logical link control sub-layer with the ability to transmit user and control data in logical channels. This is accomplished using two MAC internal services: The Time Framing Service and the Medium Access Service.

6.3.3.1 Medium Access Sub-Layer Time Framing Service

OFDM symbols are organized into OFDM frames, OFMD segments, and OFDM tiles. However, the medium access sub-layer has no knowledge of the physical layer framing structures. In fact, it does not even use them, as all data is transmitted in physical layer service data PHY-SDUs protected by Forward Error Correction *FEC*. Therefore, the medium access sub-layer has to be provided with an abstraction of the physical layer framing.

Consecutive RL PHY-SDUs and FL PHY-SDUs are presented to the MAC as time slots that can be used for transmissions. The physical layer provides three time slots on the reverse link (Random Access slot RA, Dedicated Control slot DC, and Data slot) and three time slots on the forward link (Broadcast Control slot *BC*, Common Control Slot *CC*, and Data slot). This slot structure is used by the MAC to provide logical channels to its users in the logical link control layer. The physical layer maps slots to PHY-SDUs. The size of the slots (and therefore the capacity of the logical channels) can be configured by the ground-station LME to match changing demands.

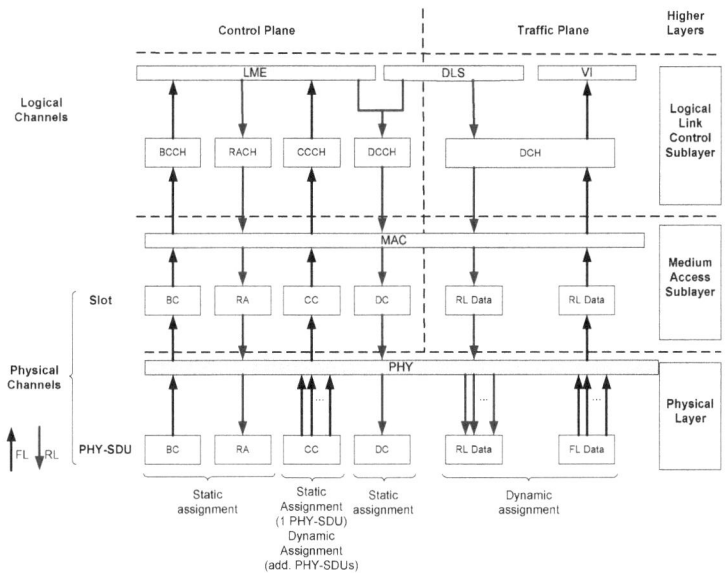

Figure 6-62: L-DACS 1 logical channel mapping (aircraft-station perspective).

Control plane transmissions on the reverse link are performed over the logical dedicated control channel *DCCH* conveyed in the DC slot. Forward link control information is transmitted in the common control channel mapped into the CC slot. The random access channel *RACH* and the broadcast control channel BCCH are used for mobility signaling (cell-entry and handover) and use the RA and BC slots, respectively.

Control channels are statically mapped to PHY-SDUs while user plane channels are mapped dynamically i.e. prior to utilizing the system for data or voice communication an aircraft-station has to register with a ground-station in order to receive a static assignment for its dedicated control channel.

Bidirectional exchange of user data between the ground-station and the aircraft-station is performed by the Data Link Service *DLS* entity using the logical data channel *DCH* for user plane transmissions. The DCH is transmitted in the Data slot. Within this slot different users are dynamically assigned resources. The mapping of logical channels to physical layer slots and PHY-SDUs in displayed in Figure 6-62. Note the significant simplification of the author's new system design in comparison to B-AMC (cf. Figure 6-20).

6.3.3.2 Medium Access Sub-Layer Medium Access Service

The medium access service supports the transmission of user and control data over logical channels. It manages the access of the logical link control sub-layer entities (DLS, LME, and VI) to the time slots conveying the logical channels. L-DACS 1 uses FDD with separated forward link and reverse link channels to provide full-duplex communication, that is, FL and RL medium access have to be managed separately.

Since the forward link is exclusively used by the ground-station, no sophisticated multiple access scheme is required in this direction. The ground-station is the only user of the FL time slots. It can therefore allocate FL channel resources (i.e. FL PHY-SDUs within TDM slots) locally according to the required quality of service.

The RL uses a bandwidth on demand scheme. Aircraft-stations have to request channel resources (i.e. RL PHY-SDUs) from the GS before they can transmit their data channel DCH in the RL Data slot. The coding and modulation of PHY-SDUs in the RL Data slot can either be fixed for the entire L-DACS 1 cell or be changed dynamically by the ground-station LME.

Before an aircraft-station can transmit on the RL it has to make a resource request. Resource requests are issued by the data link service DLS in the logical link control sub-layer to the ground-station over the dedicated control channel *DCCH* to the ground-station. Access to the DCCH is deterministic and contention free as each aircraft-station has a recurring dedicated RL PHY-SDU for its DCCH within the DC slot. This PHY-SDU is identified using a Control Offset (CO) which is assigned to the aircraft-station at cell-entry.

Within each common control channel *CCCH* (transmitted in the CC slot) the valid control offsets for the next DC slot are announced as Control Offset Start *COS* and Control Offset End *COE*. Each RL PHY-SDU in the DC slot is associated with one control offset (COS: first PHY-SDU in DC, …, COE: last PHY-SDU in DC), thus the aircraft-station can immediately identify the RL PHY-SDU dedicated to its DCCH. The values for COS and COE (i.e. number and owners of DCCH channels in the current DC slot) may be chosen by the ground-station within the limits of the maximum DC segment size (up to 52 PHY-SDUs). COS and COE values should be assigned in round-robin as this approach scales linearly (cf. section 6.2.3.4). The resource request over the DCCH is illustrated in Figure 6-63.

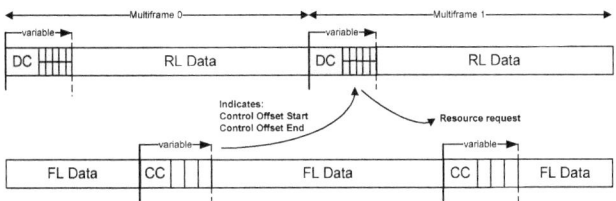

Figure 6-63: RL resource request over the DCCH.

After the DLS entities of all aircraft stations have sent their resource requests in the DCCH the ground-station collects these requests and computes a suitable resource allocation. The position, modulation, and coding of each aircraft-station's resources (i.e. PHY-SDUs) in the Data slot is announced by the ground-station in the common control channel *CCCH*. Aircraft-stations receiving a resource allocation may now use the assigned resources.

The medium access service and the physical layer, knowing the position and modulation of the allocation, maps the transmitted user data to the appropriate PHY-SDUs in the RL Data slot. Note that the ground-station also announces the allocation of FL resources in the CCCH to inform receiving aircraft-stations of the modulation and coding of FL PHY-SDUs in the FL Data slot. Since the coding and modulation of the CCCH is always the same aircraft-stations can always receive this information. The concept of the FL and RL resource allocation is illustrated in Figure 6-64.

Note that the size of the CC slot is variable. It can therefore be increased to provide the capacity necessary to transmit all resource allocations.

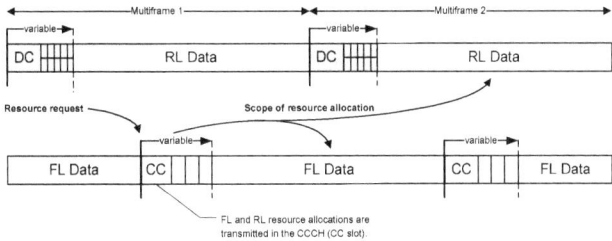

Figure 6-64: RL resource allocation over the CCCH.

The L-DACS 1 medium access sub-layer does neither generate nor process the control messages transferred over the RACH, BCCH, DCCH and CCCH itself. Resource requests, resource allocations, acknowledgements, etc. are generated and consumed only by the LLC sub-layer. The format of these control messages is specific for each logical channel and documented in the L-DACS 1 specification [1][32].

The only exceptions from this rule are the FL and RL resource allocations of the CCCH, which are stored in the MAC. This is done to ensure that outgoing data is transmitted in the correct (i.e. allocated) PHY-SDUs and to determine the source of incoming transmissions from the allocations i.e. FL and RL resource allocation messages are used as MAC headers for MAC-PDUs in the Data slots. However, these headers are transmitted in advance in the CC slot with the most robust coding and modulation. Thus no further MAC-PDU format is necessary.

6.3.3.3 Reverse Link Medium Access Sub-Layer Analysis

The size of the CC and DC slots are variable. The optimal CC slot length is the smallest number of CC PHY-SDUs sufficient to convey all forward link control messages. Determining the optimal DC slot size is less trivial. However, the minimum DC slot size can be derived from the 95% percentile latency requirements according to the following design approach: If the physical layer is configured to provide a DLS packet error rate of less than five percent, 95% of the DLS packets can be delivered without a retransmission. The 95% percentile of the higher layer latency is then (approximately) equal to the MAC latency in this case i.e. if the MAC latency can be given as a function of the DC slot length, the minimum DC slot length can be derived from the latency requirements[81].

The duration of a RL packet transmission TX_{RL} is bounded by

$$TX_{RL} \leq T_{MAC} + T_{Transmission}$$

where T_{MAC} is the medium access latency (resource request + resource allocation), and $T_{Transmission}$ is the transmission time of the RL packet itself.

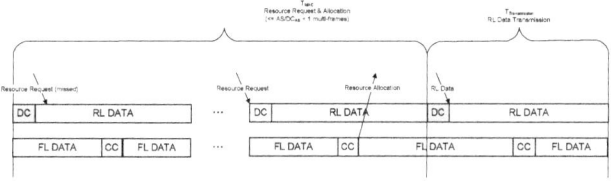

Figure 6-65: Maximum length of RL packet transmission.

An aircraft-station can send a resource request only in its dedicated DC tile. In the worst case, if the AS just missed this tile, it has therefore to wait for the current multi-frame and one complete reservation cycle to make a request. This is illustrated in Figure 6-65.

---

[81] This approach neglects the fragmentation of large higher layer packets. However, as the most stringent latency requirements apply to the smallest packets, it is suitable to provide a valid estimate of the minimum DC slot size.

The corresponding resource allocation should[82] be transmitted in the next CC slot, which is within the last multi-frame of the reservation cycle. Thus T_{MAC} is bounded by the length of the reservation cycle.

$$T_{MAC} \leq \left\lceil \frac{AS}{DC_{AS}} \cdot MF \right\rceil + MF$$

where AS is the number or registered aircraft stations, DC_{AS} is the number of aircraft stations per DC, and MF is the average length of the multi-frame (60 milliseconds neglecting the RA/BC slot).

It is assumed that RL packets a small enough to be transmitted in one multi-frame i.e. $T_{Transmission}$ = 60 milliseconds. Under the assumption that the packet error rate is less than 5% the 95% percentile of TX_{RL} will then be below

$$TX_{RL95} \leq \left\lceil \frac{AS}{DC_{AS}} \cdot MF \right\rceil + 2 \cdot MF$$

as 95% of the packets will be successfully transmitted in this time. The 5% erroneous packets require additional time for a retransmission.

Putting the equations together the DC slot length required to meet a 95% percentile requirement L can be calculated from:

$$TX_{RL95} \leq \left\lceil \frac{AS}{DC_{AS}} \cdot MF \right\rceil + 2 \cdot MF \leq L$$

Note that the calculation of the MAC latency is much simpler than in the case of B-AMC due to the removal of the BSS queues in the medium access sub-layer. The minimum DC slot length to meet the requirement L with AS aircraft stations is thus:

$$DC_{AS} \geq \frac{MF \cdot AS}{L - 2 \cdot MF}$$

The results of this calculation for the simplified evaluation scenarios and the requirements in Table 5-16 are displayed in Table 6-24. Note that all minimum slot lengths are below the maximum physical layer DC slot size of 52 tiles i.e. the author's formal analysis indicates that the L-DACS 1 medium access sub-layer is capable to fulfill all stated latency requirements.

---

[82] Sending the allocation in the next CC is not strictly required in the specification [1], but strongly recommended in the L-DACS1 guidance material [29]. If the system is not overloaded there is, however, no reason to delay the allocation anyway.

Table 6-24: L-DACS 1 minimum DC slot size in tiles.

Scenario	PIAC	Minimum DC slot size (PHY-SDUs)			
		ATS Only, with A-EXEC	ATS+AOC, with A-EXEC	ATS Only, without A-EXEC	ATS+AOC, without A-EXEC
APTZone	26	-	-	2	2
APTSurface	264	-	-	13	13
TMASmall	44	5	5	3	3
TMALarge	53	6	6	3	3
ENRSmall	45	5	5	3	3
ENRMedium	62	6	6	3	3
ENRLarge	204	20	20	10	10
ENRSuperLarge	512	50	50	24	24

6.3.3.4 Medium Access Sub-Layer Error Containment

L-DACS 1 is a data link technology for safety related communication. It is important for such a system to be robust against errors. Resilience and reliability in the user plane are provided by the data link service protocols in the DLS. Error robustness in the control plane is realized in the medium access sub-layer using an error containment scheme introduced by the author.

Control messages are generated by the entities of the logical link control sub-layer and transmitted over the logical channels provided by the MAC. The MAC maps the logical control channels to physical layer slots i.e. the forward link common control channel **CCCH** is mapped to the CC slots, while the return link dedicated control channel **DCCH** is mapped to the DC slot.

Unlike user data packets control messages cannot be automatically retransmitted in the general case (e.g. it is not possible to retransmit a lost resource allocation in the next multi-frame). The logical link control sub-layer has therefore to decide for each message separately whether it should be retransmitted or discarded. However, lost or retransmitted control messages delay the operation of the data link protocol significantly and should therefore be mitigated. The L-DACS 1 medium access sub-layer was designed to provide error mitigation by error containment i.e. the consequences of a transmission error are reduced as far as possible.

Error containment is realized in slightly different approaches on the forward link and the return link. The reverse link control channels are transmitted over the DCCH in the DC slot. Figure 6-66 displays the internal structure of the DC slot. Each DC slot starts at the beginning of the multi-frame with a known number of synchronization symbols. These symbols can be ignored in the context of this section. The remainder of the DC slot is used for PHY-SDUs with the default (i.e. most robust) modulation and coding. Each aircraft-station is assigned one PHY-SDU within this slot to transmit its DCCH.

The maximum size of the DC slot is 52 PHY-SDUs. If the number of aircraft-stations is larger than 52 the DC cycle is spread over several DC slots.

Reverse link PHY-SDUs have a payload size of 112 bit. Within its dedicated PHY-SDU each aircraft-station may send its control messages (designated M*1*, ..., M*n* in Figure 6-66). The messages are encoded in a simple type, length, value TLV scheme and secured with a 16 bit CRC [**32**]. Unused bits are padded with zeros. The benefit of this approach is that the effects of each transmission error are contained within each PHY-SDU and do not concern other user's control messages.

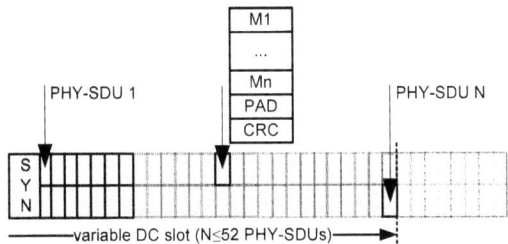

Figure 6-66: Internal structure of DC slot.

While there are not many alternatives to this approach on the reverse link, similar error containment would be desirable on the forward link, too. It is useful for this purpose to analyze the mechanisms of the reverse link approach.

Reverse link error containment works for two reasons: The first reason is the application of error detecting codes to small chunks of data. If an error is detected, the affected data can be identified and only a small amount of data has to be discarded. The remaining PHY-SDUs, which are known to be correct by their CRCs, can still be used. The second reason is that all PHY-SDUs have constant size i.e. even if a PHY-SDU is destroyed the start of the next one is still known. The protocol does therefore not lose the synchronization of message boundaries (i.e. PHY-SDU boundaries) through errors.

On the basis of the understanding of these mechanisms the reverse link error containment approach can be mapped to the forward link: Control messages transmitted in the CC slot are of constant size (48 bit) to ensure message synchronization after errors. Each message is protected with its own CRC to contain errors to as few messages as possible. This approach is illustrated in Figure 6-67.

The first message of each CC slot is the Slot Descriptor SD. This message provides a special case, as this is the only case where a transmission error has consequences for other messages. The slot descriptor describes the layout of the current CC slot (i.e. its length in PHY-SDUs) and of the next DC slot (i.e. DC slot length in PHY-SDUs, control offset start, and control offset end) i.e. if the slot descriptor is destroyed the current CC slot and the next DC slot are lost.

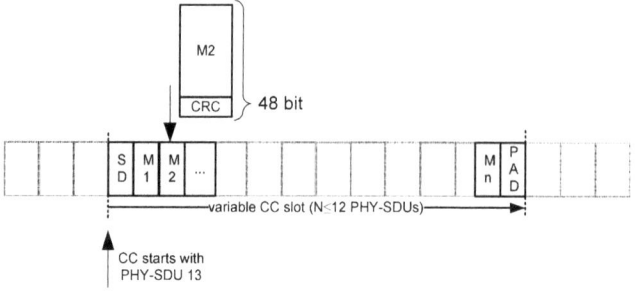

Figure 6-67: Internal structure of CC slot.

Table 6-25 and Table 6-26 present simulation results to assess the effectiveness of the L-DACS 1 error containment. The simulations were performed by the author with varying bit error rates form $5 * 10^{-9}$ to $4 * 10^{-4}$. The simulation scenario comprised 100 aircraft-stations, each transmitting 125 Byte DLS-SDUs at 1 kbit/s in the FL and RL direction to create load on the control channels.

Table 6-25 displays the MAC sub-layer loss for the dedicated control channel DCCH and the data channel DCH on the reverse link. All measurements are given with the 95% confidence interval. The LLC sub-layer protocols are not taken into account.

The results show clearly that the author's error containment in the DCCH provides significant gains. While the error rate of the DLS-PDUs rises sharply with increasing bit error rate, the message error rate of the control channel stays at a moderate level. At the typical working point of L-DACS 1 (10^{-5} bit error rate) only 1 out of 500 DCCH transmissions is lost.

Table 6-25: RL loss per logical channel.

BER	5.00e-09	5.00e-08	5.00e-07	5.00e-06	1.00e-05	5.00e-05	1.00e-04	2.00e-04	4.00e-04	
DCCH	0.01 ± 0.00	0.01 ± 0.00	0.02 ± 0.01	0.09 ± 0.01	0.17 ± 0.01	0.81 ± 0.02	1.56 ± 0.05	3.11 ± 0.07	6.24 ± 0.11	%
DCH	0.00 ± 0.00	0.01 ± 0.00	0.05 ± 0.01	0.56 ± 0.02	1.08 ± 0.04	5.32 ± 0.07	10.26 ± 0.09	19.25 ± 0.09	33.74 ± 0.11	

Table 6-26 shows that the concept of error containment can indeed be successfully transferred to the forward link CCCH. Due to the smaller size of the FL control messages (48 bit in comparison to 112 bit DC PHY-SDUs) the effect is even more pronounced.

Note that the results include the effects of lost slot descriptors i.e. if the CC slot descriptor is erroneous the simulation counts all messages (user and control plane) of this forward link multi-frame and the next reverse link multi-frame as lost.

Table 6-26: FL loss per logical channel.

BER	5.00e-09	5.00e-08	5.00e-07	5.00e-06	1.00e-05	5.00e-05	1.00e-04	2.00e-04	4.00e-04	
CCCH	0.00 ± 0.00	0.00 ± 0.00	0.01 ± 0.00	0.05 ± 0.01	0.09 ± 0.01	0.45 ± 0.01	0.83 ± 0.04	1.67 ± 0.05	3.60 ± 0.08	%
DCH	0.00 ± 0.00	0.01 ± 0.00	0.06 ± 0.01	0.58 ± 0.03	1.16 ± 0.02	5.65 ± 0.06	10.84 ± 0.08	20.36 ± 0.05	36.49 ± 0.18	

Both results indicate that error containment significantly increases the resilience of the L-DACS 1 control channels. Under typical bit error rates the message error rate of the forward link and reverse link control channels is at a very low level. Only 1 in 500 or 1000 messages is lost, respectively. The message formats of the forward link and reverse link MAC messages can be found in [1] and [32].

6.3.3.5 Medium Access Sub-Layer Link Monitoring
Even with the most sophisticated error handling real systems do fail from time to time. Thus, it is an important aspect of resilience to make system failures detectable in due time. The author introduced the L-DACS 1 link monitoring mechanism for this purpose. The aircraft-station and ground-station LME each maintain a keep-alive timer. Whenever a control or data message is received from the peer system the timer is reset. This is usually the case as the CCCH and the DCCH are transmitted in regular intervals. In the unlikely event that no useful data can be sent an empty keep-alive message is transmitted.

If the keep-alive timer goes off (usually after a few MAC cycle lengths) the LME knows that the link must have broken down and can inform the higher layers immediately[83].

6.3.4 Logical Link Control Sub-Layer
The L-DACS 1 Data Link Service DLS protocols are based on the lessons learnt from the evaluation of B-AMC just like the design of the B-AMC MAC was based on the lessons learnt from B-VHF. The author's major contribution to the L-DACS 1 DLS protocols was the complete re-design of the user plane LLC protocols. The HDLC based sliding window protocol of B-AMC was replaced by a two-layer credit-based ARQ protocol. These changes led to a significantly simplified and algorithmically much more robust LLC design.

---

[83] This offers significant benefits in the case of mobile IPv6 as the network layer need not rely on the IPv6 movement detection which has significantly higher time-outs.

The DLS has two major functions: The segmentation and reassembly of SNDCP-PDUs, and their acknowledged and unacknowledged transmission. In addition, the DLS performs the local quality of service management using separate queues for different service classes. If a resource grant is received, the input queues are served according to their priorities. This guarantees high priority queues to get prioritised medium access.

6.3.4.1 Data Link Service Architecture

The general function of the Data Link Service DLS is to provide acknowledged and unacknowledged bidirectional exchange of DLS service data units DLS-SDUs over the point-to-point reverse link or point-to-multipoint forward link. There is one DLS in the aircraft-station and one peer DLS for each aircraft-station in the ground-station.

The aircraft-station's DLS requests reverse link transmission capacity for each of its service classes periodically from the ground-station over the DCCH. The ground-station's DLS requests forward link transmission capacities directly from the radio resource management function of its local LME. When a resource allocation is granted, that is, a reverse-link allocation message is received in the DCCH (in the AS case) or a forward-link allocation is signaled by the LME (in the GS case), the DLS quality of service function distributes this transmission capacity among different service classes. L-DACS 1 supports eight service classes. The highest two classes are reserved for packet mode voice transmissions (e.g. VoIP or native digital voice channels) and link management data[84].

The provisioning of quality of service is distributed between the local quality of service function in the DLS and the radio resource management function in the ground-station's link management entity. The radio resource management provides centralized management of quality of service among different aircraft-stations, while the quality of

---

[84] The table below displays the mapping of COCRv2 service classes to L-DACS 1 service classes as it was used in this document:

Priority	TD95-FRS (ms)	COCR classes
LLC_CoS_7	-	Reserved for LME.
LLC_CoS_6	-	Reserved for voice.
LLC_CoS_5	400	DB-A
	740	DG-B
	1200	DB-B, DB-C, DB-D, DB-E, DB-F
	1400	DG-C
LLC_CoS_4	2400	DG-D
	3800	DG-E
	4700	DG-F
	9200	DG-G
	9800	DG-A
LLC_CoS_3	13600	DG-H, DG-J
	26500	DG-K, DG-I
	51700	DG-L
LLC_CoS_2 LLC_CoS_1	-	Reserved for future use.

service function in the DLS arbitrates between concurrent transmission requests of the same user.

DLS service data units (i.e. user data; DLS-SDUs) are transmitted in segments (DLS-PDUs) created by the DLS segmentation function in response to resource allocations. The transmission of large SDUs is interruptible at segment boundaries for the transmission of privileged SDUs. The transmission of the segments of the unprivileged SDU is resumed afterwards. DLS fragments have four Byte headers (five Bytes if it is the last fragment of a DLS-SDU), a two Byte cyclic redundancy checksum, and contain only data form a single service data unit. The header format of DLS-PDUs is documented in the specification [1]. The transmission of DLS-PDUs within a resource allocation is illustrated in Figure 6-68. Note that an error in one DLS-PDU will prevent the reception of all following DLS-PDUs within the same resource allocation as the DLS header information (i.e. DLS-PDU length) cannot be trusted.

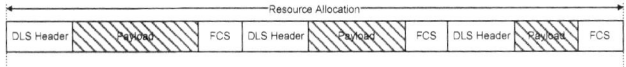

Figure 6-68: DLS-PDUs within one resource allocation.

DLS fragments are transmitted over the data channel *DCH*. If an acknowledged transmission was requested and if no acknowledgement was received within a specified time, the sending DLS automatically initiates a re-transmission. After a certain number of retries, the sending DLS may, however, abandon the attempt and inform its client of the failure. If the sending DLS receives an acknowledgement for a complete service data unit, it informs its client of the successful transmission. The complete reverse link transmission and the interaction of the DLS with the MAC in terms of primitive calls are illustrated in Figure 6-69. The complete list of L-DACS 1 primitives can be found in [1] and [32]. Note that several transmissions may take place concurrently.

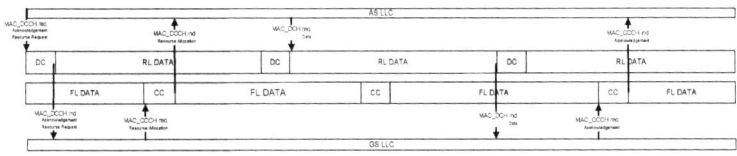

Figure 6-69: L-DACS 1 reverse link transmission.

The L-DACS 1 data link service uses a separate transmission queue and a separate sending window for each service class. This is equivalent to having one dedicated ARQ connection per class of service. The B-AMC results indicated that this may be problematic if conventional sliding-window protocols were used (e.g. HDLC as proposed in the original B-AMC specification or the custom B-AMC selective reject protocol of the enhanced specification). The reason for this is that the connections of the aircraft-station compete for the same resources in the DCH. In fact, the B-AMC performance assessment showed clearly that the management of multiple sending windows is extremely difficult to optimize and has a major impact on the overall system performance.

For this reason L-DACS 1 does not use a window-based ARQ protocol, but utilizes a credit-based approach. Whenever the data link service receives a resource allocation, this credit is distributed by the local quality of service function in the DLS among the different connections. This eliminates the need for the aircraft-station to estimate the window size[85]. Instead, the transmission window sizes of all aircraft-stations are computed by the ground-station radio resource management. This eliminates the possibility of congestion within the system completely as the channel load can be centrally controlled by the ground-station. (Congestion is of course still possible in the queues above the DSL in the protocol stack.)

Due to the facts, that DLS-PDUs cannot experience congestion and that acknowledgements are sent over variable sized dedicated control channels, which can be adjusted to provided the required capacity (i.e. control messages cannot experience congestion either), optimal ARQ timer management becomes possible: Acknowledgements can only arrive in control channels. However, the position of the relevant control channels, CCCH and DCCH, is known in advance from the slot structure. Thus it is sufficient if the DLS counts the appearance of control channel slots for timer management. If no acknowledgement is received in the expected control channel slot, the data link service can be sure that either the data packet or the acknowledgement was lost and initiate a retransmission.

6.3.4.2 *Data Link Service ARQ Functional Model*
The author used a selective repeat ARQ in the B-AMC DLS because this is the most efficient protocol variant. It causes no unnecessary retransmissions as only packets known to be lost (by NAK or time-out) are retransmitted. However, selective repeat is difficult[86] to implement if packet sizes vary[87]. L-DACS 1 seeks to make DLS-PDUs as large as possible to keep overhead low, but the maximum DLS-PDU size is defined by the resource allocation size, which changes with each resource assignment. In addition, the maximum DLS-PDU size may also be restricted by the desired DLS-PDU error rate. If L-DACS 1 is tuned for 5% DLS-PDU error rate (cf. section 6.3.4.4) the DLS-PDU size may therefore vary with the radio channel conditions. Another reason making the

---

[85] Note that credit based window management eliminates only the need to *estimate* the *transmission window* size. The *maximum window size* is, however, determined by the maximum sequence number (i.e. the size of the according header field).

[86] Note that complex code is costly to certify.

[87] A retransmission may not be possible without further segmentation or padding if the DLS-PDU size changed between the first transmission and the retransmission.

use of selective repeat ARQ unattractive is the embedding of DLS-PDUs into resource allocations (cf. Figure 6-68) allowing only in-order reception.

Instead of plain selective repeat the author decided therefore to use a two-layered ARQ approach offering comparable efficiency[88] in L-DACS 1. The higher level (***SARQ***) implements a window-based[89] selective repeat protocol operating on complete DLS-SDUs (i.e. higher layer packets). By working on complete DLS-SDUs the problem of varying packet sizes is effectively eliminated. However, the segmentation of packets to appropriate sizes is not possible anymore. Segmentation and reassembly of packets to the required DLS-PDU size is therefore performed by an embedded go-back-n protocol ***GBN*** operating on DLS-PDUs. Go-back-n matches also naturally with the in-order reception of DLS-PDUs within a resource allocation. The higher layer SARQ protocol is only used to enforce DLS-SDU order and to eliminate duplicates while the lower level GBN protocol provides the reliable transfer of DLS-PDUs. The functional model of this approach is displayed in Figure 6-70.

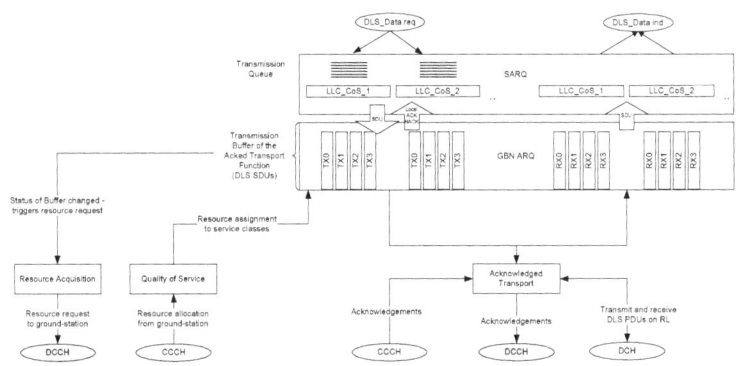

Figure 6-70: Functional Model of the L-DACS 1 AS DLS.

The sending SARQ stores DLS-SDUs received from the higher layers (i.e. SNDCP and above) into DLS transmission queues according to their service class (LLC_CoS_1, ...). Each service class has a defined number of transmission buffers called the transmission window (TX0, ..., TX3). The SARQ protocol fills these transmission buffers with DLS-SDUs from the queue with one DLS-SDU per buffer. The receiving SARQ offers the same number of receive buffers for each service class. Received DLS-SDUs are only accepted if they lie within the receive window (i.e. belong to a known buffer RX0,... ,

---

[88] LTE uses a similar approach, however, with a stop-and-go HARQ protocol in the second layer [**85**] [**86**] [**88**].

[89] The window has only the function to prevent a sequence number wrap-around.

RX3). By this the SARQ can assure that received DLS-SDUs are processed in the correct order and can avoid the generation of duplicate packets.

The lower level GBN is embedded in the transmission and reception buffers of the SARQ protocol (TX0, ..., TX3, and RX0, ..., RX3) i.e. there are as many concurrent GBN transmissions as SARQ transmit buffers[90]. The GBN ARQ implements a credit-based go-back-n protocol. It manages the segmentation and reassembly of DLS-SDUs into DLS-PDUs and provides error recovery by retransmissions. Note that the GBN protocol operates in fixed timing relations to the MAC sub-layer to achieve optimal timer management.

The DLS performs the local priority management by using separate queues for different service classes. If a resource grant is received, transmission buffers are served according to their class of service. This guarantees high priority queues prioritised medium access.

Note that that the throughput of the DLS is limited by the sending window of the SARQ protocol (i.e. the maximum sequence number of the SARQ protocol). The transmission of a complete DLS-SDU takes at least three multi-frames (request, transmission, acknowledgement) before the SARQ protocol may shift the window. With 16.6 multi-frames per second this is equivalent to approximately 5 DLS-SDU transmissions per second and GBN (assuming the DLS-SDUs are small enough to be transmitted in one step). With four concurrent GBN transmissions this is equivalent to a maximum throughput of 20 DLS-SDUs per second. As there is one SARQ for each class of service the total maximum throughput is 160 DLS-SDUs per second (using all eight service classes).

6.3.4.3 Data Link Service ARQ Data Transmission

Two-layered ARQ protocols have been recognized as a practicable design option for emerging wireless communication standards [77][78]. They have, however, not been described in the literature extensively. The operation of the L-DACS 1 ARQ protocol shall therefore be described in more detail in this and the next two sections.

Figure 6-71 illustrates the transfer of a DLS-SDU between two peer DLS entities. In the first step the higher layer (i.e. SNDCP) requests the transmission of a DLS-SDU from the sending DLS by issuing a DLS_DATA.req primitive. The DLS-SDU is stored in the DLS transmission queue of the appropriate service class.

---

[90] L-DACS 1 uses 3 bit sequence numbers for DLS-SDUs (called packet identifier PID in the specification). This results in a maximum window size of 4 transmission buffers to prevent PID wrap-around. Note that the SARQ protocol and the go-back-n protocol use different sequence numbers. SARQ PIDs apply to DLS-SDUs. Go-back-b sequence numbers denote the Byte offset within the DLS-SDU.

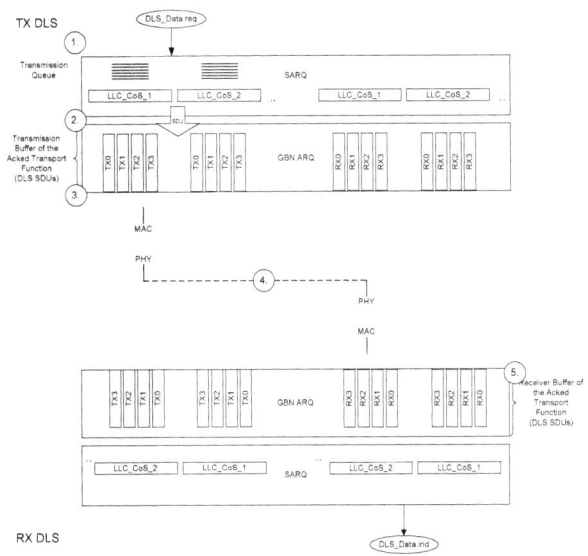

Figure 6-71: L-DACS 1 DLS ARQ transfer of user data.

Secondly, when a transmission buffer becomes available, the SARQ protocol moves the DLS-SDU from the queue into the transmission buffer. L-DACS1 uses up to four transmission buffers, thus one service class is able to transmit up to four different DLS-SDUs in parallel.

In the third step the transmitting DLS calculates the resource request for each transmission buffer and forwards the overall resource request either to the ground-station via the DCCH if the DLS is located in an aircraft-station or internally to the RRM function of the LME if the DLS is located in the ground-station. When the DLS receives a resource allocation, it starts processing the transmission buffers. The GBN ARQ function splits the DLS-SDU into DLS-PDUs according to the maximal DLS-PDU size and the resource allocation size (cf. Section 6.3.4.4). This procedure is repeated for each transmission buffer until the allocation has been used up.

Fourth, the DLS forwards the generated DLS-PDUs to its MAC, which transfers the DLS-PDUs via the data channel DCH. The receiving MAC forwards the received DLS-PDUs to the peer DLS.

In the last step the receiving DLS evaluates the cyclic redundancy checksum CRC of the DLS-PDU. If the CRC is invalid, the DLS-PDU is discarded. Otherwise, if the CRC is valid, the DLS-PDU is forwarded to the appropriate receive buffer. The GBN ARQ function keeps track of the next expected sequence number (i.e. byte offset in the DLS-SDU) i.e. the received DLS-PDU is either added to the receiver buffers according to its sequence number or discarded if the sequence number is not as expected. Whenever the GBN ARQ function processes a DLS-PDU, it generates and requests the transfer of an acknowledgement to inform the sending peer DLS.

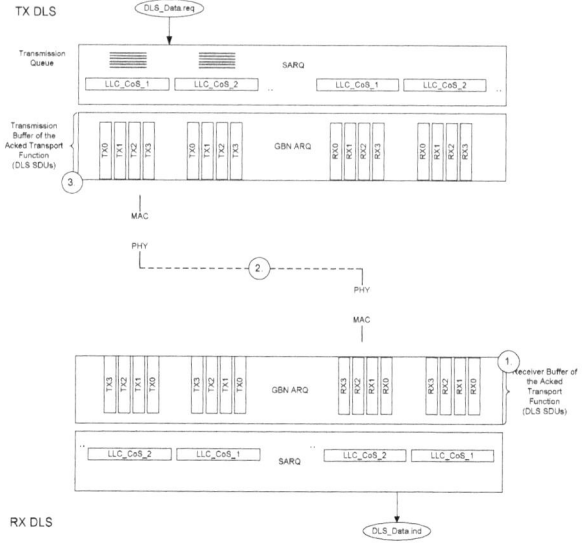

Figure 6-72: L-DACS 1 DLS ARQ transfer of an acknowledgement.

Figure 6-72 illustrates the generation and transfer an acknowledgement. If the GBN ARQ function received a DLS-PDU it generates a corresponding acknowledgement. Note that this acknowledgement may acknowledge a higher sequence number than the received DLS-PDU carried if the received packet was a retransmission of an earlier packet.

In the second step the DLS forwards the generated acknowledgement to its MAC via the DCCH or CCCH, respectively. The receiving MAC forwards the acknowledgement to the peer DLS.

The GBN ARQ function processes the received acknowledgement in the third step and updates its transmission buffer. If no acknowledgement for the DLS-PDU has been received within due time (cf. section 6.3.6.3.2) the retransmission timer expires and the transmission buffer is reset.

If the receiver buffer has assembled of the complete DLS-SDU the GBN ARQ function signals the SARQ function the error free reception. To ensure the order of the DLS-SDUs, the SARQ protocol keeps track of expected packet by means of a DLS-SDU identifier analogue to the DLS-PDU sequence number. The SARQ accepts only the expected DLS-SDU. In this case the SARQ forwards the DLS-SDU to the higher layers and shifts the receive window. Otherwise the DLS-SDU remains in the receiver buffer until it is expected by the SARQ.

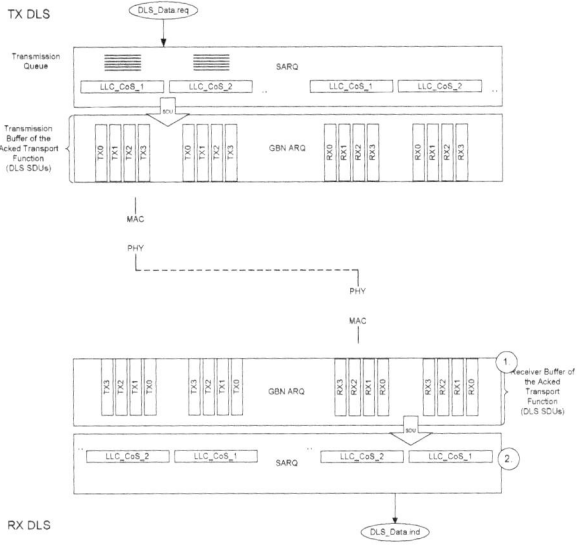

Figure 6-73: L-DACS 1 DLS ARQ processing of received user data.

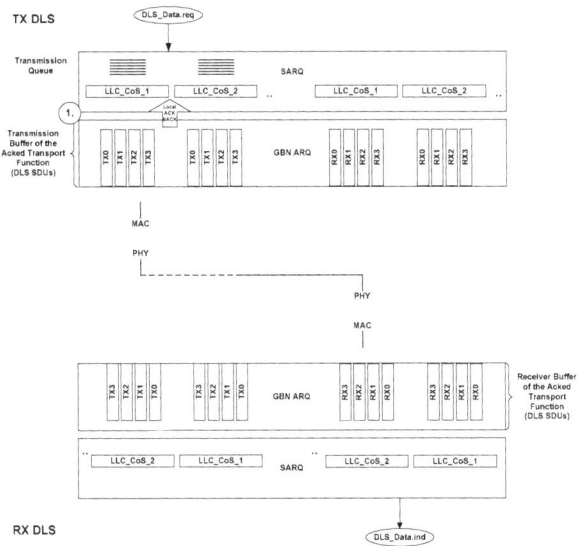

Figure 6-74: L-DACS 1 DLS ARQ local ACK and NAK.

If the SARQ function accepted the received DLS-SDU it forwards the DLS-SDU to the higher layers by triggering the DLS_DATA.ind primitive.

If a transmission buffer is completely acknowledged the GBN ARQ signals a local acknowledgement to the SARQ protocol. The SARQ removes the corresponding DLS-SDU from the transmission buffer and shifts the sending window.

Alternatively, if a maximum defined number of retransmission is exceeded the GBN ARQ sends a local NAK message to the SARQ. The SARQ function may then discard the DLS-SDU and report the error to the higher layers.

6.3.4.4 Data Link Service Segmentation and Reassembly

The DLS GBN protocol performs the segmentation and reassembly of DLS-SDUs to DLS-PDUs. The size of the DLS-PDUs is variable within the limits of the resource allocation size and the desired DLS-PDU error rate.

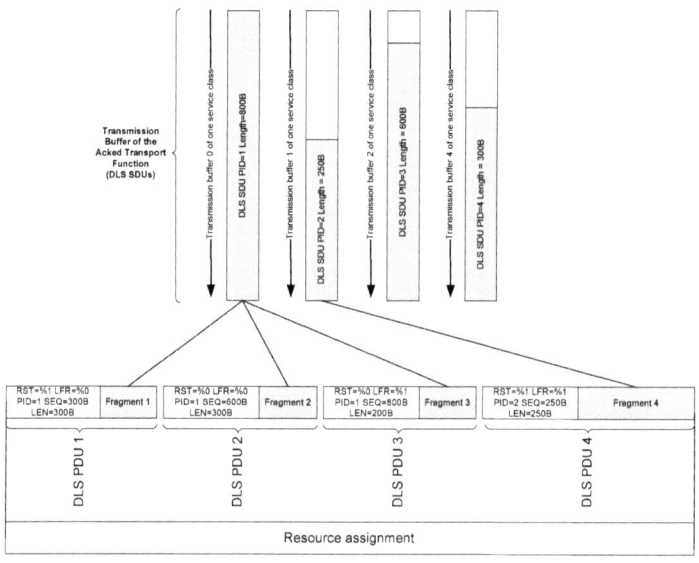

Figure 6-75: L-DACS 1 DLS segmentation.

The DLS monitors its transmission buffers and requests the required channel resources from the ground-station LME. On reception of a resource grant from the ground-station radio resource management the requesting DLS creates one or several DLS-PDUs according to the size of the resource grant. The DLS-PDU size is selected such that a single DLS-PDU or a number of DLS-PDUs fit exactly into the resource allocation without splitting DLS-PDUs over several allocations. This approach avoids the sub-optimal fragmentation encountered in B-AMC (cf. section 6.2.6.3.1). Figure 6-75 illustrates this concept[91] for one service class.

The size of the DLS-PDU fragments is not only determined by the size of the DLS-SDU and the size of the resource allocation, but also by the maximum desired DLS-PDU error rate. For a given bit error rate the DLS-PDU error rate increases with the size of the packet i.e. it is not desirable to generated too large DLS-PDUs as they are more susceptible to bit errors and cause increased retransmissions.

If the desired DLS-PDU error rate is set to 5% according to section 6.3.3.3 the maximum DLS-PDU size can be calculated as a function of the bit error rate. Figure 6-76 displays the DLS-PDU size and the expected frame error rate FER (i.e. DLS-PDU error rate). Note that the DLS-PDU size was limited to the L-DACS 1 MTU size of 1505 Byte.

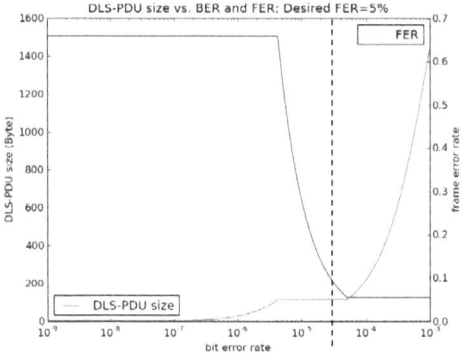

Figure 6-76: L-DACS 1 maximum DLS-PDU size for 5% error rate.

For low bit error rates (below $5 * 10^{-6}$) the maximum tolerable DLS-PDU size is larger than the maximum packet size supported by the L-DACS 1 protocol[92]. The FER is below 5% in this case. For very high bit error rates (above $5 * 10^{-5}$) the maximum DLS-PDU size would be too small for the protocol to operate with reasonable overhead. The minimum DLS-PDU size is therefore kept at 125 Byte (approximately 10% overhead) although the FER is above 5% in this case. Note that the working point of L-DACS 1 is

---

[91] The header fields displayed in the figure are: PID: SARQ packet identifier. RST: GBN first fragment flag. LFR: GBN last fragment flag. SEQ: GBN sequence number. LEN: GBN fragment length. The complete header format is defined in [1] and [30].

[92] The maximum transfer unit of L-DACS 1 was set to 1505 Byte to support Ethernet based on-board networks. Larger MTU sizes add no benefits as the higher layer packet size would be limited to this value by the on-board Ethernet anyway.

assumed to lie at 10^{-5} bit error rate (indicated by the vertical line in Figure 6-76). This is equivalent to a maximum DLS-PDU size of 641 Bytes.

6.3.4.5 Data Link Service ARQ Timer Management

DLS timer management was identified as crucial for the overall protocol performance in the B-AMC evaluation. It was therefore proposed by the author to couple the DLS timer management to the MAC time framing to achieve near optimal performance. Thus, the L-DACS 1 GBN protocol operates in fixed timing relations to the medium access sub-layer.

Depending on the physical layer implementation there are two optimal acknowledgement opportunities for a DLS-PDU transmitted in a Data slot: The first opportunity is to acknowledge the DLS-PDU in the control channel slot of the same multi-frame. However, this is only possible if the physical layer implementation allows the partial decoding of data slots. The second opportunity is to use the first control channel slot after the current multi-frame.

The retransmission timer defines the maximum number of missed acknowledgement opportunities, before a retransmission is triggered i.e. according to the last paragraph, the DLS retransmission timer should time out after not more than two missed acknowledgement opportunities.

Figure 6-77 illustrates the DLS retransmission timer on the reverse link. After the aircraft-station has sent a DLS-PDU in the RL Data slot there are two possible acknowledgment opportunities on the forward link. The first opportunity could be in the CC slot during the RL Data slot of the transmission if the physical layer supports the immediate forwarding of received data. However, only the CC slot in the next multi-frame is an acknowledgement opportunity available independently of the physical layer implementation. The DLS retransmission timer is therefore set to the end of this acknowledgement opportunity.

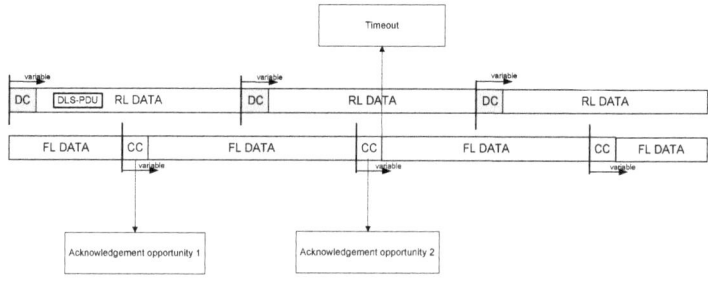

Figure 6-77: L-DACS 1 RL DLS retransmission timer.

Figure 6-78 displays the same concept for the forward link DLS retransmission timer. There are two acknowledgement opportunities on the reverse link after the DLS Data

PDU is sent. The first opportunity could be in the DC slot during the FL Data slot of the transmission. The second acknowledgement opportunity is the next appearance of the receiving aircraft-station's DCCH. According to the number of registered aircraft-stations not every AS is able to send its DC in each multi-frame. The ground-station has therefore to check the assignment of the aircraft-station's control offsets CO to identify valid acknowledgement opportunities. The timeout is therefore set to the end of the next DC slot where the aircraft-stations DCCH is transmitted.

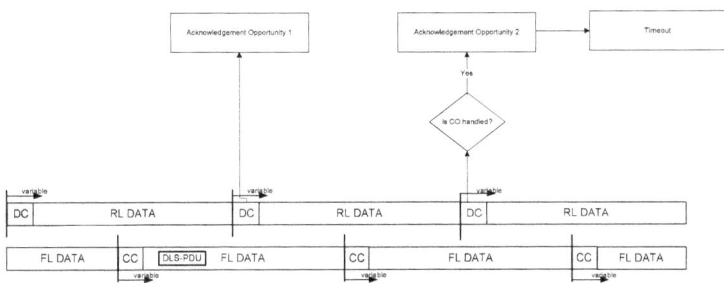

Figure 6-78: L-DACS 1 FL DLS retransmission timer.

Note that the first DC slot can always be counted as an acknowledgement opportunity, as the acknowledgement has to be sent in the next DC slot in any case.

6.3.4.6 Data Link Service ARQ Buffer Management

The use of go-back-n ARQ in L-DACS 1 introduces an optimization problem not present in B-AMC. Selective repeat achieves optimal retransmission efficiency as only packets known to be lost are retransmitted i.e. the retransmission overhead of selective repeat ARQ is equal to the packet error rate. This is not the case with go-back-n ARQ. If a packet is lost this protocol variant will retransmit the lost packet and all following packets within the transmission window (hence the name go-back-n). For large window sizes this may increase the retransmission overhead significantly.

An obvious solution to this problem is to keep the go-back-n window size as small as possible. Indeed, if the window size is set to one packet[93], the retransmission overhead is equal to the packet error rate, which is the optimum. However, this is also the case with the lowest throughput.

Note that lowering the throughput per ARQ instance need not decrease the overall system throughput for sufficiently large user populations. The overall system throughput can be kept at the same level by multiplexing. Using smaller go-back-n transmission windows a larger number of users may transmit concurrently instead of a

---

[93] This is also known as stop-and-go ARQ.

small number of users with large go-back-n windows. The overall goodput even increases as the retransmission overhead is decreased.

A similar approach would be to increase the number of parallel go-back-n transmissions per user (i.e. to increase the selective repeat sending window). However, this would require significant changes to the control message formats and was therefore identified as an item of future research.

Note also that the throughput is one transmission window's worth of packets per round-trip time i.e. decreasing the round-trip time is also a possibility to increase the throughput[94], however, in the case of L-DACS 1 the round-trip time is fixed and rather large with at least three multi-frames (cf. Figure 6-65 and Figure 6-69). This makes larger window sizes more attractive for L-DACS 1. It should, however, be noted that increasing the GBN window size beyond the maximum DLS-SDU size has no effect.

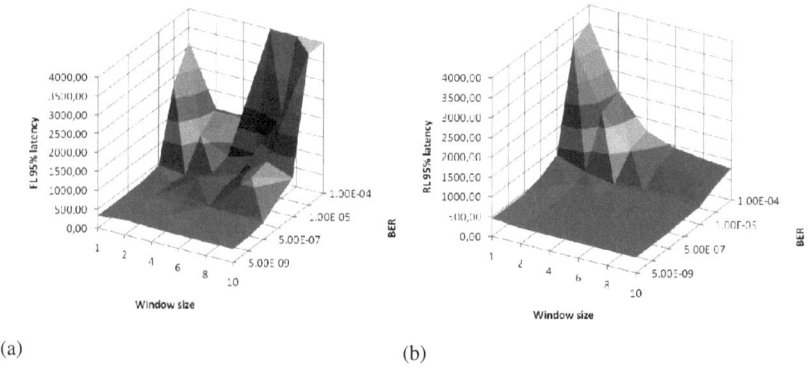

(a)   (b)

Figure 6-79: 95% percentile of latency vs. GBN window size and bit error rate.

Figure 6-79 shows the measured 95% percentile of the one-way latency for L-DACS 1 with different GBN windows sizes and under varying bit error rates. The simulation scenario was ENR.200 with COCRv2 data traffic. The simulation scenario is described in more detail in section 6.2.4.7.

The reverse link results show that the latency decreases with increasing GBN window size due to the higher throughput as expected. GBN window sizes of more than four DLS-PDUs offer no significant performance gain as the window is already larger than most RL packets in this case.

The forward link results show the superposition of two effects. For GBN window sizes up to four DLS-PDUs the latency improves as expected. However, for larger window

---

[94] This is the reason why LTE uses stop-and-wait HARQ with extremely short frame lengths (in the order of few milliseconds) [85] [86] [88].

sizes the performance drops dramatically. This is caused by the growing retransmission overhead congesting the forward link.

Figure 6-80 displays the measured retransmission overhead of the forward and reverse link. The overhead increases from the optimal value (which is the packet error rate) to almost 50% with increasing GBN windows size. The graph shows only the DCH retransmission overhead, other logical channels are not included. Note that the retransmission overhead depends strongly on the size of the transmitted packets. A different application mix may therefore result in differing overhead statistics.

The reverse link is only lightly loaded and can therefore convey the additional data easily. However, the forward link capacity is not sufficient to carry the retransmission overhead of large GBN windows[95].

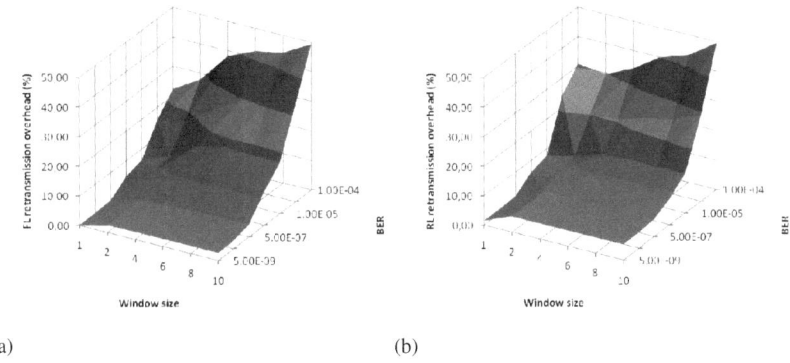

(a) (b)

Figure 6-80: Retransmission overhead vs. GBN window size and bit error rate.

Parameter optimization was not in the focus of the author's work. The window size has therefore been set to values indicated by the performance estimation presented above. The GBN window is set to four DLS-PDUs. This causes acceptable retransmission overhead in the investigated scenarios (approximately 15% at BER 10^{-5}; the optimum is 5%) with nearly minimal latencies. Note that the presented results do not take the effects of network layer fragmentation into account. Depending on the size of the N-PDUs the optimal GBN window size may change.

6.3.4.7 Link Management Entity Resource Allocation
Channel resources for transmission have to be requested by the DLS from the radio resource management in the ground-station LME. The ground-station DLS makes these requests locally using an internal interface, while the aircraft-station DLS has to make

---

[95] The higher layer offered load of the ENR.200 scenario is 195.78 kbit/s i.e. 50% overhead would completely saturate the channel which would result in serious congestion due to the high burstiness of the traffic.

its request over the dedicated control channel DCCH. The radio resource management stores these requests to calculate an appropriate resource allocation. Note that the aircraft-station DLS makes separate resource requests for each class of service.

The resource allocation for the next forward link and reverse link data slots is then calculated after the end of the DC slot when the LME has collected the resource requests of all aircraft-stations serviced in this multi-frame. The gap between the DC slot and the CC slot is used to calculate the assignment and to prepare it for transmission in the CC (i.e. generate FL and RL allocation control messages; cf. Figure 6-64).

The allocation algorithm has not been defined in the L-DACS 1 specification, but is left open to the implementer. The simulations presented in this thesis use a comparatively simple resource allocation algorithm. This algorithm respects the priorities of the different classes of service and is fair between requests of the same priority.

The resource allocation of the forward link and reverse link are calculated independently, but following the same approach: In the first step the resource requests are sorted according to their priority and class of service: High priorities before low priorities, and acknowledged transmissions before unacknowledged transmissions. In the second step resource allocations are granted in round-robin within each class of service. If the class has been completely serviced the next class is served. The algorithm assigns the largest possible allocation limited by the size of the data slot.

For the reverse link allocations an additional restriction is introduced to reduce the duty cycle and the interference generated by the system. The maximum size of the resource allocation is limited to 16 PHY-SDUs. This is equivalent to a maximum reverse link sending time of 5.76 milliseconds. Note that this restriction has no formal motivation. It was assumed as a working hypothesis in the physical layer development. Its size can, however, be configured. Note that only the sum of all resource allocations is transmitted to the user as it can be locally distributed by the DLS quality of service function according to the transmitted requests.

6.3.4.8 *Data Link Service ARQ Performance*

The performance of the reliable data link service was investigated by the author under varying bit error rates form $5 * 10^{-9}$ to $4 * 10^{-4}$. The simulation scenario comprised 100 aircraft-stations, each transmitting 1 kbit/s in the FL and RL direction. This load is well below the capacity limits of L-DACS 1. The L-DACS 1 SDU size was set to 125 Byte (cf. section 5.3). This is equivalent to a DLS-PDU size of 135 Byte (3 Byte SNDCP header; 7 Byte DLS-PDU header). The maximum reverse link allocation was set to 16 PHY-SDUs per multi-frame. Note that the results in this section are presented according to the physical layer bit error rate and not according to the MAC sub-layer frame (i.e. transport channel) error rate as in the case of B-AMC. However, in order to make the results comparable the bit error rates have been chosen equivalent to the frame error rates of section 6.2.4.7.

Figure 6-81 shows the data link layer load increases with the rising bit error rate as expected. However, the breakdown of the reverse link ARQ protocol sending rate for high bit error rates as displayed by B-AMC (cf. Figure 6-35 (b)) has disappeared in Figure 6-81 (b). The L-DACS 1 ARQ protocol behaves as expected for all investigated error rates. The 95% confidence intervals of the measurements are indicated by error-bars in the graph.

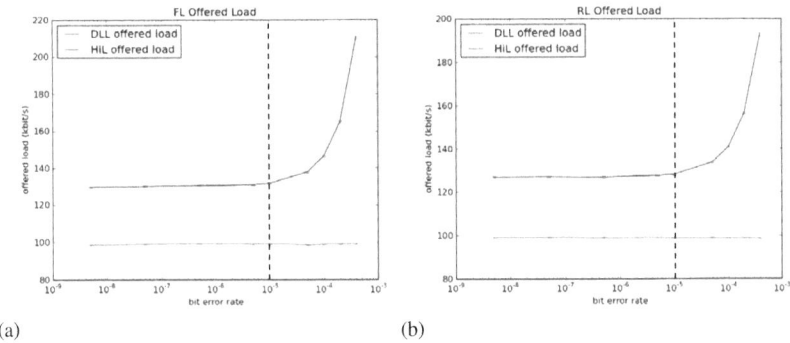

Figure 6-81: Offered load; 100 AS, 100 kbit/s FL, 100 kbit/s RL, varying BER.

Figure 6-82 indicates that the 95% percentile of the one-way latency rises sharply with increasing bit error rates as already observed in the B-AMC results. However, in the case of L-DACS1 the increase in latency is one order of magnitude smaller. This can mainly be explained by the optimized approach to timer management and the removal of the BSS queue from the system. The most stringent latency requirement (740 milliseconds) is indicated by the horizontal dashed line.

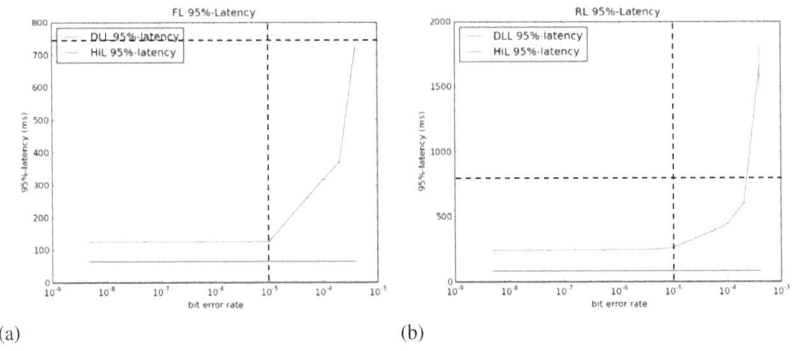

Figure 6-82: 95% percentile of latency; 100 AS, 100 kbit/s FL, 100 kbit/s RL, varying BER.

Figure 6-83 indicates that the L-DACS1 interface queue is stable (at one DLS-SDU size) in all cases. DLS-PDUs are no longer queued, therefore the DLL queue length in always zero. This is another significant improvement over the B-AMC ARQ protocol which experienced significant queuing delays for high frame error rates.

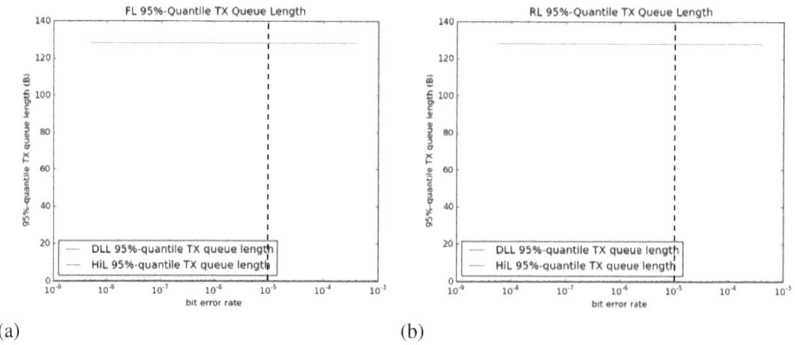

(a)   (b)

Figure 6-83: 95% percentile of queue length; 100 AS, 100 kbit/s FL, 100 kbit/s RL, varying BER.

Figure 6-84 displays the DLS-PDU and DLS-SDU error rates. The DLS-PDU error rate increases with the bit error rate as expected. The DLS-SDU error rate is zero in all cases. This indicates the stable operation of the L-DACS 1 ARQ protocols in all investigated bit rates. In particular the results indicate that the desired DLS-PDU error rate of 5% (cf. section 6.3.3.3; indicated by the horizontal dashed line) is a viable working point of the system.

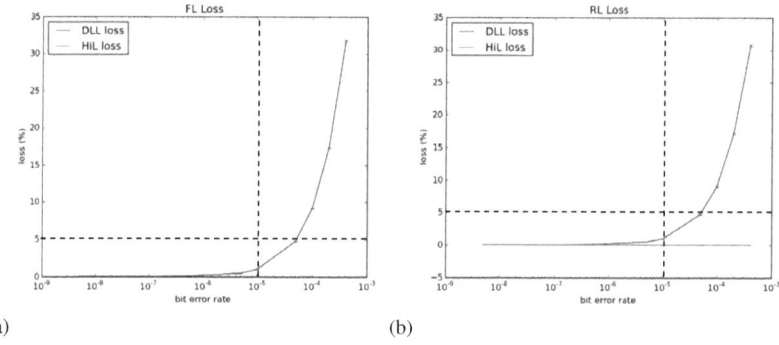

(a)   (b)

Figure 6-84: DLS-PDU error rate; 100 AS, 100 kbit/s FL, 100 kbit/s RL, varying BER.

In summary the presented results indicate a significant improvement of the author's L-DACS 1 ARQ design over the B-AMC ARQ protocol. The optimized reliable DLS transport service works correctly and without losses in all investigated cases. The latency requirement plotted in Figure 6-82 (b) indicates that the working point of the L-DACS 1 reverse link should lie below the bit error rate of 10^{-4} (one order of magnitude better than B-AMC). The bit error rate used in the L-DACS 1 performance evaluations (10^{-5}) is however the same as used with B-AMC to make the result comparable. It is marked by the vertical dotted line.

6.3.5 Performance Evaluation

The performance evaluation of the L-DACS 1 protocol was carried out by the author in a computer simulation implementing the medium access sub-layer and the logical link control sub-layer according to the methodology described in section 5.5. In total 5317 simulations were carried out. This section presents the discussion of selected simulation results according to the evaluation criteria stated in section 5.6.

6.3.5.1 Simulation Parameters

The author's L-DACS 1 simulation implemented the L-DACS 1 protocol according to [1], [32], and the descriptions given in the previous sections.

The simplified scenarios were simulated using a higher layer packet size of 125 Byte (cf. section 5.3) with a single class of service. Each higher layer packet is extended by a 3 Byte SNDCP header and at least one 7 Byte DLS-PDU header (assuming minimal fragmentation). Together these headers add 10 Bytes of overhead to each higher layer packet which is equivalent to 8% overhead. This is comparable to the 10% overhead assumed in the B-AMC evaluation. The simulation duration was set to 500 seconds plus 5 additional seconds of follow up time. Each scenario was simulated ten times with different random seeds.

The detailed scenarios were simulated using TMA.x and ENR.x simulation session traces as input. The service classes defined in [46] were mapped to three L-DACS 1 priorities according to their TD95-FRS latency requirements: Services with a latency requirement below two seconds, services with a latency requirement below ten seconds, and the remaining services. Table 6-3 displays this mapping. Note that LLC_CoS_5 is the highest priority and LLC_CoS_3 is the lowest priority.

The broadcast service classes of the FL use the unreliable multicast DLS transport service. The addressed service classes use the reliable DLS transport protocol (i.e. ARQ).

The maximum DLS-PDU size was set to 641 Byte which is equivalent to a maximum DLS-PDU error rate of 5%. The maximum window size of the lower layer go-back-n protocol was set to 4 DLS-PDUs. The simulation duration was 3600 seconds plus 100 seconds of follow up time.

Both types of simulation scenarios used the same medium access sub-layer and physical layer settings. If not stated otherwise the DC slot size was set to 52 tiles. The maximum reverse link allocation size was set to 16 PHY-SDUs per aircraft-station and multi-frame. This is equivalent to a maximum reverse link sending duration of 5.76 milliseconds per multi-frame not taking the DC slot into account.

Table 6-27: L-DACS 1 mapping of COCRv2 service classes to priorities.

Class of Service (CoS)	Expiration Time (ET) (s)	95% percentile (TD95-FRS) (s)	Priority	ARQ
DG-A	-	9.8	LLC_CoS_4	Yes
DG-B	1.6	0.74	LLC_CoS_5	Yes
DG-C	5.0	1.4	LLC_CoS_5	Yes
DG-D	7.8	2.4	LLC_CoS_4	Yes
DG-E	8.0	3.8	LLC_CoS_4	Yes
DG-F	12.0	4.7	LLC_CoS_4	Yes
DG-G	24.0	9.2	LLC_CoS_4	Yes
DG-H	32.0	13.6	LLC_CoS_3	Yes
DG-I	57.6	26.5	LLC_CoS_3	Yes
DG-J	-	13.6	LLC_CoS_3	Yes
DG-K	-	26.5	LLC_CoS_3	Yes
DG-L	-	51.7	LLC_CoS_3	Yes
DB-A	3.2	0.4	LLC_CoS_5	No
DB-B	4.8	1.2	LLC_CoS_5	No
DB-C	8.0	1.2	LLC_CoS_5	No
DB-D	3.2	1.2	LLC_CoS_5	No
DB-E	8.0	1.2	LLC_CoS_5	No
DB-F	16.0	1.2	LLC_CoS_5	No

The physical layer bit error rate was set to 10^{-5} after FEC. Unlike the B-AMC simulations bit errors are simulated for all logical channels. With the exception of the "ENR Large ATS+AOC with A-EXEC", ENR.225 and ENR.250 scenarios the default coding and modulation was used. The first two scenarios use ACM type 2 (QPSK, coding rate 2/3) coding. ENR.250 uses ACM type 4 (16QAM, coding rate 1/2). The "ENR Super Large ATS+AOC with A-EXEC" and "ENR Super Large ATS+AOC with-out A-EXEC" are actually out of the scope of L-DACS 1, but were included into the simulations with ACM type 4 coding and modulation. Results using non-default ACM settings are indicated in *italic* font.

6.3.5.2 Responsiveness
- Ground-to-air (FL) one-way latency of user-data.
- Air-to-ground (RL) one-way latency of user-data.
- Do the 95%-percentile values of the one-way latency satisfy the requirements of Table 5-12 and Table 5-13: **yes**/no?

The responsiveness of the L-DACS 1 protocol was evaluated using the detailed evaluation scenarios of section 5.4. Table 6-28 presents the evaluation results for the

TMA.x scenarios. Just like it was the case with B-AMC the TD95-FRS requirements are fulfilled in all cases and for all service classes.

Table 6-28: L-DACS 1 responsiveness (TD95-FRS in ms).

Scenario	TMA.15		TMA.30		TMA.45		TMA.60		TMA.75	
	FL	RL	FL	RL	FL	RL	FL	RL	FL	RL
all	128	523	128	533	128	542	128	553	128	559
DB-D	127	-	127	-	127	-	127	-	127	-
DB-E	126	-	125	-	125	-	125	-	125	-
DG-A	147	219	148	220	158	232	128	234	155	235
DG-C	141	229	148	233	141	234	143	236	157	237
DG-D	196	875	184	874	197	882	222	885	242	879
DG-F	238	226	240	225	276	228	272	232	290	234
DG-J	1,664	238	1,785	249	1,893	240	1,909	257	1,857	268
DG-K	424	335	451	356	474	374	493	423	505	426

Table 6-29 and Table 6-30 display the evaluation results of the L-DACS 1 responsiveness. Unlike B-AMC L-DACS 1 is able to fulfill the TD95-FRS requirements in all ENR.x scenarios, too.

Table 6-29: L-DACS 1 responsiveness (TD95-FRS in ms).

Scenario	ENR.25		ENR.50		ENR.75		ENR.100		ENR.125	
	FL	RL	FL	RL	FL	RL	FL	RL	FL	RL
all	140	525	137	533	132	533	129	577	170	618
DB-B	132	-	129	-	127	-	124	-	139	-
DB-E	138	-	135	-	131	-	127	-	136	-
DG-A	138	174	134	179	137	175	148	220	185	233
DG-C	143	173	137	173	133	177	151	210	176	231
DG-D	227	646	229	636	223	637	236	648	294	705
DG-J	1,429	178	1,536	179	1,556	219	1,793	254	2,350	314
DG-K	139	280	143	332	169	315	172	359	226	437

Table 6-30: L-DACS 1 responsiveness (TD95-FRS in ms).

Scenario	ENR.150		ENR.175		ENR.200		ENR.225		ENR.250	
	FL	RL	FL	RL	FL	RL	FL	RL	FL	RL
all	231	661	351	680	631	813	*881*	687	*216*	*648*
DB-B	177	-	284	-	504	-	*662*	-	*179*	-
DB-E	180	-	277	-	512	-	*665*	-	*175*	-
DG-A	247	290	370	300	547	383	*424*	*411*	*219*	*493*
DG-C	225	277	341	296	528	354	*412*	*418*	*191*	*480*
DG-D	411	754	572	823	926	926	*992*	*799*	*749*	*743*
DG-J	3,095	341	4,500	365	7,120	419	*6,380*	*447*	*5,313*	*504*
DG-K	292	481	449	498	734	579	*719*	*565*	*466*	*544*

Figure 6-85 and Figure 6-86 display the results in graphical form. The results show clearly that the quality of service function of the L-DACS 1 DLS can provide a similar differentiation of service classes as the priority function of the B-AMC BSS. If we compare the responsiveness of the forward link in the ENR.x scenarios (Figure 6-39 (a) and Figure 6-86 (a)) the differences in the B-AMC and L-DACS 1 approaches to prioritization become apparent.

In the case of B-AMC the transport channels of all users were managed by one priority queue in the BSS. This has the effect that higher service classes are always preferred over lower service classes regardless of the user. Using B-AMC the responsiveness of the DG-C service class is stable in all scenarios as it always preferred in the BSS queue.

In the case of L-DACS 1 priorities are managed by the DLS quality of service function within the allocation of each user. It is for this reason that the latency of the DG-C service increases analogue to the latency of the other service classes with the number of users per scenario. Note that the y axis uses a logarithmic scale.

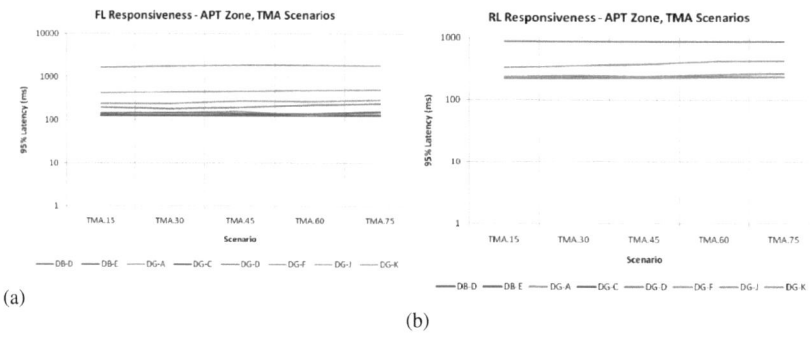

Figure 6-85: L-DACS 1 responsiveness TMA.x scenarios (TD95-FRS in ms).

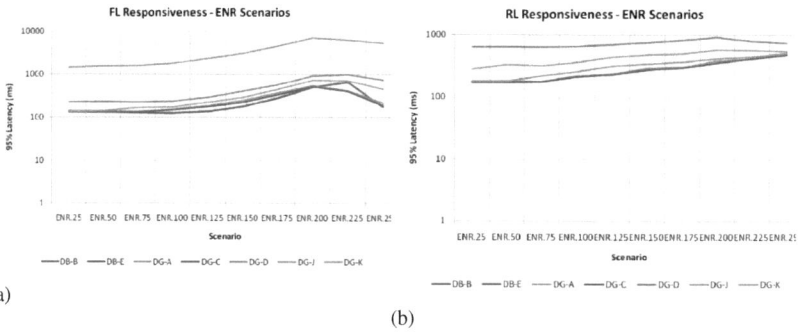

Figure 6-86: L-DACS 1 responsiveness ENR.x scenarios (TD95-FRS in ms).

Figure 6-87 displays the measured forward link responsiveness in the ENR.200 scenario. Figure 6-87 (a) is a scatter plot of the measurements (simulation time vs. measured higher layer latency Figure 6-87 (b) presents the distribution histogram of the measured values. The average and the 95% percentile of the measurements are indicated by green and red lines in both graphs.

The measured latency values of the L-DACS 1 forward link are generally higher than the B-AMC values (cf. Figure 6-40; note the change of scale). This is due to the fact that the L-DACS 1 simulations assumed a less capable physical layer. It was expected that the L-DACS 1 physical layer would decode only complete slots. This increases the minimal observable latency to one FL Data slot length. In addition, forward link DLS-PDUs have to be scheduled and announced in the CCCH in L-DACS 1 (which was not the case in B-AMC) which adds a scheduling delay not present in the previous protocol. Although the minimum of the measurements increased, the maximum observed latency values of L-DACS 1 are significantly lower than in B-AMC due to the optimized DLS timer management.

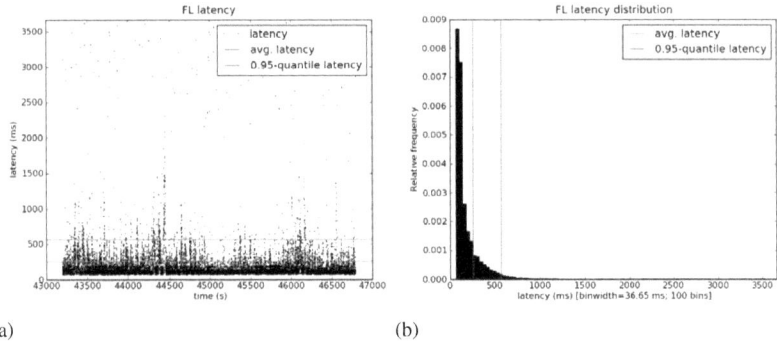

(a) (b)

Figure 6-87: L-DACS 1 FL responsiveness ENR.200 (TD95-FRS in ms).

Figure 6-88 displays the scatter plot and the distribution of the L-DACS 1 reverse link latency measurements. The ENR.200 scenario has a maximum number of 229 aircraft-stations which results in a 264 milliseconds medium access cycle according to section 6.3.3.3. These medium access intervals can be clearly distinguished in Figure 6-88 (a) analogue to the B-AMC measurements in Figure 6-41 (a) (note the change of scale).

When Figure 6-88 (a) and Figure 6-41 (a) are compared the effects of the optimized DLS timer management and flow control become apparent. Unlike in B-AMC there is no significant gap in the distribution of the latency measurements which indicates near optimal timer management. In addition, the maximum observed latency values are reduced by almost 1000 milliseconds.

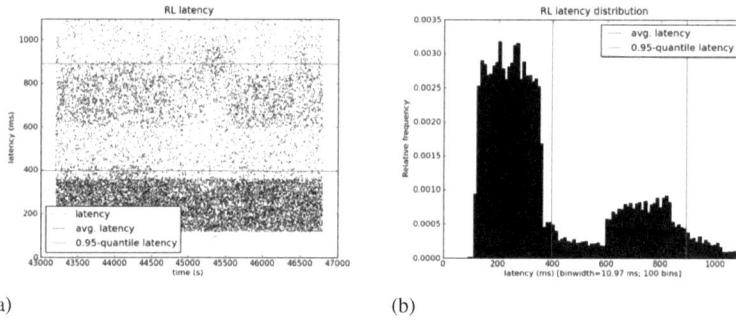

(a) (b)

Figure 6-88: L-DACS 1 RL responsiveness ENR.200 (TD95-FRS in ms).

6.3.5.3 Reliability

- Continuity of addressed user-data.
- Continuity of broadcast user-data.
- Does the system continuity satisfy the requirements of Table 5-14 and Table 5-15: yes/**no**?

The continuity of L-DACS 1 was evaluated by means of the detailed evaluation scenarios. Table 6-31 displays the continuity results for the TMA.x scenarios. Unlike B-AMC L-DACS 1 is able to meet all continuity requirements of the addressed service classes due to the improved DSL timer management. The optimized timer management reduces the overall latency significantly (e.g. compare Table 6-6 and Table 6-30) which reduces the number of expired packets below the required values.

Table 6-31: L-DACS 1 reliability (continuity in %).

Scenario	TMA.15		TMA.30		TMA.45		TMA.60		TMA.75	
	FL	RL	FL	RL	FL	RL	FL	RL	FL	RL
all	99.94	100.0	99.93	100.0	99.93	100.0	99.93	100.0	99.92	100.0
DB-D	99.62	100.0	99.59	100.0	99.61	100.0	99.63	100.0	99.58	100.0
DB-E	99.49	100.0	99.55	100.0	99.61	100.0	99.54	100.0	99.60	100.0
DG-A	100.0	100.0	100.0	100.0	100.0	100.0	100.0	100.0	100.0	100.0
DG-C	100.0	100.0	100.0	100.0	100.0	100.0	100.0	100.0	100.0	100.0
DG-D	100.0	100.0	100.0	100.0	100.0	100.0	100.0	100.0	100.0	100.0
DG-F	100.0	100.0	100.0	100.0	100.0	100.0	100.0	100.0	100.0	100.0
DG-J	100.0	100.0	100.0	100.0	100.0	100.0	100.0	100.0	100.0	100.0
DG-K	100.0	100.0	100.0	100.0	100.0	100.0	100.0	100.0	100.0	100.0

Table 6-32 and Table 6-33 present the continuity results for the ENR.x scenarios. The evaluation criteria of the addressed service classes can always be fulfilled by the reliable DLS transport service. However, the continuity requirement of the broadcast services cannot be fulfilled in the TMA.x and the ENR.x scenarios. Increasing the continuity of the broadcast service classes would require the introduction of stronger forward error correction for these services as retransmissions are not possible.

Table 6-32: L-DACS 1 reliability (continuity in %).

Scenario	ENR.25		ENR.50		ENR.75		ENR.100		ENR.125	
	FL	RL	FL	RL	FL	RL	FL	RL	FL	RL
all	99.96	100.0	99.97	100.0	99.97	100.0	99.97	100.0	99.97	100.0
DB-B	99.53	100.0	99.50	100.0	99.56	100.0	99.66	100.0	99.65	100.0
DB-E	99.53	100.0	99.62	100.0	99.61	100.0	99.53	100.0	99.61	100.0
DG-A	100.0	100.0	100.0	100.0	100.0	100.0	100.0	100.0	100.0	100.0
DG-C	100.0	100.0	100.0	100.0	100.0	100.0	100.0	100.0	100.0	100.0
DG-D	100.0	100.0	100.0	100.0	100.0	100.0	100.0	100.0	100.0	100.0
DG-J	100.0	100.0	100.0	100.0	100.0	100.0	100.0	100.0	100.0	100.0
DG-K	100.0	100.0	100.0	100.0	100.0	100.0	100.0	100.0	100.0	100.0

Table 6-33: L-DACS 1 reliability (continuity in %).

Scenario	ENR.150		ENR.175		ENR.200		ENR.225		ENR.250	
	FL	RL	FL	RL	FL	RL	FL	RL	FL	RL
all	99.97	100.0	99.97	100.0	99.97	100.0	99.97	100.0	99.97	100.0
DB-B	99.57	100.0	99.58	100.0	99.61	100.0	99.60	100.0	99.61	100.0
DB-E	99.62	100.0	99.62	100.0	99.58	100.0	99.59	100.0	99.60	100.0
DG-A	100.0	100.0	100.0	100.0	100.0	100.0	100.0	100.0	100.0	100.0
DG-C	100.0	100.0	100.0	100.0	100.0	100.0	100.0	100.0	100.0	100.0
DG-D	100.0	100.0	100.0	100.0	100.0	100.0	100.0	100.0	100.0	100.0
DG-J	100.0	100.0	100.0	100.0	100.0	100.0	100.0	100.0	100.0	100.0
DG-K	100.0	100.0	100.0	100.0	100.0	100.0	100.0	100.0	100.0	100.0

6.3.5.4 Efficiency

- Ground-to-air (FL) channel utilization.
- Air-to-ground (RL) channel utilization.
- Ground-to-air (FL) channel efficiency.
- Air-to-ground (RL) channel efficiency.

Table 6-34, Table 6-35, and Table 6-36 present the measured channel efficiency of L-DACS 1 in the TMA.x and ENR.x scenarios. In contrast to the B-AMC the control message formats of the L-DACS 1 system have been defined in [1] and [32]. It is therefore not necessary to make assumptions on the load of the control channels. The L-DACS 1 results may therefore be interpreted as valid estimates of the real system efficiency and not only on the lower boundary as in the case of B-AMC.

Table 6-34: L-DACS 1 channel efficiency and utilization; TMA.x scenarios.

Scenario	TMA.15		TMA.30		TMA.45		TMA.60		TMA.75		
	FL	RL	FL	RL	FL	RL	FL	RL	FL	RL	
Ch. efficiency	57%	16%	57%	18%	57%	20%	59%	22%	58%	24%	%
Ch. utilization	23%	9%	23%	9%	24%	10%	24%	10%	25%	10%	%

Table 6-35: L-DACS 1 channel efficiency and utilization; ENR.x scenarios.

Scenario	ENR.25		ENR.50		ENR.75		ENR.100		ENR.125		
	FL	RL	FL	RL	FL	RL	FL	RL	FL	RL	
Ch.efficiency	34%	16%	47%	18%	51%	18%	57%	21%	65%	28%	%
Ch.utilization	4%	1%	9%	3%	17%	6%	27%	9%	37%	11%	%

Table 6-36: L-DACS 1 channel efficiency and utilization; ENR.x scenarios.

Scenario	ENR.150		ENR.175		ENR.200		ENR.225		ENR.250		
	FL	RL	FL	RL	FL	RL	FL	RL	FL	RL	
Ch. efficiency	70%	37%	73%	44%	80%	54%	77%	57%	77%	60%	%
Ch. utilization	49%	12%	63%	14%	76%	15%	76%	14%	60%	10%	%

Figure 6-89 displays the results of the TMA.x scenarios in graphical form. The L-DACS 1 channel is only very lightly loaded in both directions: Less than 23% on the forward link and approximately 9% on the reverse link. Under this light load the channel efficiency of the L-DACS 1 system is more than 60% on the forward link and 23% on the reverse link. This is not very high, however, a significant improvement over the lower boundaries identified in B-AMC (FL:48%; RL:9%).

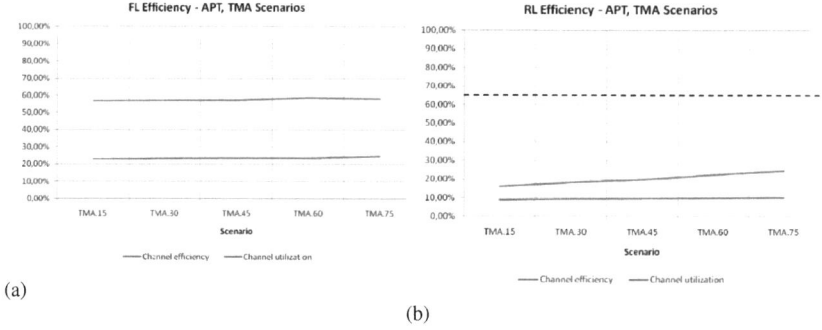

(a) (b)

Figure 6-89: L-DACS 1 efficiency; TMA.X scenarios.

Figure 6-90 displays the efficiency measurements of the ENR.x scenarios in graphical form. On the forward link the L-DACS 1 channel is utilized up to 75%. This is a slight improvement gained by the variable CC slot size. B-AMC utilized the channel up to 80%. Under the highest observed load L-DACS 1 achieves a channel efficiency of 80% at a DLS-PDU retransmission overhead of 15%. Note that the ENR.225 and ENR.250 scenarios use different ACM settings and have therefore differing channel capacities.

The reverse link efficiency is significantly lower. Partially this is due to the low channel utilization (less than 14%) where the nearly constant control channel overhead contributes more significantly than the user load. Note that the simulations used the maximum possible size for the DC slot of the dedicated control channel (52 of 162 reverse link tiles) which reserves 97.06 kbit/s for the dedicated control channel. This is a third of the available channel capacity, which implies that the channel efficiency of the L-DACS 1 reverse link cannot be greater than 67% with this parameter setting and ACM type 1 (marked by the dotted horizontal link in Figure 6-90 (b)). However, it should be noted that this capacity is not needed by the higher layers in the investigated evaluations scenarios. It was therefore decided to keep the maximum DC slot size as the spare capacity would not be used. The expected L-DACS 1 performance with different DC slot parameters is discussed in section 6.3.5.5.

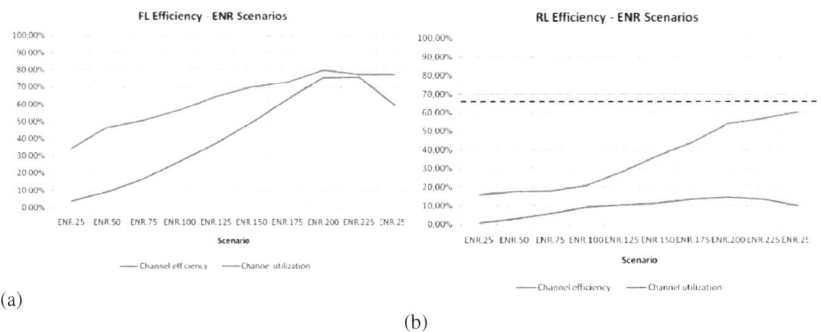

Figure 6-90: L-DACS 1 efficiency; ENR.x scenarios.

The resources of the reverse link dedicated control channel are not always completely used. In the case of B-AMC it was necessary to make assumptions on the usage of this channel. However, in the case of L-DACS 1 the actual control channel load can be measured. Figure 6-91 displays the distribution of the DC tile usage for the ENR.200 scenario. In most of the cases only the KEEP_ALIVE message and the 16 bit CRC are transmitted. If the aircraft-station makes a resource request of acknowledges received data up to 76 bit of the 112 bit tile are used. It should, however, be noted that this assumes three levels of priorities. A higher number of transmitted service classes may result in higher DC tile usage.

The high number of KEEP_ALIVE messages indicates that the size of the DC slot might be decreased without major performance losses. However, it was decided to keep the maximum DC slot size for the reasons stated above.

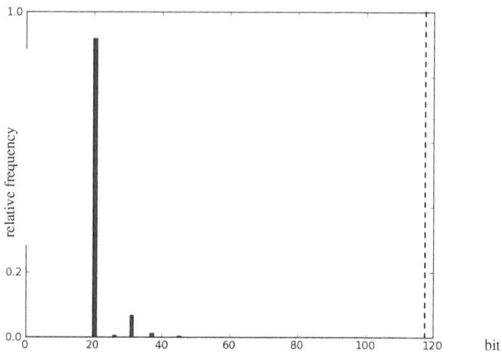

Figure 6-91: L-DACS 1 distribution of DC tile usage ENR.200.

- Interface queue length.

Table 6-37, Table 6-38, and Table 6-39 present the measurements of the L-DACS 1 DLS queue length. Unlike B-AMC there are no measurements for the BSS queue length as the BSS entity has been removed from the L-DACS 1 design.

Table 6-37: L-DACS 1 queue length; TMA.X scenarios.

Scenario	TMA.15		TMA.30		TMA.45		TMA.60		TMA.75		
	FL	RL	FL	RL	FL	RL	FL	RL	FL	RL	
Avg. q. len. (DLS)	1,147	122	1,081	128	1,035	128	968	129	905	129	B
95% q. len. (DLS)	4,080	341	4,080	341	4,080	341	4,080	376	4,080	480	B

Table 6-38: L-DACS 1 queue length; ENR.x scenarios.

Scenario	ENR.25		ENR.50		ENR.75		ENR.100		ENR.125		
	FL	RL	FL	RL	FL	RL	FL	RL	FL	RL	
Avg.q.len.(DLS)	2,040	170	2,157	207	2,106	209	2,174	222	2,215	223	B
95%q.len.(DLS)	21,080	1,383	21,080	1,383	21,080	1,383	21,080	1,383	21,080	1,383	B

Table 6-39: L-DACS 1 queue length; ENR.x scenarios.

Scenario			ENR.150		ENR.175		ENR.200		ENR.225		ENR.250		
			FL	RL	FL	RL	FL	RL	FL	RL	FL	RL	
Avg. q. len. (DLS)			2,199	216	2,094	220	2,053	218	2,028.90	217.28	1,998.61	215.38	B
95% q. len. (DLS)			21,080	1,383	21,080	1,383	21,080	1,383	21,080.0	1,383.0	21,080.0	1,383.0	B

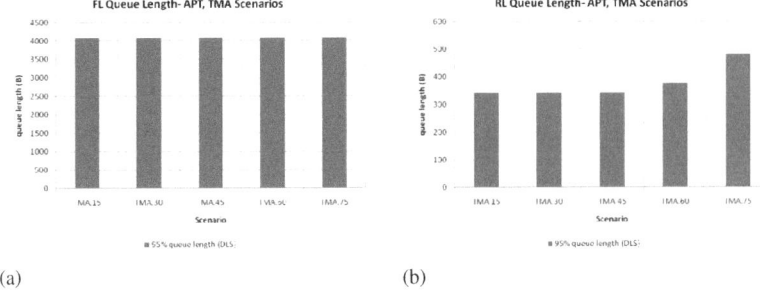

(a) (b)

Figure 6-92: L-DACS 1 queue length; TMA.X scenarios.

Figure 6-92 displays the L-DACS 1 DLS queue length in graphical form. Comparing the B-AMC results of the forward link queue length in Figure 6-44 (a) to the results in Figure 6-92 (a) below it can be seen clearly that the queue length has been significantly reduced in L-DACS 1. The aggregate B-AMC queue length of the DLS and BSS queue was over 30,000 Bytes in all TMA.x scenarios while the L-DACS 1 queue length is only in the range of 4,000 Bytes.

On the reverse link we can see a similar development. The aggregate queue length was reduced from over 1,500 Bytes to values below 500 Bytes.

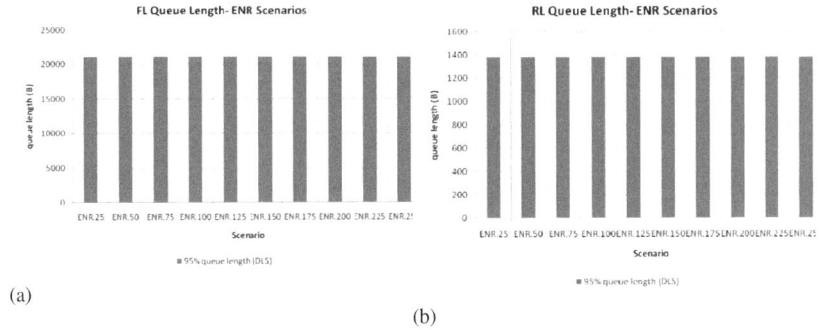

(a) (b)

Figure 6-93: L-DACS 1 queue length; ENR.X scenarios.

Figure 6-93 displays the measurements of the DLS queue in the ENR.x scenarios. The results show an analogue reduction of the L-DACS 1 queue length in comparison to the B-AMC results on the forward link. The reverse link values are similar to the B-AMC results.

- Resource distribution fairness.

Table 6-40, Table 6-41, and Table 6-42 display the measured fairness of the reverse link latency. The results indicate that L-DACS 1 achieves near-optimal fairness between different users.

Table 6-40: L-DACS 1 RL fairness TD95-FRS; TMA.x scenarios.

Scenario	TMA.15	TMA.30	TMA.45	TMA.60	TMA.75	
RL Fairness (TD95-FRS)	99.93	99.94	99.93	99.93	99.93	%

Table 6-41: L-DACS 1 RL fairness TD95-FRS; ENR.x scenarios.

Scenario	ENR.25	ENR.50	ENR.75	ENR.100	ENR.125	
RL Fairness(TD95-FRS)	99.96	99.94	99.93	99.93	99.93	%

Table 6-42: L-DACS 1 RL fairness TD95-FRS; ENR.x scenarios.

Scenario	ENR.150	ENR.175	ENR.200	ENR.225	ENR.250	
RL Fairness (TD95-FRS)	99.93	99.93	99.93	99.93	99.93	%

6.3.5.5 Scalability

- Does the system fulfill the latency requirements of Table 5-16 in all applicable scenarios: **yes**/no?

The scalability of L-DACS 1 was evaluated with the simplified evaluation scenarios. The results presented in Table 6-43 indicate that L-DACS 1 fulfils all requirements to the 95% percentile of the one-way latency in the simplified scenarios.

Note that the FL latencies are higher than in the B-AMC results as the L-DACS 1 simulations assumed a less capable physical layer. The RL 95% percentile values of the one-way latency are generally comparable to the B-AMC performance. This is not surprising as L-DACS 1 and B-AMC use the same medium access approach on the reverse link. Note that the "ENR Large ATS+AOC with A-EXEC" scenario uses ACM type 2. "ENR Super Large ATS+AOC with A-EXEC" and "ENR Super Large ATS+AOC with-out A-EXEC" use ACM type 4. These scenarios were not supported by B-AMC. Note that the PIAC in these scenarios was changed from 522 aircraft to 512 aircraft as this is the maximum supported by L-DACS 1.

Table 6-43: L-DACS 1 scalability (TD95-FRS); DC size 52.

Scenario	PIAC	95% percentile of latency (TD95-FRS)							
		ATS Only, with A-EXEC		ATS+AOC, with A-EXEC		ATS Only, without A-EXEC		ATS+AOC, without A-EXEC	
		FL	RL	FL	RL	FL	RL	FL	RL
APT Zone	26	-	-	-	-	125	412	126	412
APT Surface	264	-	-	-	-	134	178	134	179
TMA Small	44	128	180	128	180	128	180	128	180
TMA Large	53	125	187	125	187	125	187	125	187
ENR Small	45	127	180	128	180	127	180	127	180
ENR Medium	62	125	227	126	227	125	227	125	227
ENR Large	204	125	350	161	349	125	350	129	350
ENR Super Large	512	125	695	212	693	125	695	212	693

Just like in the case of B-AMC the latency requirements of the A-EXEC service (740 milliseconds) is fulfilled in all cases. This indicates that the DC slot size (and hence the dedicated control channel capacity) may be reduced. Table 6-44 displays the 95% percentile results for reduced dedicated control channel capacity. The size of the DC slot was constrained to minimum number of tiles according to Table 6-24.

Table 6-44: L-DACS 1 scalability (TD95-FRS) ; minimum DC size.

Scenario	PIAC	95% percentile of latency (TD95-FRS)							
		ATS Only, with A-EXEC		ATS+AOC, with A-EXEC		ATS Only, without A-EXEC		ATS+AOC, without A-EXEC	
		FL	RL	FL	RL	FL	RL	FL	RL
APTZone	26	-	-	-	-	141	868	145	868
APTSurface	264	-	-	-	-	139	1296	141	1296
TMASmall	44	143	639	143	639	143	988	143	988
TMALarge	53	143	636	143	636	144	1146	144	1146
ENRSmall	45	142	646	430	635	144	994	579	996
ENRMedium	62	143	724	334	719	144	1321	1472	1323
ENRLarge	204	137	706	187	708	141	1298	218	1307
ENRSuperLarge	512	126	709	207	711	136	1350	272	1350

The results show that the 95% percentile of the one-way latency changes indeed as predicted. With the exception of the ENR Medium no-A-EXEC scenario (DC is 3 tiles, TD95-FRS requirement is 1400 milliseconds) all requirements are met with the minim slots sizes. The failed requirement poses not real problem as the DC slots size can be easily increased above the minim value. It should be noted that the forward link latency also increases when the DC slot is smaller. This is caused by the ARQ transmission window which can only be shifted at the reception of a new acknowledgement in the dedicated control channel.

The results indicate that the theoretical analysis of section 6.2.3.4 provides good starting point for optimization but tends to underestimate the required DC slot size in realistic scenarios. This is caused by the fact that the estimation of section 6.2.3.4 does not take the fragmentation of large packets into account. However, the requirements are only missed by a small margin.

- Does the system provide the required level of continuity in all applicable scenarios: **yes**/no?

The evaluation of the L-DACS 1 continuity in the simplified scenarios shows that L-DACS 1 can fulfill the requirements of Table 5-16 in all cases. This is a clear improvement over B-AMC which could not provide the required continuity in all scenarios.

Table 6-45 L-DACS 1 scalability (continuity); DC size 52.

Scenario	PIAC	Continuity in %							
		ATS Only, with A-EXEC		ATS+AOC, with A-EXEC		ATS Only, without A-EXEC		ATS+AOC, without A-EXEC	
		FL	RL	FL	RL	FL	RL	FL	RL
APT Zone	26	-	-	-	-	100	100	100	100
APT Surface	264	-	-	-	-	100	100	100	100
TMA Small	44	100	100	100	100	100	100	100	100
TMA Large	53	100	100	100	100	100	100	100	100
ENR Small	45	100	100	100	100	100	100	100	100
ENR Medium	62	100	100	100	100	100	100	100	100
ENR Large	204	100	100	100	100	100	100	100	100
ENR Super Large	512	100	100	100	100	100	100	100	100

6.3.5.6 Resilience

- How does the system performance change with rising numbers of users?

Just like in the case of B-AMC the resilience of the L-DACS 1 protocol under rising numbers of users was evaluated using similar simulation settings as in the simplified scenarios. The higher layer packet size was set to 125 Bytes. The total offered load of user data was set to 100 kbit/s on the forward link and to 100 kbit/s on the reverse link distributed uniformly over the aircraft-station population. The size of the AS population varied from 16 to 240 users.

The behavior of the L-DACS 1 forward link under rising user population is displayed in Figure 6-94 (a). In comparison to B-AMC the FL latency is significantly higher (approximately 100 milliseconds). This is caused by the different assumptions of the physical layer performance (c.f. section 6.3.5.5) and the additional scheduling delay not present in B-AMC. The behavior of the FL latency is not entirely independent of the number of users as was the case with B-AMC. For populations of less than 50 aircraft-stations the measured 95% percentile of the one-way latency increases slightly. This is caused by the maximum sending window sizes of the DLS ARQ protocol which limits the peak transmission rate of the aircraft station i.e. the increased latency is caused by queuing during burst of higher layer packets as confirmed by Figure 6-95.

The reverse link behavior of the 95% percentile of the one-way latency is displayed in Figure 6-94 (b). When compared to the B-AMC results in section 6.2.5.6 and the theoretical analysis of section 6.2.3.4 and section 6.2.3.6 it becomes apparent that the L-DACS 1 latency behavior is much less influenced by the DLS protocols: The variance of the higher layer packet latency is significantly reduced. This is caused by the elimination of the round-trip time estimation. B-AMC estimated the DLS round-trip time with the 95% percentile of the measured DLS round-trip times. This approach resulted in significantly higher round-trip time estimates in the presence of high medium access variance which resulted in the latency fluctuations discussed in section 6.2.5.6. The L-DACS 1 approach is directly based on the MAC sub-layer framing and therefore far less susceptible to high medium access variance.

In addition the latency is improved by several hundreds of milliseconds for large numbers of users when compared to B-AMC (e.g. the B-AMC 95% percentile of latency is approximately 1000 milliseconds for 240 aircraft-stations). The results indicate that the tight coupling of the medium access sub-layer and the logical link control sub-layer does indeed provide an effective approach for the implementation of the DLS transport protocols.

Note that the DLS-PDU latency (labeled DLL latency in Figure 6-94) is equivalent to the delay from the resource allocation to the successful reception of the packet. Unlike B-AMC this time does not include any queuing in the medium access sub-layer as the BSS queue was removed in L-DACS 1. The 95% confidence intervals of the measurements are indicated by error bars in the graph.

Note that the results are in good accordance with the predicted performance limits of section 6.2.3.7 (maximum 280 AS for latencies below 740 milliseconds) if the protocol changes are taken into account.

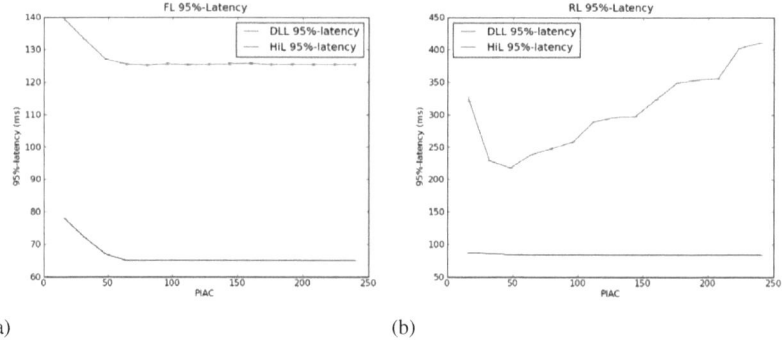

(a)   (b)

Figure 6-94: L-DACS 1 resilience under varying AS population; 95% percentile of latency. Note the significant reduction of the fluctuations caused by the variance of the DLS retransmissions when compared to B-AMC (cf. Figure 6-46 (b)).

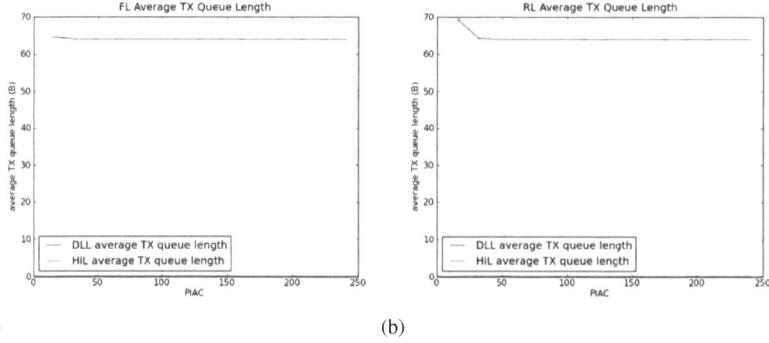

(a)   (b)

Figure 6-95: L-DACS 1 resilience under varying AS population; avg. queue length.

- How does the system performance change under rising user data load?

The behavior of L-DACS 1 under rising user data load was evaluated in a similar scenario as used above. The higher layer packet size was set to 125 Bytes. The number of aircraft-stations logged into the ground-station was set to 100 AS. The offered load of the produced by the higher layers was varied from 30 kbit/s to 300 kbit/s on the forward link and 21 kbit/s to 217 kbit/s on the reverse link. The offered load was uniformly distributed among the 100 registered aircraft-stations.

The forward link simulation results displayed in Figure 6-96 (a) indicate that the maximum achievable FL goodput is approximately 264 kbit/s which is a significant improvement over the 202.5 kbit/s achievable by B-AMC and near the predicted optimum (cf. section 6.2.3.7). Above this threshold excessive packet loss is encountered. Note that the difference between the data link layer goodput and the higher layer goodput in Figure 6-96 is caused by the overhead of the SNDCP-PDU headers, the DLS-PDU headers, and the control channels.

The maximum achievable reverse link goodput is approximately 170 kbit/s which is comparable to the 165.5 kbit/s achieved by B-AMC. However, contrary to B-AMC L-DACS 1 does not lose any packets until the maximum capacity is exceeded (Figure 6-97 (b)). The results in Figure 6-98 indicate that the L-DACS 1 interface queue does not begin to build up until this capacity limit is transgressed. Figure 6-99 indicates that L-DACS 1 can be operated with stable latency up to the identified capacity thresholds.

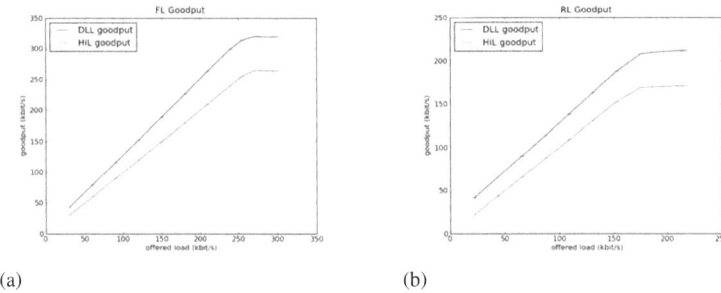

Figure 6-96: L-DACS 1 resilience under varying load; goodput.

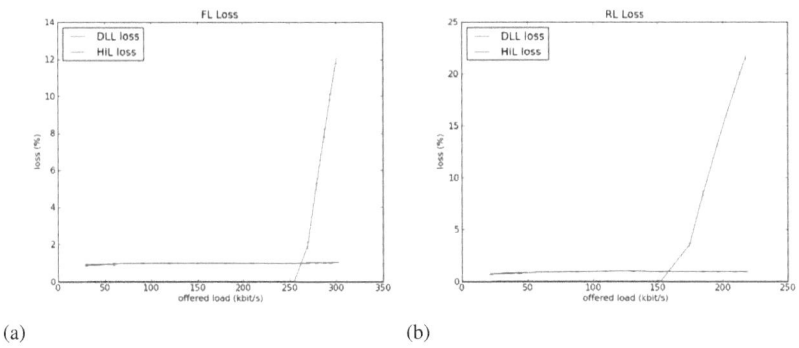

Figure 6-97: L-DACS 1 resilience under varying load; loss.

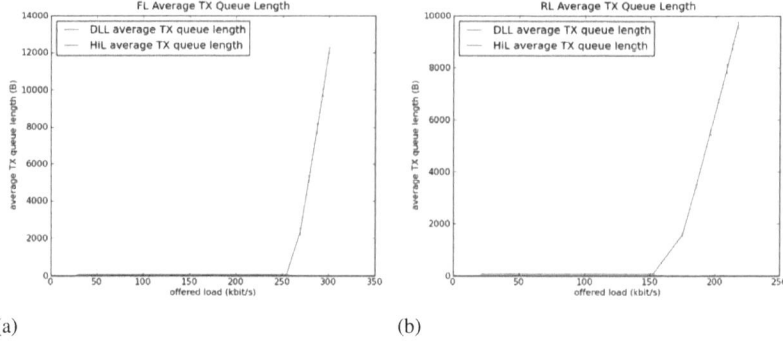

(a)   (b)

Figure 6-98: L-DACS 1 resilience under varying load; queue length.

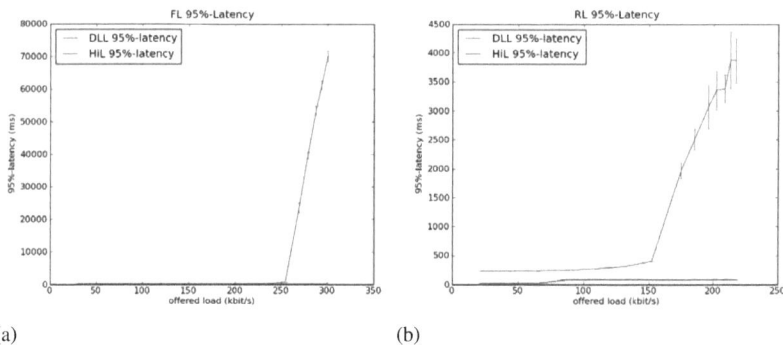

(a)   (b)

Figure 6-99: L-DACS 1 resilience under varying load; 95% latency.

6.3.6 Discussion of L-DACS1

This section summarizes and discusses the findings of the author's L-DACS 1 evaluation. The objective of the L-DACS 1 and CoLB projects was to create a *first* protocol specification enabling prototyping activities. It was not the goal of these studies to create a final product and it is expected that further refinements of the protocol will originate from these activities. The prototyping will take place in framework of the SESAR joint undertaking of the European Commission.

The focus of the author's research presented in this thesis was on the design and analysis of user plane LLC protocols suitable for a safety related system. It was the goal of his work to address the design issues identified in the B-AMC evaluation while retaining the successful concepts of the precursor protocol. The discussion of the results follows therefore loosely the discussion of the issues identified in the B-AMC analysis.

6.3.6.1 Physical Layer

The goal of the physical layer development was to develop a first specification enabling prototyping activities to clarify issues that could not be covered analytically or via modeling. This addresses mostly spectrum compatibility issues and is not in the focus of this thesis.

The physical layer design was therefore slightly modified in the course of this work. From the perspective of the data link layer development the most influential design change was the move to tile-based physical layer framing. The introduction of tile-based PHY-SDUs largely independent of the underlying OFDM frames allowed increased flexibility in the MAC framing and in the sizing of the slots conveying the logical channels.

In addition to adjustable channel sizes, the adjusted physical layer design made the use of variable sized MAC-PDUs (i.e. resource allocations) practicable. The comparatively small sizes of the forward link and reverse link PHY-SDUs offered the required granularity for efficient allocations with few padding and less overhead.

The third effect of the tile-based physical layer approach was the introduction of two adaptive coding and modulation modes into the protocol design: Cell-based ACM and user-based ACM. Adaptive coding and modulation was already discussed in B-AMC, but not realized due to the complexity of the original design. The L-DACS 1 physical layer allows now the selection of individual coding and modulation schemes for PHY-SDUs which was exploited in the new ACM modes.

6.3.6.2 Medium Access Sub-Layer

The author's focus of the B-AMC study was on the analysis and design of a swift and dependable medium access protocol suitable for safety-related communication. The concepts developed in B-AMC were retained in the L-DACS 1 design as they are deterministic, fair, contention free, and provide linear graceful degradation. However, the changes introduced in the physical layer design caused several changes in the medium-access sub-layer, too.

6.3.6.2.1 Variable Sized Logical Channels

Using MAC sub-layer slots based on variable numbers of PHY-SDUs the capacity of the logical channels can now be adjusted. The major benefit of this approach is that the L-DACS 1 control plane capacity can be adapted to the control channel load. This increases the robustness of the protocol as the required management bandwidth can be virtually guaranteed.

The reverse link medium access latency is directly related to the size of the DC slot i.e. additional reverse link data channel DCH capacity can be traded for increased medium access latency by reducing the DC slot size. The author's analysis of the L-DACS 1 medium access approach provided a formal method to derive the minimum DC slot size from the desired maximum latency. This may increase the system efficiency as less channel resources have to be statically allocated to control channels.

A minor change in the L-DACS 1 medium access sub-layer design was the merging of the B-AMC DC and SA slots into a single slot with the combined functionality by the author. This modification was fostered by the increased capacity of the reverse-link PHY-SDUs in comparison to the B-AMC T1 transport channels. Having only one control channel in the forward link and one control channel in the reverse link direction simplifies the channel mapping and the overall system architecture.

6.3.6.2.2 Error Containment and Link Monitoring

The internal behavior of the control channels was not analyzed in B-AMC. No exact message formats were defined and the simulations assumed virtually error-free control plane operation. The impact of transmission errors in the CC and DC slots was, however, considered in the L-DACS 1 design.

The author's work in the L-DACS 1 development introduced two additions to the protocol design: Error containment and link monitoring. Error containment was added to L-DACS 1 after careful analysis of the control channel error patterns. It tries to mitigate the effects of transmission errors as far as possible to increase the protocol robustness. The effectiveness of this approach was verified in the simulations.

The second addition of the author to the L-DACS 1 design was the introduction of link monitoring. This concept allows the timely detection of link failures or the loss of connectivity. This feature was introduced to make the system resilient against undetected errors.

6.3.6.2.3 Removal of MAC Queues

The author's major architectural change in the medium access sub-layer was the removal of the BSS transmission queues. The purpose of the BSS entity in the B-AMC design was to ensure prioritized medium access of competing service classes by active queue management.

The priority management of the BSS operated on fixed sized MAC-PDUs (i.e. transport channels) which generated the need for a second level of segmentation and reassembly in the MAC in addition to the segmentation and reassembly in the DLS. Removing this functionality form the medium access sub-layer provided a significant simplification of the protocol behavior. However, the priority management had now to be implemented in the DLS and the segmentation and reassembly of large packets was moved into the logical link control sub-layer, too.

The simplification of the medium access sub-layer behavior was also exploited analytically by the author to determine the minimum DC slot size.

6.3.6.3 Logical Link Control Sub-Layer

The author's major innovation of the L-DACS 1 research was the complete re-design of the user plane LLC protocols. The HDLC based sliding window protocol of B-AMC was replaced by a two-layer credit-based ARQ protocol. These changes led to a significantly simplified and algorithmically much more robust LLC design.

6.3.6.3.1 Flow Control

An additional consequence of removing the BSS from the system is that only one queue remains in the system: The interface queue of the DLS. The B-AMC DLS protocols had to use carefully tuned flow control mechanisms to avoid producing congestion in the BSS queues. This is no longer necessary with these queues removed.

The DLS sending window management was simplified by coupling it to the central resource management of the ground-station. The ground-station has a complete view of all resource needs in the system as it collects the resource requests of all users. This knowledge is used to compute the resource allocations for all aircraft-stations. The resource allocations that are periodically transmitted by the ground-station contain the complete knowledge of the available transmission resources. Consequently the size of the resource allocation is also the optimal DLS transmission window size. This is known as credit based flow management. Using this approach there is no need to estimate the size of the sending window. It is exactly known from the resource allocations of the ground-station making near to optimal flow management possible.

6.3.6.3.2 Timer Management

The B-AMC timer management was relatively complex as the DLS had no information on the medium access sub-layer status. The retransmission timer depended on complex measurements and estimations of the observed round trip time. Operating several classes of service within the same B-AMC stack efficiently was particularly difficult as the DLS shared no state with the MAC sub-layer.

The removal of the BSS from the L-DACS 1 protocol stack allowed the tight coupling of the LLC and MAC protocols. The DLS protocol operates now in fixed timing relations to the MAC frame structure to achieve near to optimal timer management. Acknowledgements and data packets are sent in slots occurring at well-known times in the frame structure. As the L-DACS 1 DLS is aware of the MAC frame structure it can perform timer management by counting transmission opportunities for data packets and acknowledgements. This approach offers much greater algorithmic robustness than time-outs based on round-trip time estimations.

6.3.6.3.3 Segmentation and Reassembly

Within B-AMC DLS-PDUs could be split over several allocations (i.e. transport channels). This increased the variance of DLS-PDU transmission times significantly if they had to be transmitted in several transport channels. It is another benefit of the tight coupling of the MAC and LLC sub-layers in L-DACS 1 that the negative effects of

DLS-SDU fragmentation could be significantly reduced by linking the DLS segmentation mechanism with the resource allocation management.

L-DACS 1 employs only one level of segmentation based on the feedback of the medium access sub-layer. DLS-PDUs are directly fragmented into the appropriate allocations size by the DLS. The intermediate step using the BSS and a second level of fragmentation is removed.

6.4 Summary

The analysis, design, and validation of the B-AMC and L-DACS 1 protocols by the author have produced a set of protocols that is backed by formal and simulation based analysis. It was the objective of the author's work to develop a protocol design providing the quality of service required for future ATM operations. It has been confirmed by the presented evaluations that this objective has been accomplished. The author's work was constrained by the current capabilities of industrial implementation and the expected operational environment i.e. the medium access protocol had to be adapted to physical layer implementation constraints (e.g. the number of concurrent OFDMA accesses supported by current hardware) and the constraints of the operational environment (e.g. the duty cycle limitations of the inlay approach had to be taken into account by the resource allocation procedure).

The author's formal analysis of the B-VHF medium access protocols indicated serious design issues. From the perspective of resilience and reliability the main problem of medium access is its non-deterministic behavior. This poses a major problem for a safety-related system as the medium access latency depends on the number of medium access attempts made by the aircraft-stations i.e. the system performance is determined by the application's data traffic pattern, which is hardly predictable and not under the control of the system.

This analysis led the author to a new medium access approach built on the lessons learnt from B-VHF. The new approach was designed by the author to provide dependable medium access for a high number of users without any dependency of the access latency on the data traffic pattern. The effect of this design is that the medium access latency is only coupled to the number of aircraft-stations served by the ground-station. The medium access performance degrades only linearly with the number of users and not exponentially as in the case of random access. In the author's protocol design the resource allocation between different users is performed centralized by the ground-station while the resource distribution between packets of different priorities is be performed locally by each user. The effect of this approach is that the medium access sub-layer now supports prioritized channel access.

Error robustness in the MAC sub-layer control plane is realized by the author using error containment in the medium access sub-layer. The effect of this design is significantly increased resilience in the control channels. At the typical working point of L-DACS 1 (bit error rate 10^{-5}) only 1 out of 500 reverse link control channel transmissions is lost. Due to the smaller size of the forward link control messages the effect is even more pronounced in this direction.

The author's analysis of the requirements towards the overall communication system performance produced the justification for the use of ARQ in the logical link control sub-layer. The DLS approach was designed and refined by the author on the basis of the critical analysis of the B-AMC performance. In the eventual L-DACS 1 protocol design the sending window management was simplified by coupling it to the central resource management of the ground-station. As the ground-station has a complete view of all resource needs in the system this has the effect that the resource allocation is also the optimal DLS transmission window size. Coupling the DLS timer management to the MAC sub-layer time framing has the effect to produce near to optimal timer management.

In terms of the overall system architecture the author's work resulted in a significant simplification of the protocol stack design. The removal of the BSS entity from the L-DACS 1 protocol stack allows the tight coupling of the LLC and MAC protocols. Another effect of this measure is that the negative effects of DLS-SDU fragmentation are significantly reduced by linking the DLS segmentation mechanism with the resource allocation management.

7 Conclusion

Air transportation is an important factor for the economic growth of the European Union, however, the current system is already approaching its capacity limits and needs to be reformed to meet the demands of further sustainable development. These limitations stem mainly from the current European Air Traffic Control *ATC* system. New concepts have been developed to overcome the limitations of the current system that do not longer *control* air traffic, but rather *manage* it. Air Traffic Management *ATM* is expected to supersede ATC in the Single European Sky. However, ATM requires sophisticated data communication capabilities as it transfers parts of the decision making from air traffic controllers to cockpit crews supported by automated procedures and algorithms. The aircrews must now be provided with timely, accurate and sufficient data to effectively collaborate in the collaborative decision making process of ATM.

In 2003, at the eleventh ICAO Air Navigation Conference it has been agreed that the aeronautical air-ground communications infrastructure has to evolve to provide the capacity and quality of service required to support ATM. FAA and EUROCONTROL, representing the regions feeling the most pressure to reform their air-ground communication infrastructure, initiated the Action Plan 17 *AP17* activity to jointly identify and assess candidates for future aeronautical communication systems. AP17 came to an end in late 2007 and the final report concluded that none of the considered technology proposals could be fully recommended for all airspace domains. The future system shall therefore be a system of systems integrating existing technologies as well as new communication systems. Within this thesis two proposals developed after AP17 for the terrestrial or continental component of the future communications infrastructure were discussed: B-AMC and L-DACS 1.

B-AMC is a technology proposal developed in a EUROCONTROL funded design study in the context of AP17. It was designed to support air-ground communication as well as direct air-air communication. The key design objective of the air-ground mode is the optimization of B-AMC for data communication while keeping support for digital voice. It should be completely transparent with automatic handovers between radio cells. The system should support operational aeronautical communication i.e. Air Traffic Services *ATS* and Aeronautical Operational Control *AOC* communications.

The author's major contribution to the development of B-AMC was the analysis and design of the medium access approach. The B-AMC medium access approach built on the lessons learnt from the author's analysis of the B-VHF protocol. The B-VHF approach was based on random access slots. However, in order to cope with significant numbers of users B-VHF required high numbers of slots, but even so the latency would rise sharply under high load. In addition to the poor performance the second problem of the random access based approach was that it is essentially non-deterministic, which poses a major problem for a safety-related system. The medium access latency depended on the number of medium access attempts of the aircraft-stations. The system performance was determined by the application's data traffic pattern, which is neither predictable nor under the control of the system. B-AMC medium access is therefore based on a new approach devised by the author to solve these problems. It was designed to provide dependable medium access to a high number of users without any dependency of the access latency on the data traffic pattern. This is realized by the introduction of a dedicated and periodic control channel for each aircraft-station. The aircraft-stations use this channel to provide the ground-station with periodic updates on their resource needs. This decouples the medium access algorithm from the data traffic pattern. Providing dedicated resources for each control channel makes medium access contention-free. The medium access latency is therefore only coupled to the number of aircraft-stations served by the ground-station.

The second technology proposal discussed in this document was ***L-DACS 1***. B-AMC was identified as the most promising L-DACS 1 candidate by EUROCONTROL. Together with the other L-DACS 1 candidates TIA-902 P34 and IEEE 802.16e WiMAX it was therefore selected to provide the technological basis for the development of the L-DACS 1 system. The L-DACS 1 design inherited its main features from the author's B-AMC system design. Like B-AMC the air-ground mode of the L-DACS 1 data link is a multi-application cellular broadband system capable of simultaneously providing various kinds of Air Traffic Services ***ATS*** and Aeronautical Operational Control ***AOC*** communication services via deployed ground-stations.

The author's major contribution to the L-DACS 1 research is the complete re-design of the user plane LLC protocols. The HDLC based sliding window protocol of B-AMC is replaced by a two-layer credit-based ARQ protocol. The sending window management is simplified by coupling it to the central resource management of the ground-station. The ground-station has a complete view of all resource needs in the system as it collects the resource requests of all users. Consequently the size of the resource allocation is also the optimal DLS transmission window size making near to optimal flow management possible. In addition to the improved flow management, the DLS protocol operates now in fixed timing relations to the MAC frame structure to achieve near to optimal timer management.

The methodology applied by the author in this thesis was as follows: In the first step the relevant requirements for future terrestrial communication systems were analyzed to derive the design goals. In the second step the analysis of existing proposals and the design of new approaches overcoming the identified shortcomings were performed. This step was iterated two times: Firstly on the basis of B-VHF resulting in the author's design of B-AMC, and secondly on the basis of B-AMC resulting in the author's design of L-DACS 1. The third step was the evaluation of the proposed solutions against the design goals identified by the author in the first step.

B-AMC and L-DACS 1 were evaluated by the author using formal analysis and computer simulations according to evaluation criteria derived from the design goals for the future radio system FRS. The primary design goals for all FRS technology proposals were defined by the high level objectives formulated in AP17 [**37**]:

- *The system development shall be facilitated and expedited through the choice of appropriate components and mature standards.*

- *The new system should be capable to operate in the L-band without interfering with existing users of the band.*

- *The system performance should meet the requirements defined in AP17 technical task 2.*

The first objective was fulfilled by the author by the evaluation of state of the art communication systems and the careful adaptation of selected concepts. The notion of physical layer tiles and medium access sub-layer allocation maps was adopted from the WiMAX standard. Two layered ARQ protocols can also be found in the upcoming LTE standard.

The second objective is mainly a physical layer design task. It is therefore not discussed in depth in this thesis. However, the suppression of out-of-band interference implies some consequences for the design of the data link layer. Most notably it requires the inclusion of configurable resource allocation limits to keep the duty cycle low.

The third design goal is broken down into a set of quantitative and qualitative evaluation criteria evaluated in B-AMC and L-DACS 1 computer simulations by the author:

Responsiveness is the capability of the system to react quickly to communication demand. It was evaluated by measuring the one-way latency of user data according to requirements defined by EUROCONTROL and FAA:

- Do the 95%-percentile values of the one-way latency satisfy the requirements of Table 5-12 and Table 5-13: **yes**

The computer simulations show that L-DACS 1 fulfils this requirement in all applicable evaluation scenarios. In addition, the author's results showed clearly that the L-DACS 1 priority management is able to provide prioritized medium access and to deliver data traffic within the specified delays of its service class.

Reliability is the ability of the system to transmit data without losing or duplicating information. It is evaluated by measuring the continuity of user data according to the requirements defined by EUROCONTROL and FAA.

- Does the system continuity satisfy the requirements of Table 5-14 and Table 5-15: **no**

The author's computer simulations showed that L-DACS 1 is able to provide the required service continuity for all unicast data link applications. The continuity requirements of the broadcast services could not be met. A possible mitigation for this issue could be the application of extremely strong forward error correction to this class of service. However, in the view of the author it is questionable if 99.996% continuity can be achieved for broadcast services with reasonable overhead.

Efficiency was evaluated quantitatively by measuring the channel utilization, channel efficiency, interface queue length, and fairness. The author's results indicate that L-DACS 1 utilizes up to 75% of the radio channel with 80% efficiency in the investigated evaluation scenarios (ENR.200). The interface queue length is in the range of the maximum packet size, pointing at near to optimal flow management. The protocol is extremely fair with over 99% fairness according to Jain's fairness index [**79**].

Scalability was evaluated according to the EUROCONTROL-defined air traffic volumes. L-DACS 1 is able to support all relevant use cases with acceptable quality of service.

- Does the system fulfill the latency requirements of Table 5-16 in all applicable scenarios: **yes**

The author's results indicate that L-DACS 1 fulfils all requirements to the 95% percentile of the one-way latency using the default protocol parameters. If the calculated minimum control channel capacity is used, the one-way latency changes as predicted: With the exception of one scenario all requirements were met with the minimum slots sizes, too.

- Does the system provide the required level of continuity in all applicable scenarios: **yes**

L-DACS 1 is able to provide the required unicast continuity in all investigated scenarios.

Resilience is the ability to provide and maintain an acceptable quality of service under adverse conditions. L-DACS 1 was evaluated in periods of excessive load and with high numbers of users. The system showed predictable service degradation under overload. System failures are immediately detected by the built-in link monitoring.

- How does the system performance change with rising numbers of users?

The author has shown analytically and by simulation that the performance of the system degrades only linearly with an increasing number of aircraft-stations per cell. L-DACS 1 exhibits therefore a form of built-in graceful degradation.

- How does the system performance change under rising user data load?

The author's results indicate that the maximum achievable goodput is near the predicted optimum and that the L-DACS 1 can be operated stable up to the identified capacity thresholds.

In summary the analysis, design, and validation of the B-AMC and L-DACS 1 protocols by the author have produced a set of protocols that is backed by formal and simulation based analysis. It was the objective of the author's work to develop a protocol design providing the quality of service required for future ATM operations. It has been confirmed by the presented evaluations that this objective has been accomplished. The author's work was constrained by the current capabilities of industrial implementation and the expected operational environment i.e. the medium access protocol had to be adapted to physical layer implementation constraints and the constraints of the operational environment. The major findings of this thesis therefore show the effectiveness of the author's L-DACS 1 user plane quality of service protocols. The relevance of the author's innovations is further underlined by the adoption of key concepts of his work within the competing L-DACS 2 technology proposal. In the context of the user plane quality of service protocols the following items are considered as areas of future work:

- Improved protocol efficiency by revised control message formats: The specified L-DACS 1 messages were based on TIA-902 P34 and not optimized for L-DACS 1. Although message formats were not in the focus of this thesis the evaluation of the protocol performance did indicate that the overall protocol efficiency may be significantly improved by revised control message formats. Note that any new control message format must support the error containment properties of the existing format (e.g. by the use of CRC hunting instead of fixed length messages).
- Improved forward link responsiveness by polling for LLC ARQ acknowledgements: The round-trip time of the forward link LLC ARQ protocol depends on the length of the medium access cycle of the dedicated control channel. By including support for polling on the dedicated control channel, the forward link ARQ round-trip time may be significantly reduced. Note that any new mechanism must not interfere with the deterministic medium access protocol (e.g. by reserving a small number of DC tiles for this purpose).
- Improved LLC ARQ parameters: The logical link control sub-layer ARQ protocol performance may be further improved by tuning the values for maximum DLS sending window size and maximum DLS service data unit size according to the lower layer bit error rate. This may, however, require modifications of the control message formats and to the sub-network depended convergence protocol on top of the L-DACS 1 protocol stack to support changing DLS-SDU sizes.

L-DACS 1 has now entered a new phase within the protocol engineering process going from the development phase to the prototyping phase. The initial specification can now be considered complete and evaluated. The next steps will be determined by the further optimization of the protocol and the evaluation of the prototype within the context of Single European Sky ATM Research Programme *SESAR*. L-DACS 1 can now be considered a mature technology proposal offering a solid baseline for the definition of the future terrestrial radio system.

8 References

[1] M Sajatovic et al., "L-DACS1 System Definition Proposal," L-DACS 1 Project, Deliverable D2 2009.

[2] QinetiQ, "Future Communications Infrastructure - Step 2: Technology Assessment Results," EUROCONTROL, 2007.

[3] M. Sajatovic et al., "L-DACS1 System Definition Proposal: Deliverable D3 - Design Specifications for L-DACS1 Prototype," L-DACS1 Project, Deliverable D3 2009.

[4] Commision of the European Communities, "European Transport Policy for 2010; Time to Decide," Brussels, 2001.

[5] European Commission. (2009, May) Transport: Single European Sky - European commission. [Online]. http://ec.europa.eu/transport/air/single_european_sky/single_european_sky_en.htm

[6] B. Korn, C. Edinger, S. Tittel, D. Kügler, and T. Pütz, "Sectorless ATM – A Concept to Increase En-Route Efficiency," in *Proc. 29th DASC*, 2009.

[7] SESAR Joint Untertaking. SESAR JU. [Online]. http://www.sesarju.eu

[8] A. Helfrick, *Principles of Avionics*, 4th ed. Leesburg, VA, USA: Avionics Communications Inc., 2007.

[9] Eleventh Air Navigation Conference, "Report of Committee B on Agenda Item 7," Montreal, 2003.

[10] B. Kamali, "An Overview of VHF Civil Radio Network and the Resolution of Spectrum Depletion," in *Proc. ICNS'10*, 2010.

[11] Eleventh Air Navigation Conference, "IATA Position on Aeronautical Air Ground Communications Needs," Montreal, 2003.

[12] EUROCONTROL/FAA, "Action Plan 17 Future Communications Study - Final Conclusions and Recomendations," 2007.

[13] B. Haindl et al., "B-VHF - A Multi-Carrier Based Broadband VHF Communications Concept for Air Traffic Management," in *Proc. of 2005 IEEE Aerospace Conference*, 2005.

[14] S. Brandes, I. Cosovic, and M. Schnell, "Techniques for Ensuring Co-existence

Between B-VHF and Legacy VHF Systems," in *Proc. of 2006 IEEE Aerospace Conference*, 2006.

[15] M. Schnell, E. Haas, M. Sajatovic, C. Rihacek, and B. Haindl, "B-VHF - An Overlay System Concept for Future ATC Communications in the VHF Band," in *Proc. 23rd DASC*, 2004.

[16] S. Brandes et al., "B-VHF - Selected Simulation Results and Final Assessment," in *Proc. 25th DASC*, 2006.

[17] I. Cosovic, S. Brandes, M. Schnell, and B. Haindl, "Physical Layer Design for a Broadband Overlay System in the VHF Band With and In-band Transition," in *Proc. 24th DASC*, 2005.

[18] S. Brandes et al., "Final Assessment of the B-VHF Overlay Concept," in *Proc. IEEE Aeospace Conference*, 2007.

[19] C.H. Rokitansky et al., "B-AMC - Aeronautical Broadband Communication in the L-band," in *Proc. CEAS European Air and Space Conference*, 2007, pp. 487 - 496.

[20] C.H. Rokitansky et al., "B-AMC A System for Future Broadband Aeronautical Multi-Carrier Communications in the L-band," in *Proc. 26th DASC*, 2007, pp. 4.D.2-1 - 4.D.2-13.

[21] M. Schnell et al., "B-AMC - Broadband Aeronautical Multi-carrier Communications," in *Proc. ICNS'08*, 2008.

[22] T. Gräupl, M. Ehammer, and C.-H. Rokitansky, "Link-Layer Quality of Service in the L-Band Digital Aeronautical Communications System B-AMC," in *Proc. 27th DASC*, 2008.

[23] A. Woogara and J. Micallef, "Analysis of B-AMC Performance," Helios, 2008.

[24] A. Woogara and J. Micallef, "Key Characteristics and Performance Comparison of B-AMC, AMACS and P34," Helios, 2008.

[25] TIA, "TIA-902," 2002/2003.

[26] IEEE, "IEEE Standard for Local and Metropolitan Area Networks - Part 16: Air Interface for Fixed Braodband, IEEE Std 802.16-2004," 2004.

[27] T. Gräupl, M. Ehammer, and C.-H. Rokitansky, "L-DACS 1 Data Link Layer Design and Performance," in *Proc. ICNS'09*, 2009.

[28] M. Schnell, S. Brandes, S. Gligorevic, M. Walter, and C. Rihacek, "Interference Mitigartion for Broadband L-DACS," in *Proc. 27th DASC*, 2008.

[29] S. Brandes, U. Epple, S. Gligorevic, and M Schnell, "Physical Layer Specification of the L-band Digital Aeronautical Communications System (L-DACS1)," in *Proc. ICNS'09*, 2009.

[30] B. Haindl et al., "Improvement of L-DACS1 Design by Combining B-AMC with P34 and WiMAX Technologies," in *Proc. ICNS'09*, 2009.

[31] M. Sajatovic and T. Gräupl, "Functional System Analysis Report," CoLB Project, Deliverable D2 2009.

[32] M. Sajatovic, T. Gräupl, and S. Zwettler, "L-DACS1 System Design Improvements," CoLB Project, Deliverable D4 2010.

[33] ICAO, "Communication Systems," ANNEX 10 Volume III, 1995.

[34] Helios Information Services Ltd., "The ATN SARPs," 2001.

[35] FANS Information Services Ltd., "Comprehensive ATN Manual (CAMAL)," 1999.

[36] ICAO. ACP-WG-I Internet Protocol Suit. [Online]. http://www.icao.int/anb/panels/ACP/wgmeetinglist.cfm?WGID=26

[37] N. Fistas, Future Aeronautical Communication System - FCI, 2009, Presentation at TAKE OFF Conference'09, Salzburg.

[38] L-DASCS 2 Project, "LDACS2 System Definition Proposal," Deliverable D2 2009.

[39] AMACS Project, "Future Communications Infrastructure - Technology Investigations Desciption of AMACS," 2007.

[40] M. Sajatovic and T. Gräupl, "Evaluation Report," CoLB Project, Deliverable D6 2011.

[41] ESA. ARTES-10 Iris. [Online]. http://telecom.esa.int/

[42] NEWSKY Project. NEWSKY. [Online]. http://www.newsky-fp6.eu

[43] L. Kleinrock, *Queueing Systems. Volume 1: Theory*.: Wiley-Interscience, 1975.

[44] F. Brooks, *The Mythical Man-Month: Essays on Software Engineering*, 2nd ed.:

Addison-Wesley, 1995.

[45] EUROCONTROL/FAA, "Evaluation Scenarios," 2007.

[46] EUROCONTROL/FAA, "Communication Operating Concept and Requirements for the Future Radio System, Ver. 2," 2007.

[47] C.-H. Rokitansky, M. Ehammer, and T. Gräupl, "Communication Capacity Assessment for the IRIS Satellite System," in *Proc. 27th DASC*, 2008.

[48] T. Gräupl et al., "Dimensioning Requirements for the ANTARES ATM Satellite Data-Link," in *Proc. ICNS'10*, 2010.

[49] C. Morlet, M. Ehammer, T. Gräupl, and C.-H. Rokitansky, "Characterisation of the Data Link Communication Air Traffic for the European Airspace," in *Proc. 29th DASC*, 2010.

[50] S. Brandes, S. Gligorevic, M. Ehammer, T. Gräupl, and R. Dittrich, "Expected B-AMC System Performance," B-AMC Project, Deliverable D5 2007.

[51] M. Ehammer, T. Gräupl, and C.-H. Rokitanksy, "Applying SOA Concepts to the Simulation of Aeronautical Wireless Communication," in *Proc CNS'08*, 2008.

[52] C.-H. Rokitansky, S. Brandes, and M. Sajatovic, "Draft B-AMC Frequency Plan," B-AMC Project (ext.), Deliverable D2 2008.

[53] EUROCONTROL, "Long-Term Forecast: IFR Flight Movements 2006-2025," 2006.

[54] T. Gräupl, "USBG Simulation Handbook," University of Salzburg, Tecnical Report X23 2009.

[55] E Allaix, T. Azzarelli, C. Morlet, H. Gonzales, and University of Salzburg, "Estimation of Information Volume Requirements for ATM under AI 1.7," ACP/WGF 20/WP 17, 2009.

[56] E. Kristiansen, S. Patella, and M. Mazzoccanti, "An application layer gateway for air traffic management," in *Proc. 26th ICSSC*, 2008.

[57] E. Gamma, R. Helm, R. Johnson, and J. Vlissides, *Design Patterns. Elements of Reusable Object-Oriented Software*, 1st ed. Amsterdam: Addison-Wesley Longman, 1995.

[58] R. Jain, D.M. Chiu, and W. Hawe, "A Quantitative Measure of Fairness and Discrimination for Resource Allocation in Shared Systems," DEC Research Report

TR-30 1984.

[59] ISO, "Information Technology - Telecommunications and information exchange between systems - High-level data link control (HDLC) procedures," ISO/IEC 13239:2002, 2002.

[60] B-VHF Project. (2006) Broadband VHF Aeronautical Communication System Based on MC-CDMA. [Online]. http://www.b-vhf.org

[61] B. Haindl and M. Schnell, "Interference on the B-VHF Overlay System," B-VHF Project, Deliverable D-09 04A02 E510.11, 2005.

[62] M. Schnell, E. Haas, C. Rihacek, and M. Sajatovic, "B-VHF - An Overlay System Concept for Future ATC Communications in teh VHF Band," in *Proc. 23rd DASC*, 2004.

[63] S. Gligorevic and A. Schlereth, "B-VHF Testbed Evaluation," B-VHF Project, Deliverable D-34, 2006.

[64] M. Ehammer and T. Gräupl, "Performance Evaluation of the Data Link Layer," B-VHF Project, Deliverable D-24 UNISBG.FBSCICOMP.2006.B-VHF.D.24, 2006.

[65] M. Ehammer and T. Gräupl, "Performance Evaluation of the Upper Layers," B-VHF Project, Deliverable D-25 UNISBG.FBSCICOMP.2006.B-VHF.D.25.0, 2006.

[66] D. Roberts and K. Miles, "DME Spectrum Characteristics and L-Band Spectrum Availabilty for an OFDM-like System," B-AMC Project, Deliverable D1 2007.

[67] M. Sajatovic et al., "B-AMC System High Level Description," B-AMC Project, Deliverable D2.1 2007.

[68] M. Sajatovic, T. Gräupl, and M. Ehammer, "B-AMC Operating Concept and Deployment Scenarios," B-AMC Project, Deliverable D2.2 2007.

[69] M. Schnell et al., "System Specification Including Standardization and Certification Considerations," B-AMC Project, Deliverable D3 2007.

[70] M. Sajatovic, "B-AMC Interference Analysis and Spectrum Requirements," B-AMC Project, Deliverable D4 2007.

[71] M. Sajatovic, "B-AMC Aircraft Integration and Ground Infrastructure," B-AMC Project, Deliverable D6 2007.

[72] S. Brandes and M. Schnell, "Proposed L-Band Interference Scenarios," B-AMC Project (ext.), Deliverable D1 2008.

[73] S. Brandes and M. Schnell, "Systematic Interference Investigations," B-AMC Project (ext.), Deliverable D3 2008.

[74] D. Roberts and K. Miles, "DME Spectrum Characterization and L-band Spectrum Availability for an OFDM-like System," Report D-1 2007.

[75] S. Brandes, I. Cosovic, and M. Schnell, "Techniques for Ensuring Co-existence Between B-VHF and Legacy VHF Systems," in *IEEE Aerospace Conference*, 2006.

[76] V. Jacobson, "Congestion Avoidance and Control," in *Proc. SIGCOMM'88*, 1988.

[77] Freescal Semiconductor, "Long Term Evolution Protocol Overview," 2008.

[78] A. Larmo et al., "The LTE Link-Layer Design," *IEEE Communications Magazine*, 2009.

[79] R. Jain, A. Durresi, and G. Babic, "Throughput Fairness Index: An Explanation," ATM_Forum/99-0045, 1999.

[80] E. Christensen, F. Curbera, G Meredith, and S. Weerawarana, "Web Services Description Language (WSDL) 1.1," NOTE-wsdl-20010315, 2001.

[81] M. Gudgin et al., "SOAP Version 1.2 Part 1: Messaging Framework (Second Edition)," REC-soap12-part1-20070427, 2007.

[82] W3C, "Extensible Markup Language (XML) 1.1 (Second Edition)," REC-xml11-20060816, 2006.

[83] Python Software Foundation. Python Programming Language -- Official Website. [Online]. http://www.python.org

[84] P Deutsch, "DEFLATE Compressed Data Format Specification version 1.3," RFC 1951, 1996.

[85] DIN, "Grundlagen der Meßtechnik - Teil 3: Auswertung von Messungen einer einzelnen Meßgröße, Meßunsicherheit," DIN 1319-3, 1996.

[86] A. Tanenbaum, *Computer Networks*, 4th ed.: Pearson Education International, 2003.

[87] ITU-R, *Radio Regulations.*, 2004.

[88] NASA, "NASA & the Next Generation Air Transportation System (NextGen)," 2007.

[89] Panel on Human Factors in Air Traffic Control Automation, *The Future of Air Traffic Control*, Christopher D. Wickens et al., Eds. Washington DC: National Academy Press, 1998.

[90] G. Bachula, Testimony of Gary R. Bachula, Vice President, Internet2 Before the United States Senate Committee on Commerce, Science and Transportation Hearing on Net Neutrality, 2006.

[91] B. Teitelbaum and S. Shalunov, "Why Premium IP Service Has Not Deployed (and Probably Never Will)," Internet2 QoS Working Group Informational Document 2006. [Online]. http://qos.internet2.edu/wg/documents-informational/20020503-premium-problems-non-architectural.html

[92] S. Brandes et al., "Physical Layer Specification of the L-band Digital Aeronautical Communications System (L-DACS1)," in *Proc. ICNS'09*, 2009.

[93] M. Meyer, H. Wiemann, M. Sagfors, J. Torsner, and Jung-Fu Cheng, "ARQ Concept for the UMTS Long-Term Evolution," in *Proc. VTC-2006 Fall*, 2006.

[94] M. Schnell et al., "Interference mitigation for broadband L-DACS," in *27th DASC*, 2009.

[95] EUROCONTROL, "Long-Term Forecast, Flight Movements 2008-2030," 2008.

[96] M. Sajatovic, "B-AMC Operating Concept and Deployment Scenarios," B-AMC Project, Deliverable D2.2 2007.

9 Appendix

9.1 SOA Simulation Service Interface

The most important single component needed by any implementation of an SOA is the interface used for communication between different services. If the interaction of computer implemented services is conducted over the public Internet, well known protocols like WSDL [80] and SOAP [81] are commonly employed. However, these protocols are tailored for the needs of enterprise applications and are difficult to apply to other problem domains. As of this writing there is currently no light-weight protocol available that is suitable for the exchange of simulation data. Therefore a new interface protocol had to be defined by the author for the exchange of data between simulation services.

The author's design goals for this interface were mainly driven by software engineering needs. First of all the interface should be based on well-known standards in order to gain synergies from existing implementations and to facilitate conformance testing. The second goal was to keep the interface as simple as possible. Ideally it would offer enough flexibility to enable the live exchange of simulation data as well as the permanent storage of results. The third goal was keep the interface extensible to allow the later addition of further capabilities.

All three design goals have been achieved by the author by defining a domain specific interface language on the basis of XML syntax [82].

Most contemporary computer programming languages support parsing and writing XML natively. This simplifies the usage of the interface considerably and provides the additional benefit of highly optimized and well-tested implementations.

The interface protocol uses mostly empty XML elements[96] of the form:

```
<event time="..." attribute1="..." attribtute2="..." />
```

Restricting the interface syntax to empty elements enables the interface protocol to trace event driven simulations with minimal effort. Each XML element corresponds naturally to one simulation event. The properties of the event are reported in the attributes of the XML element. Note that the `time` attribute is mandatory for all simulation events.

The equivalence of XML elements to simulation events is also retained when the output of one simulation service is parsed as input by another simulation service. The parsing service can re-generate all relevant simulation events directly from the input. The simplicity of this approach is best illustrated by the source code of a fully functional

---

[96] The XML terminology defines an element as empty if it contains only attributes and no body.

implementation of an interface parser in the next paragraph. The source code is given in the Python [**83**] programming language:

```
import xml.sax

class MyContentHandler(xml.sax.ContentHandler):
    def startElement(self, name, attrs):
        if name == "event1":
            time = float( attrs.getValue("time") )
            # process other attributes here
            # create event1(time) in simulation
        elif name == "event2":
            time = float( attrs.getValue("time") )
            # ...

xml.sax.parse("session_trace.xml", MyContentHandler())
```

If a simulation trace shall be stored in a file, the XML elements of the interface protocol have to be enclosed by a root XML element to create a valid stand-alone XML document. The format of a session trace file is then:

```
<?xml version="1.0" encoding="UTF-8" standalone="yes" ?>
<trace begin="…" end="…" source="…" host="…" description="…" >

<!-- service interface elements here -->

</trace>
```

The `trace` element is the XML root[97] element of the trace file and describes the stored simulation session. It reports simulation properties (start and end of simulation) and the source of the session trace (source, host, and description). The format is in C-style syntax:

```
<trace begin ="%.3f" end="%.3f" source="%s" host="%s"
description="%s" />
```

Table 9-1: <trace/> element attributes.

Attribute	Type	Unit	Example
begin	Float	Time in seconds.	begin="0.000"
end	Float	Time in seconds.	end="3600.000"
source	String	Free text.	source="L-DACS 1 protocol simulator r123"
host	String	Free text.	host="tgraeupl@seeigel.cosy.sbg.ac.at"
description	String	Free text.	description="Example."

The `begin` attribute specifies the starting time of the simulation. The time is given in seconds relative to 00:00 of the simulated day. The absolute day-time is only relevant

---

[97] The XML terminology defines the first element of the XML file as the root element.

for the detailed simulation scenarios. The `end` attribute specifies the end of the simulation. It is also given in seconds. Note that the time is always rounded to millisecond precision to avoid problems of differing rounding accuracy.

The `source`, `host` and `description` attributes describe the source of the simulation interface trace. The `source` attribute specifies the simulation service that created the session (service name and code revision). The `host` attribute reports the user and host that ran the service. The `description` attribute contains a human readable description of the simulation session.

In order to reduce the size of session traces they are stored in compressed form. Traces are compressed using the deflate algorithm [**84**] which can be applied transparently. Compressed trace files are identified with the `.xml.gz` file extension.

The format of the service interface protocol elements is documented in the next sections together with the detailed description of the simulation services. Note that only the attributes and interface elements relevant to the B-AMC and L-DACS 1 simulations are discussed in this thesis. The complete specification of the interface format, including the description of elements for other simulation trials, is available on request from the author [**54**].

9.1.1 Simplified Evaluation Scenarios

The creation and deletion of aircraft is capture in the simulation interface protocol with two XML elements. The first service interface element traces the arrival of a new aircraft in the simulation scenario. The second traces its departure. In the simplified evaluation scenarios arrival and departure coincide with the start and end of the simulation.

The `<create_flight/>` element adds a new aircraft to the simulation.

```
<create_flight time="%.3f" id="%s" />
```

It has only two relevant attributes.

Table 9-2: <create_flight/> element attributes.

Attribute	Type	Unit	Example
time	Float	Time in seconds.	time="123.456"
id	String	Free text.	id="aircraft01"

The `time` attribute specifies the time of creation of the aircraft in the simulation. All time values are given in absolute simulation time and in units of seconds. Each aircraft has a unique identifier. This identifier is given in the `id` element. Usually this is a simple alphanumeric numbering scheme.

The `<delete_flight/>` element removes an aircraft from the simulation.

```
<delete_flight time="%.3f" id="%s" />
```

It has the same two attributes as the `<create_flight/>` element. The `time` attribute specified the time of removal from the simulation scenario. The `id` attribute uniquely identifies the aircraft. Additional element attributes that are not used in this context are documented in [54].

The generation of the data traffic in the simplified scenarios is implemented as a Poisson process i.e. constant sized data packets are generated with exponentially distributed inter-arrival times. The size of the packets is chosen in accordance with the simulated protocol[98] and the mean inter-arrival time is chosen appropriately to achieve the specified user data rates[99]. Within the B-AMC and L-DACS 1 simulations packets sizes of approximately 1000 bit were used[100] as most COCR packets have comparable sizes [50]. Note that the user data rates include already any overhead introduced by higher layer protocols.

The generation of a new data packet is traced by the service interface protocol with the `<create_packet/>` element.

```
<create_packet time="%.3f" id="%s" pkt_direction="%s"
  pkt_size="%d" pkt_peer="%s" cocr_tos="%s" cocr_cos="%s"/>
```

The attributes describe the properties of the packet.

Table 9-3: <create_packet/> element attributes.

Attribute	Type	Unit	Example
time	Float	Time in seconds.	time="123.456"
id	String	Free text.	id="packet001"
pkt_direction	String	Predefined text: FL, RL.	pkt_direction="FL"
pkt_peer	String	Predefined text: Flight id.	pkt_peer="aircraft01"
pkt_size	Integer	Octets.	pkt_size="128"
cocr_tos	String	Predefined text: addressed, broadcast.	cocr_tos="addressed"

---

[98] The approach of choosing packets sizes deemed suitable for the protocol under evaluation was confirmed by one of the authors of the COCR report [41] and its companion document [40]. (Interview of the author with P. Platt, QinetiQ Malvern Technology Centre, Jun 19th 2007).

[99] The mean number of packets per time unit μ equals the quotient of the user data rate u and the packet size p.

$$\mu = \frac{u}{p}$$

Thus the mean inter-arrival time λ is

$$\lambda = \frac{1}{\mu} = \frac{p}{u}$$

[100] A detailed rationale for this packet size can be found in [44].

Attribute	Type	Unit	Example
`cocr_cos`	String	Predefined text: COCR classes of service.	cocr_cos="DG-A"

The `time` attribute specifies the time of creation of the packet. It is given in absolute simulation time in seconds. Each data packet has a unique identifier given in the `id` attribute. The identifier may have any format, however, an alphanumeric scheme is preferred.

The `pkt_direction` attribute indicates the forwarding direction of the packet: air-to-ground (reverse link **RL**) or ground-to-air (forward link **FL**). The terms "forward link" and "reverse link" have been introduced for better comprehensibility. The traditional terms "uplink" and "downlink" (as used in the COCR report [**46**]) may lead to misunderstandings. Therefore forward-link (FL) is used for data communications addressed to aircraft and reverse-link (RL) for data communications addressed to ground-stations.

The `pkt_peer` attribute specifies the source aircraft (RL direction) or the destination aircraft (FL direction). The other communication partner is always the ground-station. Aircraft are identified using the unique identifier specified in the `id` attribute of the `<create_flight/>` element. In the simplified evaluation scenarios source and destination aircraft are chosen randomly.

The remaining three attributes indicate the properties of the data packet. The `pkt_size` attribute gives the packet size in octets. The `cocr_tos` attribute specifies whether it is an `addressed` packet destined to one particular user or a `broadcast` packet destined to all aircraft in range. The `cocr_cos` attribute defines the class of service of the packet. Service classes are defined in [**46**] and discussed in section 5.6.

Unless noted differently in this thesis, packet sizes are constant in the simplified evaluation scenarios and all packets are assumed to be `addressed` packets with the same class of service.

9.1.2 Detailed Evaluation Scenarios
The detailed simulation scenarios use the same service interface protocol format as the simplified simulation scenarios.

9.1.3 Evaluation
Simulation results are added to the service interface session by the protocol simulation. The evaluation service utilizes the following interface elements to perform measurements.

The `<set_packet/>` element reports the result of a packet transmission. The transmission may have been successful or unsuccessful.

```
<set_packet  time="%f"  id="%s"  pkt_status="%s" />
```

It has three attributes.

Table 9-4: <set_packet/> element attributes.

Attribute	Type	Unit	Example
time	Float	Time in seconds.	time="123.456"
id	String	Free text.	id="packet001"
pkt_status	String	Predefined text: OK, LOST, CANCELLED.	

The `time` attribute reports the end of the transmission process. The id attribute is the unique identifier of the transmitted packet. The `pkt_status` attribute indicates the condition under which the packet was received. The value of these attribute can be one of the following values:

- OK: Indicates that the packet was received correctly.
- LOST: Indicates that the packet was lost, discarded, or received with an error that could not be recovered.

The `<set_queue/>` element reports the current length of the transmission queue (i.e. the length of the interface queue of the data link layer).

```
<set_queue time='%.3f' id='%s' q_direction='%s' q_length='%d' />
```

It has four attributes.

Table 9-5: <set_queue/> element attributes.

Attribute	Type	Unit	Example
time	Float	Time in seconds.	time="123.456"
id	String	Free text.	id="queue01"
q_direction	String	Predefined text: FL, RL.	q_direction="FL"
q_length	Integer	Octets.	q_length="128"

The `time` attribute reports the time of the measurement. The `id` attribute uniquely identifies the queue. Note that there is no `<create_queue/>` service element. The `q_direction` attribute indicates the direction of the queue: air-to-ground direction (RL) or ground-to-air direction (FL). The queue length is reported in octets in the `q_length` attribute.

The service element pairs `<create_packet/>` and `<set_packet/>` are used to trace events of COCR data packets. There is an equivalent pair of service interface elements for data link layer packets. The `<create_MACpdu/>` element reports the creation of a data link layer PDU.

```
<create_MACpdu time='%.3f' id='%s' pkt_direction='%s'
pkt_peer='%s' pkt_size='%d' pkt_priority='%s' />
```

The attributes describe the properties of the packet.

Table 9-6: <create_MACpdu/> element attributes.

Attribute	Type	Unit	Example
time	Float	Time in seconds.	time="123.456"
id	String	Free text.	id="mac_packet001"
pkt_direction	String	Predefined text: FL, RL.	pkt_direction="FL"
pkt_peer	String	Predefined text: Flight id.	pkt_peer="aircraft01"
pkt_size	Integer	Octets.	pkt_size="128"
pkt_priority	String	Free text.	pkt_priority="cos_1"

The `time` attribute specifies the time of creation of the data link layer packet. It is given in absolute simulation time in seconds. Each PDU has a unique identifier given in the `id` attribute. The `pkt_direction` attribute indicates the forwarding direction of the packet: air-to-ground (reverse link RL) or ground-to-air (forward link FL). The `pkt_peer` attribute specifies the source aircraft (RL direction) or the destination aircraft (FL direction). Aircraft are identified using the unique identifier specified in the `id` attribute of the `<create_flight/>` element. The `pkt_priority` attribute reports the data link layer class of service.

The `<set_MACpdu />` interface element indicates the completion of a data link layer packet transmission. Note that this need not coincide with the end of the transmission of the corresponding COCR packet if the higher layer packet is fragmented. Control packets of the data link layer have no equivalent COCR packets at all. The `<set_MACpdu/>` element has the same attributes as the `<set_packet/>` element.

The `<set_MACqueue/>` interface element reports the queue length of the internal queue of the data link layer. It has the same attributes as the `<set_queue/>` element.

The use of these interface elements is illustrated in Figure 9-1. Note that the `<set_packet/>` interface element may be created by several protocol entities within the protocol simulation. In the first step a COCR packet is created by the simulation scenario. This packet is put into the interface queue of the data link layer in the second step. The data link layer creates a data link layer PDU, puts it into the queue, and transmits it to the receiver. If the COCR packet is fragmented by the data link layer, steps three to five may be repeated several times before the complete COCR packet has been transmitted. Completely received COCR packets are accepted by the receiving instance in the higher layers of the protocol stack and reported to the evaluation service.

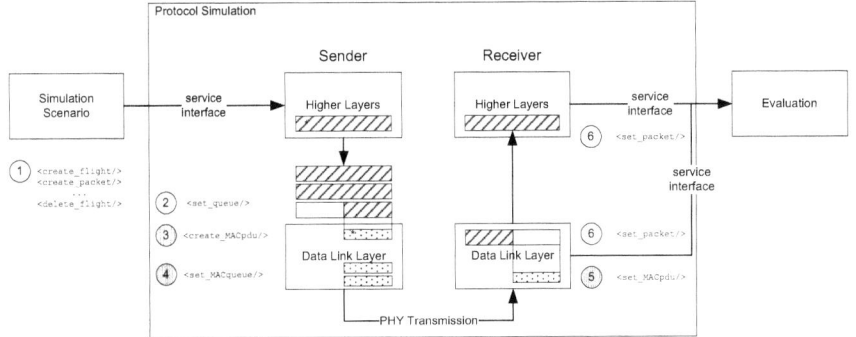

Figure 9-1: Packet transmission interface trace.

9.2 DIN1319-3 Confidence intervals

The confidence intervals of the measurements presented in this thesis were calculated according to DIN 1319-3 [85]. If an unknown value X is measured n times the true value of X lies with probability p within the confidence interval

$$[\bar{X} - u, \bar{X} + u]$$

where $\bar{X}$ is the arithmetic average of the n measurements and

$$u = t_{p,n} \frac{S_X}{\sqrt{n}}.$$

S_X is the standard deviation of the measurements and $t_{p,n}$ is Student's t-distribution according to Table 9-7.

Table 9-7: Student's t-distribution.

Number of measurements	2	3	4	5	6	10	100	>200
$p = 0.6826$	1.84	1.32	1.20	1.15	1.11	1.06	1.00	1.00
$p = 0.95$	12.71	4.30	3.18	2.78	2.57	2.26	1.98	1.96

9.3 Jain's Fairness Index

If a value x_i is measured for n users the fairness f between these users is rated according to

$$f = \frac{(\sum x_i)^2}{(n \sum x_i^2)}.$$

Jain's fairness index [58] is independent of scale, continuous, and bounded between 0 and 1. The report [79] provides an excellent discussion of the properties of this index.

9.4 Analysis of Slotted ALOHA and RDLC B-VHF sRA Access

This section gives a motivation for the use of the Random Delay Counter RDLC algorithm instead of slotted ALOHA in the B-VHF sRA medium access protocol.

Slotted ALOHA is one of the simplest medium access algorithms. An aircraft wishing to send just transmits its message. If it was not successful, it waits for a random number of slots, but not longer than an upper bound of R slots, and tries again.

Random delay counter is only slightly more complex. This algorithm is also organized in rounds of R slots. Each aircraft willing to send is allowed to do so only once per round. For this purpose it randomly chooses one specific slot r of the R slots of the round and uses it for transmission. In all other slots it has to remain silent.

We assume in both cases that all aircraft use the same setting for the parameter R and that the number of competing users is constant. In addition we assume that the aircraft have always data to send.

9.4.1 Definitions

For the definition of the analytical models we need some helper functions. We define two functions to make the notation more readable:

$$p(n) = \frac{1}{R - n + 1}$$

$$p'(n) = 1 - p(n)$$

for $1 \leq n \leq R$. With the help of these two functions both algorithms can be modeled easily.

Assume that the aircraft (willing to send a net entry request) is in slot $n-1$ of its round and has not yet tried to send a packet in the current round. Before slot n begins, it has to decide whether or not to send in it. Let the transition probabilities from slot $n - 1$ to n be

$$P(slot_{n-1} \to send\ in\ slot_n) = p(n)$$

$$P(slot_{n-1} \to do\ not\ send\ in\ slot_n) = p'(n)$$

for $1 \leq n \leq R$, if the aircraft has not sent yet and 0 otherwise.

For convenience we set slot 0 to the last slot of the previous round. Then an aircraft will send once in R slots and the probability for sending in slot n is $1/R$ for any slot $1 \leq n \leq R$.

Proof: Obviously the aircraft will send at least once in each round as $p(R) = 1$. As the sending probability is 0 after having sent once by definition, the aircraft will attempt to send at most once per round.

The probability that the aircraft is sending in slot *n* of the round is given by

$$p(n)\prod_{i=1}^{n-1} p'(i)$$

for $1 \leq n \leq R$. A short calculation shows that this expression indeed equals *1/R*. ∎

These are exactly the properties needed.

9.4.2 Slotted ALOHA Medium Access

The first variant of the medium access algorithms we are going to investigate is the basic *slotted ALOHA* scheme. In this access scheme an aircraft willing to send just puts a resource request on the sRA. If there is more than one user this will inevitably lead to collisions, after which the aircraft has to wait for a random time before it is allowed to try again. Our model describes this phase of contention for the sRA.

The Markov model is set up from the perspective of one specific (but arbitrary) aircraft. We assume that all users in the system use the same variant of slotted ALOHA, the number of waiting slots being randomly chosen from the interval $[0, R-1]$ with a uniform distribution. By this scheme each aircraft will send no later than *R* slots after the last transmission attempt. In addition, this allows us to use the functions from the previous section.

Due to the assumption that the aircraft have always resource requests to send, we can make the simplifying assumption that all aircraft remain in an infinite loop, alternating between sending attempts and waiting times.

9.4.2.1 States

During the slotted ALOHA contention period an aircraft has two distinct (classes of) states. Either it is *sending* or it is *waiting*. In our simplified model we need not differentiate between a successful transmission and a collision, so we have just one generic state

$$S$$

for *sending*.

After each sending attempt the aircraft waits for up to *R-1* slots to try again. It has to send no later than in the *R*-th slot after the last attempt so only *R-1 waiting* states are needed.

$$W_1, W_2, \ldots, W_{R-1}$$

denotes that the aircraft is waiting the *1,2, ..., R-1*-th slot now. The corresponding Markov model is illustrated in Figure 9-2.

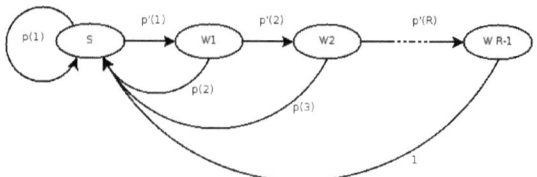

Figure 9-2: State model of slotted ALOHA B-VHF MAC in the sRA.

9.4.2.2 Transition probabilities

In this model the transition probabilities between the different states are fairly straightforward.

$$P(S \rightarrow S) = p(1)$$

$$P(S \rightarrow W_1) = p'(1)$$

$$P(W_{n-1} \rightarrow W_n) = p'(n) \quad 2 \leq n \leq R-1$$

$$P(W_n \rightarrow S) = p(n+1) \quad 1 \leq n \leq R-1$$

Note that the properties of the p function ensure that the aircraft sends within R slots after the last sending attempt with probability 1.

If we write down the transition probabilities in matrix form

	S	W_1	...	W_{R-1}
S				
W_1				
...			P_{ij}	
W_{R-1}				

we get the following transition matrix.

$$P = \begin{bmatrix} p(1) & p'(1) & & \\ p(2) & & \ddots & \\ \vdots & & & p'(R-2) \\ p(R-1) & & & p'(R-1) \\ p(R) & & & \end{bmatrix}$$

9.4.2.3 Stable Distribution

This Markov chain is aperiodic, irreducible, and finite and therefore has a stable distribution. We denote the stable distribution with π, where π has the property that

$$\pi P = \pi$$

where $\sum_i \pi_i = 1$.

To calculate the stable distribution we first calculate one eigenvector of P, x, such that

$$xP = x$$

$$(x_1 \quad \cdots \quad x_R)P = (x_1 \quad \cdots \quad x_R).$$

Which expands to

$$x_1 p(1) + x_2 p(2) + \cdots + x_R p(R) = x_1$$

$$\left.\begin{array}{rcl} x_1 p'(1) & = & x_2 \\ \vdots & & \vdots \\ x_{R-1} p'(R-1) & = & x_R \end{array}\right\} (*).$$

The first equation is just a linear combination of the equations below, therefore it is sufficient to find one solution of (*).

The equations (*) have the general form

$$x_r\, p'(r) = x_{r+1}$$

$$\to x_r\, \frac{R-r}{R-r+1} = x_{r+1} \quad 1 \le r \le R-1.$$

As this equation system is under-determined we can set one variable to an arbitrary value. Let $x_1 = 1 = R/R$ then we get the solutions

$$x_1 = \frac{R}{R}$$
$$x_2 = p'(1) x_1 = \frac{R-1}{R}$$
$$x_3 = p'(2) x_2 = \frac{R-2}{R}$$
$$\cdots$$
$$x_{R-1} = p'(R-2) x_{R-2} = \frac{2}{R}$$
$$x_R = p'(R-1) x_{R-1} = \frac{1}{R}$$

which can be abbreviated to

$$x_r = p'(r-1) x_{r-1} = \frac{R-r+1}{R}.$$

x is already a solution of the equation system, but it is not yet the stable distribution we are looking for. In order to get the stable distribution we have to normalize x, such that $\sum_i x_i = \sum_i \pi_i = 1$.

Therefore we compute

$$\sum_{r=1}^{R} x_r = \sum_{r=1}^{R} \frac{R-r+1}{R} = \frac{R}{R} + \frac{R-1}{R} + \cdots + \frac{1}{R} =$$

$$= \sum_{r=1}^{R} \frac{r}{R} = \frac{1}{R} \sum_{r=1}^{R} r = \frac{R(R-1)}{2R}.$$

We set $\pi_r = \frac{x_r}{\sum x_r}$ which implies $\sum \pi_i = 1$ and get

$$\rightarrow \pi_r = \frac{2(R-r+1)}{R(R+1)}$$

for $r = 1, \ldots, R$. Which is the stable distribution of the Markov chain?

9.4.2.4 Conclusions from the Stable Distribution

From the stable distribution we can deduce that after sufficient time

$$P\begin{pmatrix} \text{an aircraft is sending} \\ \text{its resource request in} \\ \text{slot } t \text{ of the sRA} \end{pmatrix} \xrightarrow{t \to \infty} \pi_1 = \frac{2}{R+1}.$$

From this result we can derive more properties of slotted ALOHA. If a total of *u+1* users (i.e. *u* aircraft + the selected aircraft) are involved in the resource request process (i.e. the slotted ALOHA contention), the probability that *u* users do not send in a slot converges to

$$p_{succ} = \left(1 - \frac{2}{R+1}\right)^u.$$

As the transmission of the selected aircraft can only be successful if no collision occurs, p_{succ} is the (limit of the) probability of one specific aircraft transmitting its resource request successfully.

If one or several other users are sending during the slot, the transmitted packet suffers from a collision. Therefore the probability for an unsuccessful resource request (neglecting transmission errors) converges to

$$p'_{succ} = 1 - p_{succ}.$$

If we look at the times where the selected aircraft is waiting we can deduce another set of properties of slotted ALOHA. The probability that one of the *u* competing users successfully transmits its resource request during the aircraft's waiting time converges then to

$$q_{succ} = \left(1 - \frac{2}{R+1}\right)^{u-1} \frac{2}{R+1} \binom{u}{1}.$$

This implies, of course, that the probability that no one transmits successfully becomes

$$q'_{succ} = 1 - q_{succ}.$$

If we drop the perspective used so far and do not distinguish the involved aircraft, we can derive yet another property. To this end we define

$$q(u, R) = \left(1 - \frac{2}{R+1}\right)^{u-1} \frac{2}{R+1} u \qquad (**)$$

which is just q_{succ} as a function of the number of users u and the maximum waiting time R.

From this point of view q is the probability of any user sending its resource request successfully. The throughput of slotted ALOHA is the best when $q(u)$ is maximal (R fixed). A quick calculation shows that $q(u)$ has its maximum at

$$u_{max}(R) = \frac{-1}{\ln\left(1 - \frac{2}{R+1}\right)}$$

where it takes the value

$$q(u_{max}(R), R) = \frac{-\frac{2}{R+1}}{e\left(1 - \frac{2}{R+1}\right)\ln\left(1 - \frac{2}{R+1}\right)}.$$

$u_{max}(R)$ can be approximated by $u_{max} \approx \frac{R}{2}$ which implies that the optimal round length (in terms of throughput) for u users is approximately $2u$ slots.

Figure 9-3 displays the limit of the slotted ALOHA through put as a function of the number of users u and as a function of the number of slots R. Note the region of optimal throughput along $(u, 2u)$.

If the number of users approaches infinity (i.e. large number of users) the maximum achievable throughput of resource requests converges to

$$q(u_{max}) \xrightarrow{u_{max} \to \infty} \frac{1}{e}.$$

This is a well known result and can be obtained by other methods, too (cf. [**86**]).

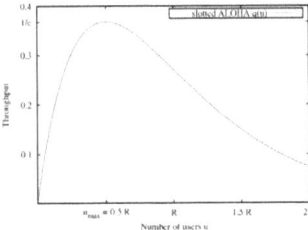
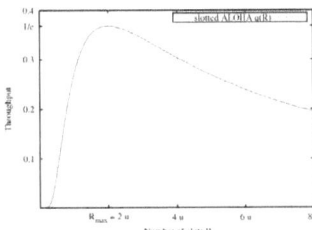

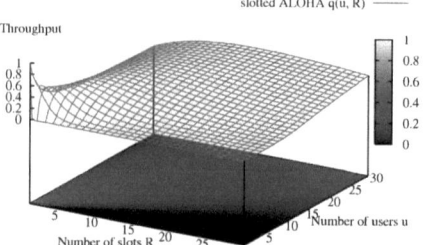

Figure 9-3: Limit of slotted ALOHA throughput (**).

9.4.3 Random Delay Counter Medium Access

The second random access scheme that was investigated for B-VHF sRA access was the *random delay counter* RDLC algorithm. Random delay counter works as follows. The slots are organized into rounds of length R, again. An aircraft willing to send, randomly chooses one of the slots of the round for transmission. If a collision occurred it has to remain idle for the rest of the round and wait for the next one to try again.

First we need to calculate the probability of sending a resource request successfully in the presence of u competing aircraft (1 specific aircraft + u others). In order not to suffer from a collision, no other aircraft may be sending in the same slot. As the probability to find one other aircraft sending in a specific slot is 1/R for RDLC (by design) we define

$$p_{succ}(u) = \left(1 - \frac{1}{R}\right)^u \text{ and}$$

$$p'_{succ}(u) = 1 - p_{succ}(u) \text{ for } u \in \mathbf{N}.$$

This gives us the probabilities for sending successfully or not[101].

The probability that one of the u competing users sends its resource request successfully during the aircraft's waiting time becomes then

$$q_{succ}(u) = \left(1 - \frac{1}{R}\right)^{u-1} \frac{1}{R} \binom{u}{1}$$

which implies, of course, that the probability that no one transmits successfully is

---

[101] This is analog to computing the probability of sending successfully in one round, which can be calculated by

$$p_{succ}(u) = \left(\frac{R-1}{R}\right)^u$$

being the probability that all competing users chose one of the R − 1 other slots (i.e. not my slot).

$$q'_{succ}(u) = 1 - q_{succ}(u).$$

From this result we can derive the function

$$q(u, R) = \left(1 - \frac{1}{R}\right)^{u-1} \frac{1}{R} u \qquad (***)$$

which is just q_{succ} as a function of the number of users u and round length R. As q is the probability of any user sending successfully, the throughput of RDLC is best when $q(u)$ is maximal (R fixed). We calculate that the maximum is at

$$u_{max}(R) = \frac{-1}{\ln\left(1 - \frac{1}{R}\right)}$$

where it takes the value

$$q(u_{max}(R), R) = \frac{-\frac{1}{R}}{e\left(1 - \frac{1}{R}\right)\ln\left(1 - \frac{1}{R}\right)}$$

$u_{max}(R)$ can be approximated by $u_{max} \approx R$ which implies that the optimal round length (in terms of throughput) for u users is approximately u slots.

Figure 9-4 displays the limit of the RDLC through put as a function of the number of users u and as a function of the number of slots R. Note the region of optimal throughput along (u, u).

If the number of users approaches infinity the maximal achievable throughput of RDLC converges to

$$q(u_{max}) \xrightarrow{u_{max} \to \infty} \frac{1}{e}.$$

The calculation is analog to the previous section.

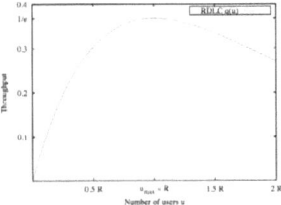
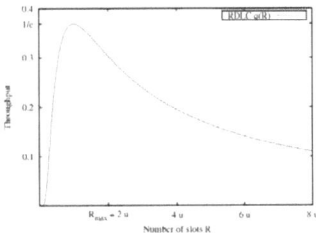

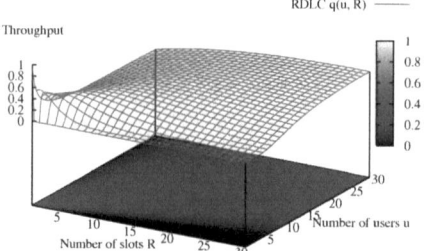

Figure 9-4: Limit of slotted RDLC throughput (***).

9.4.4 Conclusion

The decision of the B-VHF project to use RLDC medium access for the sRA instead of slotted ALOHA can be motivated (among other reasons) by the properties of RDLC, which requires less slots to achieve the same limit throughput. Figure 9-5 displays a comparison of both sRA MAC approaches according to the number of available sRA slots.

The same analytical results were used to derive the required number of sRA slots from the B-VHF user data traffic pattern.

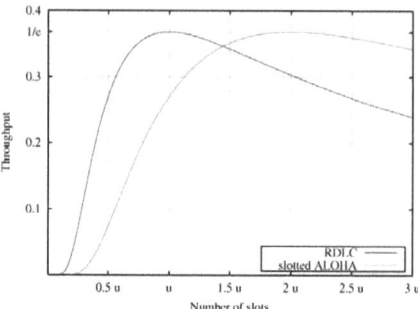

Figure 9-5: Comparison of slotted ALOHA and RDLC.

i want morebooks!

Buy your books fast and straightforward online - at one of world's fastest growing online book stores! Environmentally sound due to Print-on-Demand technologies.

Buy your books online at
www.get-morebooks.com

Kaufen Sie Ihre Bücher schnell und unkompliziert online – auf einer der am schnellsten wachsenden Buchhandelsplattformen weltweit! Dank Print-On-Demand umwelt- und ressourcenschonend produziert.

Bücher schneller online kaufen
www.morebooks.de

VDM Verlagsservicegesellschaft mbH
Heinrich-Böcking-Str. 6-8   Telefon: +49 681 3720 174   info@vdm-vsg.de
D - 66121 Saarbrücken   Telefax: +49 681 3720 1749   www.vdm-vsg.de

Printed by Books on Demand GmbH, Norderstedt / Germany